Doctrines of Salvation

JOSEPH FIELDING SMITH

DOCTRINES
OF
SALVATION

Sermons and Writings of
JOSEPH FIELDING SMITH

Compiled by
BRUCE R. McCONKIE

Volume 1

Bookcraft
Salt Lake City, Utah

Copyright
Bookcraft
1954

ISBN 0-88494-036-5

25 26 27 28 29 30   89 88 87 86 85 84 83

Lithographed in the United States of America
PUBLISHERS PRESS
Salt Lake City, Utah

PREFACE

Joseph Fielding Smith is the leading gospel scholar and the greatest doctrinal teacher of this generation. Few men in this dispensation have approached him in gospel knowledge or surpassed him in spiritual insight. His is the faith and the knowledge of his father, President Joseph F. Smith, and his grandfather, the Patriarch Hyrum Smith.

It was inevitable, therefore, that his sermons and writings should form the basis of a substantial contribution to the literature of the Church. This first-of-three volumes should find ready acceptance among gospel students everywhere.

Source of the material is the published sermons and articles of President Smith as found in the various periodicals of the Church; also, the thousands upon thousands of personal letters he has written to give answers to questions raised by searchers who could not find the desired information in any published work.

It follows that a host of answers will be found herein to gospel questions frequently asked, but seldom answered with the authoritative finality of the oracles of God. When President Smith speaks, it is not as the scribes.

The student will do well to read the scriptural references listed in the footnotes, and to approach his study in a spirit of faith and prayerful search for ultimate truth.

To many I express deep appreciation for help and encouragement: Chiefly, to President Joseph Fielding Smith, himself, for his scriptural insight, his plain teachings, and his power of expression; to Elder Oscar W. McConkie, my father, for much counsel and for many helpful suggestions; to Elder Milton R. Hunter of the First Council of the Seventy, for like assistance; to Joseph Fielding Smith, Jr., for setting the type and making many valued suggestions; to Velma Harvey and Shirley Stone Storrs, for typing the mountain of manuscripts from which the gems here published were selected; and to Harold Lundstrom, for a painstaking and careful reading of the proof.

—Bruce R. McConkie

Salt Lake City, Utah
November 10, 1954.

CONTENTS

CHAPTER 1. CHARACTER, ATTRIBUTES, AND PERFECTIONS OF GOD

The Godhead (1). Modern Knowledge of God (2). How God Progresses (5). How God Does Not Progress (7). How God is Everlasting (10). Reverence for God (12). Did the Father Eat with Abraham? (16). Did Jacob Wrestle with an Angel? (17).

CHAPTER 2. THE SON OF GOD

The Only Begotten Son (18). Advent and Mission of Christ Foretold (20). Our Advocate and Our Mediator (26). Christ the Father and the Son (28). Christ Only Hath Power of Immortality (30). Christ Worked Out His Own Salvation (32). Teach that Christ was More than a Man (33). Historicity of Jesus (34). Appearance of the Lord to Brother of Jared (37).

CHAPTER 3. THE HOLY GHOST, LIGHT OF CHRIST, AND SECOND COMFORTER

The Holy Ghost (38). Gift of the Holy Ghost (39). Holy Ghost a Sure Witness of Truth (43). The Holy Spirit of Promise (45). The Holy Ghost Led All the Prophets (45). The Sin Against the Holy Ghost (47). The Light of Christ (49). The Second Comforter (55).

CHAPTER 4. OUR FIRST AND SECOND ESTATES

Pre-existence of Man (56). Pre-existence of all Creatures (62). The War in Heaven (64). Mortality (66). Free Agency in Both Estates (70).

CHAPTER 5. THE EARTH: ITS CREATION AND DESTINY

Many Earths and Their Salvation (72). The Lord's Blueprint of Creation (74). Physical Creation of all Things (75). Age of the Earth (78). The Telestial Earth (82). The Terrestrial Earth (84). The Celestial Earth (87).

CHAPTER 6. MICHAEL OUR PRINCE

Creation of Adam (90). Adam: First Man and First Flesh (92). Adam Commanded to Replenish the Earth (93). Adam: Intelligent and Civilized (94). The Adam-God Theory (96).

CHAPTER 7. THE FALL OF ADAM

Status of Adam before the Fall (107). Status of Adam after the Fall (111). Fall of Adam a Blessing (113). "No Adam, No Fall; No Fall, No Atonement" (116).

CHAPTER 8. THE ATONEMENT OF CHRIST

Atonement Based on the Fall (121). Atonement Ransoms Us from the Fall (123). Christ Had Life in Himself (127). The Price Christ Paid for Us (129). Atonement and Our Lack of Gratitude (131). The Doctrine of Blood Atonement (133). Infinite Scope of Atonement (138).

CHAPTER 9. EVOLUTION

Origin of Life (139). Evolution and Religion Cannot Be Harmonized (141). Intelligence of the Ancients (144). The Devolution Not Evolution of Civilization (148).

CHAPTER 10. EVERLASTING COVENANTS

Nature of Gospel Covenants (152). The New and Everlasting Covenant (156). The Gospel Covenant (159). Gospel Dispensations (160). The Abrahamic Covenant (164).

CHAPTER 11. THE RESTORATION OF ALL THINGS

A Marvelous Work and a Wonder (167). Elias, Elijah and the Restoration (170). World-wide Scope of the Restoration (174).

CHAPTER 12. JOSEPH SMITH: PROPHET OF THE RESTORATION

Nature of the Prophetic Calling (184). The Divine Mission of Joseph Smith (188). The Messenger of the Restoration (191). Details Proving Truth of Prophet's Mission (195). Personal Sentiments about Joseph Smith (199).

CHAPTER 13. THE DIVINE LAW OF WITNESSES

Nature and History of Law of Witnesses (203). Joseph Smith and the Law of Witnesses (210). Joseph and Hyrum: Joint Witnesses (216). Witnesses of the Book of Mormon (222).

CHAPTER 14. THE CHURCH AND KINGDOM

The Kingdom of God on Earth (229). The Kingdom Set Up on Earth (230). The Saints: A Peculiar People (234). Privileges and Duties of Saints (236). The Kingdom: Its Organization and Gifts (238). The Kingdom to Stand Forever (240).

CHAPTER 15. ORIGIN AND DESTINY OF THE "REORGANIZED" CHURCH

Origin of Early Apostate Cults (247). Succession in the Presidency (254). Fruits of the "Reorganization" (261). The "Reorganites" vs. Salvation for the Dead (263).

CHAPTER 16. THE LAW OF REVELATION

Eternal Nature of Revelation (274). Revelation in the Church Today (279). False Spirits and False Revelations (283).

CHAPTER 17. GAINING THE KNOWLEDGE THAT SAVES

Nature of Saving Knowledge (290). Gaining Truth and Light from the Spirit (293). Search the Scriptures (301).

CHAPTER 18. TEACHING THE GOSPEL

Raising the Warning Voice (307). Teaching in the Church (311). Teaching Our Children (316). Testing Truth of All Revelations (320).

VOLUME II CONTAINS THE FOLLOWING CHAPTERS:
1. Salvation. 2. The Degrees of Glory. 3. Exaltation. 4. Celestial Marriage. 5. Sins Against the Marriage Covenant. 6. Elijah: The Man and the Prophet. 7. Elijah: His Mission and Sealing Power. 8. Salvation Universal. 9. Salvation for the Dead. 10. Salvation for the Living. 11. The Divine Law of Record Keeping. 12. Spiritual Life and Death. 13. The Law of Temple Building. 14. Law of the Resurrection. 15. Salvation and the Resurrection. 16. Faith Unto Salvation. 17. Baptism and Salvation. 18. The Sacrament and Salvation.

VOLUME III CONTAINS THE FOLLOWING CHAPTERS:
1. Signs Preceding Second Coming. 2. Signs of the Times. 3. War and the Second Coming. 4. The Millennium and New Jerusalem. 5. Priesthood: God's Eternal Power. 6. Priesthood Organization. 7. Keys and Covenant of Priesthood. 8. The Holy Apostleship. 9. Patriarchs, Blessings, and Administrations. 10. Books the Lord Approves. 11. Coming Forth of Book of Mormon. 12. A Voice from Cumorah. 13. Israel: God's Covenant Race. 14. The Apostate World. 15. Apostasy from Latter-day Kingdom. 16. Kingdoms of This World. 17. Exodus of Modern Israel. 18. Mormon Pioneers and Colonization.

Chapter 1

CHARACTER, ATTRIBUTES, AND PERFECTIONS OF GOD

THE GODHEAD

The Supreme Council. "We believe in God, the Eternal Father, and in His Son, Jesus Christ, and in the Holy Ghost."[1]

We accept these three personages as the supreme governing council in the heavens. The Father and the Son have tabernacles of flesh and bones, and the Holy Ghost is a personage of Spirit.[2] We worship the Father in the name of the Son, who is the Mediator between God and man, and his is the only name given whereby man can be saved.[3] We accept Jesus as the Only Begotten Son of the Father in the flesh, although we are all his offspring in the spirit, and therefore his children.[4]

Fatherhood of God. We are taught in the scriptures that God is literally, and not in a figurative sense, our very Eternal Father. The words of our Redeemer spoken to Mary near the tomb from which he had risen and gained the victory over death, are most sublime and filled with glorious meaning: "Touch me not; for I am not yet ascended to my Father: but go to my brethren, and say unto them, I ascend unto my Father, and your Father; and to my God and your God."[5] In these words the truth of the Fatherhood of God is emphatically pronounced by his Only Begotten Son, who declares that he is our brother and that we have the same Eternal Father.[6]

---

[1] First Article of Faith.
[2] D. & C. 130:22.
[3] D. & C. 18:23.
[4] *Origin of the "Reorganized" Church,* p. 82; Acts 17:28-29.
[5] John 20:17.
[6] *Church News,* June 12, 1949, p. 21.

MODERN KNOWLEDGE OF GOD

APOSTATE CONCEPTS OF GOD. In the year 1820, when the First Vision was received, the universal doctrine in the Protestant as well as the Catholic world, relating to the Godhead, in substance, was as follows:

"There is but one only living and true God who is infinite in being and perfection, a most pure spirit, invisible, without body, parts, or passions, immutable, immense, eternal, incomprehensible, almighty, most wise, most holy, most free, most absolute, working all things according to the counsel of his own immutable and most righteous will."[7]

JOSEPH SMITH RESTORED KNOWLEDGE OF GOD. The vision of Joseph Smith made it clear that the Father and the Son are separate personages, having bodies as tangible as the body of man. It was further revealed to him that the Holy Ghost is a personage of Spirit, distinct and separate from the personalities of the Father and the Son.

SCRIPTURES SHOW PERSONALITY OF GOD. This all-important truth staggered the world; yet, when we consider the clear expressions of holy writ, it is a most astounding and wonderful fact that man could have gone so far astray. The Savior said, "My Father is greater than I,"[8] and he invited his disciples, after his resurrection, to handle him and see that it was he, for, said he, "A spirit hath not flesh and bones, as ye see me have."[9] The apostles clearly understood the distinct entities of the Father, Son, and Holy Ghost, to which they constantly referred in their epistles; and Paul informed the Corinthians of the fact that when all things are subjected to the Father, "Then shall the Son also himself be subject unto him that put all things under him, that God may be all in all."[10]

---

[7] Presbyterian Confession of Faith, ch. 2.
[8] John 14:28.
[9] Luke 24:39.
[10] 1 Cor. 15:28.

Joseph Smith beheld the Father and the Son; therefore he could testify with personal knowledge that the scriptures were true wherein we read: "So God created man in his own image, in the image of God created he him; male and female created he them."[11] This was to be understood literally, and not in some mystical or figurative sense.[12]

GAINING KNOWLEDGE ABOUT GOD. I know, as these my brethren know, that God lives; that Jesus Christ is the Only Begotten Son of God in the flesh, and the Redeemer of the world. But I have not learned all that there is to know about him and our Father; neither have you; for in this mortal life it is impossible for us fully to comprehend the mission of our Lord and Redeemer, to know him and just who and what he is, and the extent of the great work he accomplished. But if we shall be worthy to enter into the presence of God the Father and Jesus Christ his Son and there be crowned with exaltation, it will be necessary for us to know them in the fulness. However, until we do enter into their presence and receive this great blessing, we will not fully know the only true God and Jesus Christ whom he has sent.[13]

ANY RIGHTEOUS MAN CAN SEE GOD. The Lord has established all things in order and has given us a perfect system. We cannot improve upon it. If we would carry out that which the Lord has revealed, as he has revealed it, then all things would be perfect; for the organization is a perfect organization: the theory of it, the plan of it, is without flaw. If we followed all the orders that have been given to us in the priesthood and otherwise; if we would put into practice the great doctrines which have been revealed in the revelations contained in the holy scriptures, it would only be a matter of a very short time until this great people would be in the same condition, absolutely, as were the people in the

---
[11]Gen. 1:27.
[12]*Era*, vol. 23, pp. 496-497.
[13]Conf. Rep., Oct., 1925, p. 112; John 17:3.

city of Enoch. We would be able to walk with God, we would be able to behold his face, because then faith would abound in the hearts of the people to the extent that it would be impossible for the Lord to withhold himself, and he would reveal himself unto us as he has done in times past.[14]

GOSPEL AND PRIESTHOOD NEEDED TO SEE GOD. We cannot tie the hands of the Lord. The Father and the Son appeared to the Prophet Joseph Smith before the Church was organized and the priesthood restored to the earth. Under those conditions the Lord could appear to one who sought for light as he did in the case of Joseph Smith.

Now that the Church is organized, and the power of the priesthood is here, no one can see the face of God, even the Father, without the blessings of the gospel and the authority of the priesthood.[15]

WALKING WITH GOD. The statement that men anciently "walked with God" we accept, of course, as a figure of speech. It means that they were in perfect harmony and at the same time receiving constant guidance and revelation from the Lord. It does not mean that they were privileged to walk along the streets, for instance, as Jesus walked with the two disciples after his resurrection.[16]

FEAR THE LORD. The Lord is merciful and kind and does not require of those who serve him that they be afraid and tremble before him. There is no delight in his heart in the "fear" of the wicked because of their sins. Most scriptural passages which tell us to "fear the Lord" have no reference to fright.

The word "fear" has more than the one meaning which we so universally use. The scriptural meaning is "to have reverential awe." In Young's *Concordance of*

---

[14]Conf. Rep., Apr., 1921, p. 40; Joseph Fielding Smith, *Teachings of the Prophet Joseph Smith*, pp. 8-9; Ether 3:17-20; 4:7.

[15]D. & C. 84:22.
[16]Gen. 5:22-24; 6:9; Micah 6:8

CHARACTER, ATTRIBUTES, AND PERFECTIONS OF GOD

the Bible, under the word "fear" we find several meanings, such as "terror," from the Hebrew word "emah"; "dread" from the Hebrew "pachdah"; "reverence" from the Hebrew "yare." So we see that the word "fear" as used in the English language, had different shades of meaning in the Hebrew, and that language used different words to connote those shades of meaning.

LOVE THE LORD. When the Lord requires that we "fear" him and keep his commandments, he means that we should pay to him that homage and reverence which we owe to our Eternal Father and his Son Jesus Christ. To fear the Lord is to love him. That is the sense in which the word is used. The Lord is not asking us to be afraid of him, but to draw near unto him, and the greatest of all the commandments is, that we love him.[17]

HOW GOD PROGRESSES

GOD HAS ALL POWER AND WISDOM. My grandfather, Hyrum Smith, at the conference of the Church, April, 1844, in the course of his remarks said: "I want to put down all false influences. If I thought I should be saved and any in the congregation be lost, I should not be happy. For this purpose Jesus effected a resurrection. Our Savior is competent to save all from death and hell [i.e. by repentance]. I can prove it out of the revelations. *I would not serve a God that had not all wisdom and all power."*

Do we believe that God has all "wisdom"? If so, in that, he is absolute. If there is something he does not know, then he is not absolute in "wisdom," and to think such a thing is absurd. Does he have all "power"? If so then there is nothing in which he lacks. If he is lacking in "wisdom" and in "power" then he is not supreme and there must be something greater than he is, and this is absurd.

---

[17]D. & C. 45:39; 76:5; Acts 10:34-35; Ps. 111:10; 112:1; Prov. 1:7; Eccles. 12:13.

JOSEPH SMITH TEACHES OMNIPOTENCE OF GOD. In the Lectures on Faith, which appeared in the earlier editions of the *Doctrine and Covenants*, we find the following which was prepared by the Prophet Joseph Smith: *"There are two personages [i.e. of flesh and bones] who constitute the great, matchless, governing, and supreme, power over all things,* by whom all things were created and made, that are created and made, whether visible or invisible, whether in heaven, on earth, or in the earth, under the earth, or throughout the immensity of space. They are the Father and the Son—*the Father being a personage of spirit,*[18] *glory, and power, possessing all perfection and fulness, the Son,* who was in the bosom of the Father, a personage of tabernacle, made or fashioned like unto man, or being in the form and likeness of man, or rather man was formed after his likeness and in his image; he is also the express image and likeness of the personage of the Father, possessing all the fulness of the Father, or the same fulness with the Father."[19]

"*God is the only supreme governor and independent being in whom all fulness and perfection dwell; who is omnipotent, omnipresent, and omniscient;* without beginning of days or end of life; and that in him every good gift and every good principle dwell."[20]

"*Without the knowledge of all things God would not be able to save any portion of his creatures;* for it is by reason of the knowledge which he has of all things, from the beginning to the end, that enables him to give that understanding to his creatures by which they are made partakers of eternal life; and *if it were not for the idea existing in the minds of men that God had all knowl-*

---

[18]The Father and the Son are personages of spirit and of tabernacle. As here used these expressions are synonymous and interchangeable. Both personages have resurrected bodies. A resurrected body of flesh and bones is a spiritual body in scriptural terminology. Thus Paul says: "It is sown a natural body; it is raised a spiritual body. There is a natural body, and there is a spiritual body. And so it is written, The first man Adam was made a living soul; the last Adam was made a quickening spirit." 1 Cor. 15:44-45. Thus also the Lord says: "For notwithstanding they die, they also shall rise again, a spiritual body." D. & C. 88:27. B. R. M.
[19]Lectures on Faith, lec. 5, para. 2.   [20]*Ibid.*, lec. 2, para. 2.

CHARACTER, ATTRIBUTES, AND PERFECTIONS OF GOD

edge it would be impossible for them to exercise faith in him."[21]

PROGRESSION BY INCREASING HIS CREATIONS. The Book of Moses informs us that the great work of the Father is in creating worlds and peopling them, and "there is no end to my works, neither to my words," he says, "For behold, this is my work and my glory—to bring to pass the immortality and eternal life of man,"[22] *and in this is his progression.*

Commenting on this the Prophet Joseph Smith has said: "What did Jesus do? Why; I do the things I saw my Father do when worlds come rolling into existence. My Father worked out his kingdom with fear and trembling, and I must do the same [that is Christ must do the same]; and *when I get my kingdom, I shall present it to my Father,* so that he may obtain kingdom upon kingdom, and *it will exalt him in glory. He will then take a higher exaltation, and I [Christ]* will take his place, and thereby become exalted myself. So that Jesus treads in the tracks of his Father, and inherits what God did before; and God is thus glorified and exalted in the salvation and exaltation of all his children."[23]

Do you not see that it is in this manner that our Eternal Father is progressing? Not by seeking knowledge which he does not have, for such a thought cannot be maintained in the light of scripture. It is not through ignorance and learning hidden truth that he progresses, for *if there are truths which he does not know, then these things are greater than he, and this cannot be.* Why can't we learn wisdom and believe what the Lord has revealed?

HOW GOD DOES NOT PROGRESS

FALSE NOTIONS ABOUT GOD'S PROGRESSION. It seems very strange to me that members of the Church will hold to the doctrine, "God increases in knowledge

---
[21]*Ibid.,* lec. 4, para. 11.
[22]Moses 1:38-39.
[23]Smith, *op. cit.,* pp. 347-348.

as time goes on." Or that they can believe (as a recently published article says): "If absolute perfection were attainable, there would eventually come a time when those who had chosen the better way would reach the ultimate; and if the ultimate could be gained, progression would cease. This cannot be, for as before specified nothing in nature remains at a standstill. When progression abdicates the throne, retrogression is the degrading successor."

But, how does anyone know? Where has the Lord ever revealed to us that he is lacking in knowledge? That he is still learning new truth; discovering new laws that are unknown to him? I think this kind of doctrine is very dangerous. I don't know where the Lord has ever declared such a thing. It is not contained in any revelation that I have read. Man's opinion unaided by the revelations of the Lord, does not make it so.

PERFECTION OF GOD NOT "RELATIVE." I believe that *God knows all things* and that *his understanding is perfect, not "relative."* I have never seen or heard of any revealed fact to the contrary. I believe that our Heavenly Father and his Son Jesus Christ are *perfect.* I offer no excuse for the simplicity of my faith.

Who dares say that the quality of "virtue" is limited with our Father and his Son? *Is their truthfulness only "relative"? Could they be more truthful? More honorable? More virtuous or loving?* How foolish such questions are, and how much more foolish would be the answer if we said: "Yes, the Lord is limited in his truthfulness, honor, virtue." Well, if he is absolute in these qualities, is he on the road of retrogression in them? According to the argument this must be so if the absolute is reached. Then why should we say that his knowledge is limited and that hidden law and truths abound which he has not discovered. Who made those laws and where do they come from?

CHARACTER, ATTRIBUTES, AND PERFECTIONS OF GOD

SCRIPTURES PROVE OMNIPOTENCE OF GOD. I believe, literally, what is written in these scriptures:

"O how great the holiness of our God! For *he knoweth all things, and there is not anything save he knows it.*"[24]

"Thus saith the Lord your God, even *Jesus Christ, the Great I AM, Alpha and Omega,* the beginning and the end, the same which looked upon the wide expanse of eternity, and all the seraphic hosts of heaven, before the world was made;

"*The same which knoweth all things,* for all things are present before mine eyes."[25]

"And now, verily I say unto you, I was in the beginning with the Father, and am the Firstborn; . . .

"The Spirit of truth is of God. I am the Spirit of truth, and John bore record of me, saying: *He received a fulness of truth, yea, even of all truth.*"[26]

"Now have we not reason to rejoice? Yea, I say unto you, there never were men that had so great reason to rejoice as we, since the world began; yea, and my joy is carried away, even unto boasting in my God; for *he has all power, all wisdom, and all understanding; he comprehendeth all things,* and he is a merciful Being, even unto salvation, to those who will repent and believe on his name."[27]

"Praise ye the Lord: for it is good to sing praises unto our God; for it is pleasant; and praise is comely. . . .

"*Great is our Lord, and of great power: his understanding is infinite.*"[28]

"*He comprehendeth all things,* and all things are before him, and all things are round about him; and he is above all things, and in all things, and is through all things, and is round about all things; and all things are by him, and of him, even God, for ever and ever."

---
[24] 2 Ne. 9:20.
[25] *D. & C.* 38:1-2; 88:7-13.
[26] *D. & C.* 93:21, 26.
[27] Alma 26:35.
[28] Ps. 147:1, 5.

The next verse (42) is very significant in revealing to us something regarding the laws:

"And again, verily I say unto you, *he hath given a law unto all things*, by which they move in their times and their seasons."[29]

GOD PROGRESSES BECAUSE OF KNOWLEDGE. It is not because the Lord is ignorant of law and truth that he is able to progress, but *because* of his knowledge and wisdom. The Lord is constantly using his knowledge in his work. And his great work is in bringing to pass the immortality and eternal life of man. By the creation of worlds and peopling them, by building and extending, he progresses, but *not* because the fulness of truth is not understood by him.[30]

WILL GOD DESTROY HIMSELF? I cannot comprehend God in his perfection having to spend time discovering laws and truth he does not know. Such a thought to me is destructive, not progressive. Should there be truth which God has not discovered, when may he discover it, and, like a chemist who mixes certain elements and blows himself up, *when will the Almighty find some hidden truth or law which will shatter all?* Is there not a danger that some other personage may discover some greater truth than our Father knows? If such could be the case, what would become of God?

HOW GOD IS EVERLASTING

GOD IS AN EXALTED MAN. Some people are troubled over the statements of the Prophet Joseph Smith as found in the King Follett sermon delivered in Nauvoo in 1844. The matter that seems such a mystery is the statement that our Father in heaven at one time passed through a life and death and is an exalted man. This is one of the mysteries, and to some it appears to contradict other statements in the scriptures. Naturally there are many

---

[29]*D. & C.* 88:41-42.   [30]*D. & C.* 84:38; 93:16-17; Matt. 28:18; Moro. 7:22.

CHARACTER, ATTRIBUTES, AND PERFECTIONS OF GOD

things that we will not comprehend while in this mortal life and we will not be able to fathom all of the difficulties that lie before us. Our understanding is limited and we judge according to the things we know and with which we are familiar. The things of eternity we will not understand until we reach the goal of eternal life, when all things will be made clear.

We read in the scriptures that God is "infinite and eternal, from everlasting to everlasting the same unchangeable God";[31] that he is "the same yesterday, today, and forever";[32] that he "is unchangeable from all eternity to all eternity."[33] How does this conform to the Prophet's teaching: "God himself was once as we are now, and is an exalted man, . . . that he was once a man like us; yea, that God himself, the Father of us all, dwelt on an earth, the same as Jesus Christ himself did"?[34]

CHRIST BORN; YET FROM EVERLASTING. Now I suppose that we all understand the fact that Jesus Christ was Jehovah, who led Israel in the days of Abraham and Moses, and in fact from the days of Adam. Also that Jehovah, or Jesus Christ, as a personage of Spirit appeared to the Brother of Jared, and that he was born a babe in this world and grew to manhood in this world and therefore he did not always have a tangible body. Yet Jesus says of himself that he is "the first and the last,"[35] and that he is "the beginning and the end, the same which looked upon the wide expanse of eternity, and all the seraphic hosts of heaven, before the world was made."[36]

The Prophet says: "If Jesus Christ was the Son of God, and John discovered that God the Father of Jesus Christ had a Father, you may suppose that he had a Father also." Then he asks: "Where was there ever a son without a father? And where was there ever a father

---
[31]D. & C. 20:17.
[32]Morm. 9:9.
[33]Moro. 8:18.
[34]Smith, op. cit., pp. 345-346.
[35]D. & C. 110:4.
[36]D. & C. 38:1; Micah 5:2.

without first being a son?"[37] He points out that the Savior declared that he would do the things his Father did, that is, lay down his life and take it again.[38]

Let me ask, are we not taught that we as sons of God may become like him?[39] Is not this a glorious thought? Yet we have to pass through mortality and receive the resurrection and then go on to perfection just as our Father did before us. The Prophet taught that our Father had a Father and so on. Is not this a reasonable thought, especially when we remember that the promises are made to us that we may become like him?

How God is from Eternity to Eternity. However, the thing that seems so puzzling is the statement that God is "the same yesterday, today and forever"; that he is "from all eternity to all eternity." Well, is not this true, and is there any conflict with the thought that he has passed through the same states that we are destined to do? *From eternity to eternity means from the spirit existence through the probation which we are in, and then back again to the eternal existence which will follow.* Surely this is everlasting, for when we receive the resurrection, we will never die. We all existed in the first eternity. I think I can say of myself and others, we are *from* eternity; and *we will be to eternity everlasting, if we receive the exaltation.* The intelligent part of man was never created but always existed. That is true of each of us as well as it is of God, yet we are born sons and daughters of God in the spirit and are destined to exist forever. *Those who become like God will also be from eternity to eternity.*[40]

REVERENCE FOR GOD

Profaning Name of Deity. We should hold the name of Deity in the most sacred and solemn respect.[41] Few things are so distressing or shock the feelings of a

---
[37]Smith, op. cit., p. 373.
[38]Smith, op. cit., p. 346.
[39]1 John 3:1-3.
[40]Pers. Corresp.
[41]D. & C. 63:60-64; Ex. 20:7; Lev. 22:32; Deut. 5:11.

refined person more than to hear some uncouth, ignorant, or filthy creature bandy around the name of Deity. Some individuals have become so profane that it appears almost impossible for them to speak two or three sentences without the emphasis—as they think—of a vulgar or blasphemous oath. There are some individuals also who seem to think, at least that is the impression they leave upon others, that it is a manly accomplishment and elevates them from the common run of mankind if they can use blasphemous language.

PROFANITY IS FILTHINESS. A person is known as much by his language as he is by the company he keeps. People who swear and profane belong to the same class as do those who think, or leave the impression that they think, that to have a cigaret, cigar, or pipe in their mouth, lends dignity and manliness—do we have to say also womanliness?—to their character. Filthiness in any form is degrading and soul-destroying and should be avoided as a deadly poison by every member of the Church.

BLASPHEMY IN COMMON CONVERSATION. Good stories have been frequently ruined simply because the authors have not understood the propriety of the use of sacred names. When blasphemous expressions are placed in the mouths of otherwise respectable characters, instead of enhancing the story they detract from its value and interest. How strange it is that some people, and good people at that, think that to use some expression involving the name of the Lord, adds interest, wit, or power to their stories! How often this is seen in the moving pictures, even in shows that otherwise are commendable.

But all such expressions in the theatre, and the use of tobacco and liquor, are detrimental to the morals and spirituality of those who witness them, and especially is it true in the case of the youth of tender years whose character is in the formative stage. It is a shame that such expressions are found so frequently, even in the so-called higher class publications which come into the homes of Latter-day Saints.

Above all other peoples on the earth, the Latter-day Saints should hold in the utmost sacredness and reverence all things that are holy. The people of the world have not been trained as we have been in such matters, notwithstanding there are many honest, devout, and refined people in the world. But we have the guidance of the Holy Spirit and the revelations of the Lord, and he has solemnly taught us in our own day our duty in relation to all such things.

SOME HYMNS PROFANE DEITY. Even in some of the sacred hymns that are universally used, the frequent and familiar use of the name of the Lord enters, and spoils their use so far as we are concerned. A few hymns of this nature, with noble, uplifting thoughts, have found their way into the musical exercises of the Latter-day Saints.

PROPER USE OF LORD'S NAME. There are times, of course, when the use of the name of Deity is perfectly proper. The Lord has given us such examples in the blessings on the sacrament and the ordinance of baptism. The same is true in the conferring of the priesthood, for, as we have been taught, all things are to be done in the name of the Son; all our prayers should be addressed to the Father and brought to a close in the name of the Son.

IMPROPER USE OF LORD'S NAME IN PRAYERS. Even in this, however, we frequently hear improper expressions that jar on the sensitiveness of refined ears. Running the risk of criticism, I would like to call attention to a few expressions which it would be better not to use. At times we hear a very earnest, fervent prayer given in the spirit of pure humility and innocence, closed with this expression: "for Christ's sake. Amen." I never hear this expression that it does not bring to my mind the similar use by blasphemers on the streets. Of course, in the prayer, such a thing as an improper expression was not intended and never entered the mind of the one who prayed.

PRAYER IS FOR OUR SAKE. Then again, we do not pray or conduct exercises for his sake, but for our own. Our Redeemer has done everything that is essential for our salvation, and he has taught us that if we serve him with all our soul, and all our days, yet we are unprofitable servants and have done only that which it was our duty to do. Paul says we were bought with a price, and we are not our own.[42] Our Redeemer has a perfect right to command us, and all that we do is for our own sakes. He can do without us, but we cannot do without him. We are told that we are unprofitable servants,[43] and so we are, if we think of trying to pay our Savior back for what he has done for us, for that we never can do; and we cannot by any number of acts, or a full life of faithful service, place our Savior in our debt.

PRAY IN NAME OF CHRIST. How much better it is in our worship, and in our praying when we come to a conclusion, to end what we are doing, with a simple, humble statement, as we have been commanded to do, that it is done "in the name" of Jesus Christ, our Lord![44]

CHRIST OUR ELDER BROTHER. Another expression finding its place among us, especially on the part of speakers and writers on gospel themes, is to refer to our Lord as *the* Christ. Of course there is, and can be, no other. We have been given the information, however, that his name is Jesus Christ, and that he is the Only Begotten of the Father in the flesh, but the Firstborn in the spirit. He is our Elder Brother and was honored by the Father with the fulness of authority and power as a member of the grand Presidency, of Father, Son, and Holy Ghost. He was commissioned, before the world was framed, to come to this earth and here offer himself a sacrifice, through the shedding of his blood for the sins

---

[42] 1 Cor. 6:20; 7:23.
[43] Mosiah 2:20-25; Luke 17:5-10.
[44] *D. & C.* 18:18, 40; 20:29; 24:5; 42:3; 46:31; 50:29; 93:19; John 14:13-14; 15:16; 16:23-26.

of mankind, on condition of their true repentance, and for the transgression of our first parents which brought our fallen, mortal state.

WHEN TO USE TITLE: "THE CHRIST." The name *Christ* is a title comparable to the title *Messiah* and meaning *The Anointed One,* and has reference to the *office* of our Savior. If the remarks of a speaker have reference to the nature and calling of our Lord in the office which he holds, then the definite article preceding the name is in perfect order. However, when we are speaking of the Redeemer in some other sense than by reference to his official title, it is well for us not to use the article, but the whole name of our Lord, or, even better still, in order to avoid the too frequent repetition, we can say our *Redeemer* or *Savior* or *the Lord.*

The great lesson for us to learn, in all our preaching, writing, and conversations, is to use the titles of Deity sparingly, not with familiarity, or with lack of reverence.[45]

DID THE FATHER EAT WITH ABRAHAM?

LORD APPEARED TO ABRAHAM. We are not justified in teaching that our Heavenly Father, with other heavenly persons, came down, dusty and weary, and ate with Abraham. This is not taught in the 18th chapter of Genesis. The first verse of that chapter should read as follows: "And the Lord appeared unto him in the plains of Mamre." That is a complete thought. The second part of this paragraph has nothing to do with the Lord's appearing to Abraham, and there should be another paragraph or sentence saying: "And he sat in the tent door in the heat of the day; and he lifted up his eyes and looked, and, lo, three men stood by him." These three men were mortals. They had bodies and were able to eat, to bathe, and sit and rest from their weariness. Not one of these three was the *Lord.*

ABRAHAM ENTERTAINED HIS BRETHREN. I will

---
[45]*Era,* vol. 44, pp. 525, 572, 573, 575.

CHARACTER, ATTRIBUTES, AND PERFECTIONS OF GOD 17

give you a key: It was natural for the English to translate, as in verse three, and say "My Lord" in referring to a distinguished individual, because that is the way they recognized distinguished characters; but you will notice that the word *Lord* in the third paragraph is spelled with one capital and three small letters which indicates that it was not *the Lord* that was meant. Now in verses 13, 14, 17-20, you will find all of the letters in capitals and that does refer to THE LORD. Now according to the Prophet's revision of this scripture, the third verse reads as follows: "My brethren, if now I have found favor in your sight, pass not away I pray you from thy servant."[46]

DID JACOB WRESTLE WITH AN ANGEL?

MESSENGER BLESSES JACOB. Who wrestled with Jacob on Mount Peniel? The scriptures say it was a man. The Bible interpreters say it was an angel. More than likely it was a messenger sent to Jacob to give him the blessing. To think he wrestled and held an angel who couldn't get away, is out of the question. The term *angel* as used in the scriptures, at times, refers to messengers who are sent with some important instruction. Later in this chapter when Jacob said he had beheld the Lord, that did not have reference to his wrestling.[47]

---
[46]Gen. 18:1-20; *Inspired Version,* Gen. 18:1-19. [47]Pers. Corresp.; Gen. 32:24-30.

CHAPTER 2

THE SON OF GOD

THE ONLY BEGOTTEN SON

THE FIRSTBORN. Our Father in heaven is the Father of Jesus Christ, both in the spirit and in the flesh. Our Savior is the Firstborn in the spirit,[1] the Only Begotten in the flesh.[2]

CHRIST NOT BEGOTTEN OF HOLY GHOST. I believe firmly that Jesus Christ is the Only Begotten Son of God in the flesh. He taught this doctrine to his disciples.[3] He did not teach them that he was the Son of the Holy Ghost, but the Son of the Father. Truly, all things are done by the *power* of the Holy Ghost. It was through this power that Jesus was brought into this world, but not as the Son of the Holy Ghost, but the Son of God. Jesus is greater than the Holy Spirit, which is subject unto him,[4] but his Father is greater than he![5] He has said it. Christ was begotten of God. He was not born without the aid of Man, and *that Man was God!*

CHRIST NOT REINCARNATED. Christ was born a babe at Bethlehem. That is where he got his body, and the only physical body, or body of flesh and bones, that he ever had or ever will have. The doctrine of reincarnation is, says the Prophet Joseph, the doctrine of the devil![6] Of course the devil will teach people any doctrine that will contradict the truth. The great works accomplished by our Redeemer before he was born, including the creation of worlds at the command of his Father, were accomplished by him in his spirit existence.[7]

---

[1] D. & C. 93:21; Col. 1:15; Rom. 8:29.
[2] D. & C. 20:21; 29:42, 46; 49:5.
[3] John 3:18.
[4] John 15:26; 16:7.
[5] John 14:28.
[6] Joseph Fielding Smith, Teachings of the Prophet Joseph Smith, pp. 104-105.
[7] Pers. Corresp.; Ether 3:6-16; Moses 1:31-33; John 1:1-14; Heb. 1:1-4.

THE SON OF GOD

FALSE "REORGANITE" DOCTRINE ABOUT BIRTH OF CHRIST. "Reorganites" claim that Brigham Young went astray and apostatized because he declared that Jesus Christ was not begotten of the Holy Ghost. "Reorganites" claim that he was begotten of the Holy Ghost, and they make the statement that the scriptures so teach. But they do err not understanding the scriptures. They tell us the *Book of Mormon* states that Jesus was begotten of the Holy Ghost. I challenge the statement. The *Book of Mormon* teaches no such thing! Neither does the *Bible*. It is true there is one passage that states so, but we must consider it in the light of other passages with which it is in conflict.

CHRIST CONCEIVED BY POWER OF HOLY GHOST. The *Book of Mormon* says: "And behold, he shall be born of Mary, at Jerusalem which is the land of our forefathers, she being a virgin, a precious and chosen vessel, who shall be overshadowed and conceive *by the power* of the Holy Ghost, and bring forth a son, yea, even the Son of God."[8]

With this Luke agrees: "Then said Mary unto the angel, How shall this be, seeing I know not a man? And the angel answered and said unto her, The Holy Ghost shall come upon thee, and *the power of the Highest* shall overshadow thee: therefore also that holy thing which shall be born of thee shall be called the Son of God."[9]

In Matthew it reads "of the Holy Ghost,"[10] which evidently means "power of the Holy Ghost," to agree with the *Book of Mormon* and with Luke.

CHRIST NOT SON OF THE HOLY GHOST. If "Reorganites" are correct, then Jesus is not the Only Begotten Son of the Father, but the Son of the Holy Ghost. This will not do for it conflicts with the scriptures. The Prophet taught that the Father, Son, and Holy Ghost were three separate personages, and that Jesus was the

---
[8]Alma 7:10.
[9]Luke 1:34-35.
[10]Matt. 1:18.

Only Begotten of the Father. In the Book of Genesis (*Inspired Version*), Jesus is spoken of throughout as the *Only Begotten of the Father* not less than 12 times, and in the *Book of Mormon* at least five times, and a great number of times in the *Doctrine and Covenants;* and in these scriptures he is spoken of as the Son of God innumerable times.

Now, if he is the *Only Begotten* of the Father in flesh, he must be the Son of the Father and not the Son of the Holy Ghost. Yet, to be consistent, "Reorganites" must claim that Jesus is the Son of the Holy Ghost and not the Son of God the Father. Their alternative—if it can be called such—must be, then, the stand of Mr. William H. Kelley, "president" of their "apostles," who gave a written statement in answer to the question put to him by the writer, September 10, 1903: "You say that Jesus Christ, the Son of God, was begotten of the Holy Ghost. Is he the Son of the Holy Ghost?"

Mr. Kelley signed his answer as follows: "*I do not know.* Wm. H. Kelley."

Just think of this for a moment. Here is a man professing to be the chief of the special witnesses for Christ, declaring that he does not know whether Jesus is the Son of God the Father or the Son of the Holy Ghost. And the Savior declared it so plainly that he was the Son of the Father, his Only Begotten, and was so acknowledged by the Father throughout the scriptures. "And this is life eternal, that they might know thee the only true God, and Jesus Christ, whom thou hast sent."[11]

ADVENT AND MISSION OF CHRIST FORETOLD

SHILOH PROPHECY. When Jacob blessed his son Judah, he declared that the scepter should not depart from Judah until Shiloh come.[12] Who is Shiloh? He is Christ. And Judah had the scepter in Israel or Judah, until the days of Christ.

---

[11]*Origin of the "Reorganized" Church,* pp. 91-93; John 17:3.   [12]Gen. 49:10.

THE SON OF GOD

Joseph who was sold into Egypt foretold the delivery of Israel from that land by Moses. In that prophecy he says that Christ is Shilo. He said: "The Lord God will raise up . . . unto thee, whom my father Jacob hath named Israel, a prophet; (*not the Messiah who is called Shilo;*) and this prophet shall deliver my people out of Egypt in the days of thy bondage."[13]

The Shiloh prophecy has reference to the authority which should in course of time be conferred upon the descendants, or tribe of Judah, when Israel became established in the land of their inheritance. This authority was to be that of kingly rule or exercise of authority in making and enforcing the law.

FULFILLMENT OF SHILOH PROPHECY. This prophecy was fulfilled, for after Judah came to power in Israel, when David was exalted to the throne, that tribe held authority until the time of the coming of Christ. Even after the division of the kingdom into the two kingdoms, Judah and Israel, still kings of Judah sat on the throne until the time of the captivity 600 years before Christ.

Judah continued even during the captivity and after the return to Palestine 70 years later to have lawgivers for the Jews. Daniel and others in Babylon held power, and as prophets directed the people. When they returned under Zorababbel (who was the legal descendant of David, and who acted as governor of Jerusalem), and when Ezra and others rebuilt the temple and Jerusalem, they were still directed by lawgivers. Eventually the Sanhedrin was established and it continued in this capacity until after the death of Christ, when in the destruction of Jerusalem and the scattering of the Jews that authority ceased on the earth; and the Jews had no lawgiver unto whom they could turn. It is true that there were times when these lawgivers were iniquitous and did wrong, but nevertheless this prophecy was fulfilled.[14]

---

[13]Pers. Corresp.; *Inspired Version*, Gen. 50:24. [14]*Church News*, Sept. 23, 1933, pp. 3, 8.

BRAZEN SERPENT A SIMILITUDE OF CHRIST. In the third chapter of John, we have the account of the Lord's conversation with Nicodemus in which the Lord said: "And as Moses lifted up the serpent in the wilderness, even so must the Son of man be lifted up: That whosoever believeth in him should not perish, but have eternal life."[15] Do you recall how in the wilderness when they came among the serpents, the Lord told Moses to put a brazen serpent upon a pole and they who looked upon it should be healed, for some of them were dying when bitten? That was done in the similitude of our Lord's being lifted upon the cross, so that all who believed in him should not perish.[16]

ANIMAL SACRIFICE A SIMILITUDE OF CHRIST. When the Israelites left Egypt, the Lord gave them the passover.[17] They were to take a lamb without blemish; they were not to break any of its bones. They were to kill it, cook it, and eat it with bitter herbs and unleavened bread. This feast they were to remember annually thereafter until Christ should come. This was also in the similitude of the sacrifice of Jesus Christ. If you stop to consider it, it was at the time of the passover that our Lord was taken and crucified in fulfillment of the promises that had been made that he would come to be our Redeemer.[18]

All these things point to his coming and to his ministry. In fact sacrifice goes right back to the days of Adam. Animal sacrifices were to be without blemish, for it was in the similitude of the sacrifice of Jesus Christ, and pointed to his coming. We do not learn much in the Book of Genesis what sacrifice was for, because the plain things pertaining to sacrifice have been removed.[19]

When Noah came out of the Ark the first thing that he did was to take a clean animal and offer sacrifice,

---

[15]John 3:14-15.
[16]Nu. 21:6-9; Alma 33:19-20; Hela. 8:13-15.
[17]Ex. 12:3-51.
[18]Matt. 26:17-75; 27:1-50; Mark 14:12-72; 15:1-38; Luke 22:7-71; 23:1-46; 1 Cor. 5:7.
[19]1 Ne. 13:24-26.

THE SON OF GOD

although animals were scarce. In the Book of Moses in the *Pearl of Great Price*, we get the full understanding why sacrifice was practiced.[20] It is because it pointed to the sacrifice of Jesus Christ, and every animal had to be without spot or blemish. When Christ was crucified, he was placed on the cross between two thieves. The bones of the thieves were broken, but not the bones of the Savior.

ISAIAH FORETELLS LIFE OF CHRIST. I want to read to you the 53rd chapter of Isaiah. Now *Bible* commentators will tell you that this has nothing to do with the life of Jesus Christ. To them this story is one concerning suffering Israel. I want to tell you that it is a story, a synopsis of the life of our Redeemer, revealed to Isaiah 700 years before the Lord was born. If you have the proper discernment you will discover this. I am going to make some comments on it as I read it.

HE OUTWARDLY APPEARED AS OTHER MEN. "Who hath believed our report? and to whom is the arm of the Lord revealed? For he shall grow up before him as a tender plant, and as a root out of a dry ground: he hath no form nor comeliness; and when we shall see him, there is no beauty that we should desire him."

What is the meaning of that? Did not Christ grow up as a tender plant? There was nothing about him to cause people to single him out. In appearance he was like men; and so it is expressed here by the prophet that he had no form or comeliness, that is, he was not so distinctive, so different from others that people would recognize him as the Son of God. He appeared as a mortal man.

CHRIST A MAN OF SORROWS. "He is despised and rejected of men; a man of sorrows, and acquainted with grief: and we hid as it were our faces from him; he was despised, and we esteemed him not. Surely he hath

---
[20]Moses 5:5-8.

borne our griefs, and carried our sorrows: yet we did esteem him stricken, smitten of God, and afflicted."

Was not Christ a man of sorrows? Was he not rejected of men? Was he not acquainted with grief? Did not the people (figuratively) hide their faces from him? Did not the people esteem him not? Surely he knew our griefs and carried our sorrows, but he was thought to be stricken of God and forsaken by him. Did not the people say that? How true all these things are!

HIS SUFFERING FORETOLD. "But he was wounded for our transgressions, he was bruised for our iniquities: the chastisement of our peace was upon him; and with his stripes we are healed."

Now this is poetic language of course. Why should it not be? But can't you get the true picture? Was he not wounded for our transgressions and bruised for our iniquities? Was he not chastised for us, and if we will believe on him, are we not healed with his stripes?

"All we like sheep have gone astray; we have turned every one to his own way; and the Lord hath laid on him the iniquity of us all."

Does not the gospel teach us that he carried the burden of our sins and that we as sheep have strayed away?

"He was oppressed, and he was afflicted, yet he opened not his mouth: he is brought as a lamb to the slaughter, and as a sheep before her shearers is dumb, so he openeth not his mouth."

Is this not true of Christ? Can you not read it in the gospels?

"He was taken from prison and from judgment: and who shall declare his generation? for he was cut off out of the land of the living: for the transgression of my people was he stricken."

It was for our transgressions that he died. And who are mentioned as his generation? Those who accept him and keep his commandments.

THE SON OF GOD

"And he made his grave with the wicked, and with the rich in his death; because he had done no violence, neither was any deceit in his mouth."

Was he not buried among the wicked, and was not the sepulchre in which he was placed one belonging to the rich? Surely there was no deceit in his mouth for he was perfect.

HE SHALL SEE HIS SEED. "Yet it pleased the Lord to bruise him; he hath put him to grief: when thou shalt make his soul an offering for sin, he shall see his seed, he shall prolong his days, and the pleasure of the Lord shall prosper in his hand."

The Father "so loved the world, that he gave his only begotten Son, that whosoever believeth in him should not perish, but have everlasting life."[21]

"He shall see of the travail of his soul, and shall be satisfied: by his knowledge shall my righteous servant justify many; for he shall bear their iniquities. Therefore will I divide him a portion with the great, and he shall divide the spoil with the strong; because he hath poured out his soul unto death; and he was numbered with the transgressors; and he bare the sin of many, and made intercession for the transgressors."[22]

THE SEED OF CHRIST. Is this not just as clear as sunshine, at least to those who have the inspiration of the Spirit of the Lord? In the 15th chapter of Mosiah, Abinadi comments on this chapter in Isaiah and makes it plain. He declares that the seed of Christ are those who believe in him.[23] Christ was numbered with the transgressors and he bare the sins of many, but he made intercession for the transgressors, and through their repentance gives unto them eternal life.

In relation to his seed, I wish to quote the words of King Benjamin in the 5th chapter of Mosiah: "And now, because of the covenant which ye have made ye

[21]John 3:16.
[22]Isa. 53:1-12.
[23]Mosiah 14:1-12; 15:1-20.

shall be called the children of Christ, his sons, and his daughters; for behold, this day he hath spiritually begotten you; for ye say that your hearts are changed through faith on his name; therefore, ye are born of him and have become his sons and his daughters."[24]

These and all who have made such covenants are the "seed" of Christ.[25]

OUR ADVOCATE AND OUR MEDIATOR

FATHER PRESENT IN EDEN. When Adam was in the Garden of Eden he was in the presence of the Father and was taught by him. He learned his language. He was as familiar with our Eternal Father in that garden as we are with our fathers in mortal life. The first part of Genesis dealing with the creation and with Adam in the Garden of Eden is when the Father was present with him.[26]

After he partook of the forbidden fruit, Adam and Eve were cast out of that garden and likewise out of the presence of the Father. He was banished because of his transgression, and became spiritually dead—that is, he was shut out from the presence of God.[27]

CHRIST STANDS BETWEEN MAN AND THE FATHER. Then Jesus Christ came upon the scene as the Mediator between man and God, and the Advocate for man with the Father. He pleads our cause. As our Mediator, through his ministry, he labors to reconcile us, to bring us into agreement with God his Father.[28]

An advocate is one who defends or pleads for or in behalf of another. A mediator is one who reconciles or brings about agreement between parties.

That is part of his great mission. He stands between the Father and man. When he was upon earth, he prayed frequently for his disciples, pleading with his

---
[24]Mosiah 5:7.
[25]*Church News*, July 23, 1952, pp. 5, 14.
[26]Gen. 1, 2, 3; Moses 2, 3, 4.
[27]D. & C. 29:41-42.
[28]D. & C. 29:5; 45:3-4; 62:1; 76:69; 107:18-19; 2 Ne. 2:9-10; Moro. 7:27-28; Rom. 8:34; Gal. 3:19-20; 1 Tim. 2:5-6; Heb. 7:25; 1 John 2:1.

THE SON OF GOD

Father in their behalf,[29] and he has been pleading ever since, and he stands between us and God our Father.

JEHOVAH GIVES ALL REVELATION. All revelation since the fall has come through Jesus Christ, who is the Jehovah of the Old Testament. In all of the scriptures, where God is mentioned and where he has appeared, it was Jehovah who talked with Abraham, with Noah, Enoch, Moses and all the prophets. He is the God of Israel, the Holy One of Israel; the one who led that nation out of Egyptian bondage, and who gave and fulfilled the Law of Moses.[30] The Father has never dealt with man directly and personally since the fall, and he has never appeared except to introduce and bear record of the Son. Thus the *Inspired Version* records that "no man hath seen God at any time, except he hath borne record of the Son."[31]

Exodus 6:3 in the King James version is a mistranslation. It reads: "And I appeared unto Abraham, unto Isaac, and unto Jacob, by the name of God Almighty, but by my name JEHOVAH was I not known to them." Now we know that Jehovah is Christ, and here is a statement that it was not our Savior who appeared to these ancient prophets. However, in the revision of the scriptures by the Prophet Joseph, the passage reads as follows: "And I appeared unto Abraham, unto Isaac, and unto Jacob. I am the Lord God Almighty; the Lord JEHOVAH. And was not my name known unto them?"[32]

CHRIST MAY SPEAK AS THE FATHER. In giving revelations our Savior speaks at times for himself; at other times for the Father, and in the Father's name, as though he were the Father, and yet it is Jesus Christ, our Redeemer who gives the message. So, we see, in *Doctrine and Covenants* 29:1, that he introduces himself as "Jesus Christ, your Redeemer," but in the closing

---
[29]Luke 22:31-32; John 17:11-26.   [31]*Inspired Version*, John 1:19.
[30]1 Ne. 19:10; 3 Ne. 11:10, 14; 15:2-9.   [32]*Ibid.*, Ex. 6:3.

part of the revelation he speaks for the Father, and in the Father's name as though he were the Father,[33] and yet it is still Jesus who is speaking, for the Father has put his name on him for that purpose.

FIRST VISION AND REVELATION. We have a wonderful illustration of how revelation comes through Christ presented to us in the Vision given to the Prophet Joseph Smith. The Father and the Son appeared unto him, but it was not the Father who answered his question! The Father introduced Joseph to his Son, and it was the Son who answered the important question and gave the instruction.[34]

Had Joseph Smith come home from the grove and declared that the Father and the Son appeared to him and that the Father spoke to him and answered his question while the Son stood silently by, then we could have accepted the story as a fraud. Joseph Smith was too young and inexperienced to know this at the time, but he made no mistake, and his story was in perfect harmony with divine truth, with the divine law that Christ is the Mediator between God and man.

CHRIST THE FATHER AND THE SON

FATHER BECAUSE OF THE ATONEMENT. Our scriptures teach that Jesus Christ is both the Father and the Son.[35] The simple truth is that he is the Son of God by birth, both in the spirit and in the flesh. He is the Father because of the work that he has performed.

The difference between our Savior and the rest of us is that we have had fathers who were mortal and therefore subject to death. Our Savior did not have a mortal Father and therefore death was subject to him. He had power to lay down his life and to take it again, but we do not have power to lay down our lives and to

---

[33]D. & C. 29:42, 46.
[34]Joseph Smith 2:17-20.

[35]"The Father and the Son: A Doctrinal Exposition by the First Presidency and the Twelve," cited in Joseph Fielding Smith, *Man: His Origin and Destiny*, pp. 117-129.

take them again.[36] It is through the atonement of Jesus Christ that we receive eternal life, through the resurrection of the dead and obedience to the principles of the gospel.

The Savior becomes our Father, in the sense in which this term is used in the scriptures, because he offers us life, eternal life, through the atonement which he made for us. In the wonderful instruction given by King Benjamin we find this: "And now, because of the covenant which ye have made ye shall be called *the children of Christ, his sons, and his daughters;* for behold, this day *he hath spiritually begotten you;* for ye say that your hearts are changed through faith on his name; therefore, *ye are born of him and have become his sons and his daughters.*"[37]

So, we become the children, sons and daughters of Jesus Christ, through our covenants of obedience to him. Because of his divine authority and sacrifice on the cross, we become spiritually begotten sons and daughters, and he is our Father.

FATHER BY DIVINE INVESTITURE OF AUTHORITY. Christ is also our Father because his Father has given him of his fulness; that is, he has received a fulness of the glory of the Father. This is taught in *Doctrine and Covenants* 93:1-5, 16-17, and also by Abinadi in the 15th chapter of Mosiah. Abinadi's statement that he is "the Father, because he was conceived by the power of God," harmonizes with the Lord's own words in section 93 that he is the Father because he has received of the fulness of the Father. Christ says he is the Son because, "I was in the world and made flesh my tabernacle, and dwelt among the sons of men." Abinadi expresses this truth by saying he is "the Son because of the flesh."

The Father has honored Christ by placing his name upon him, so that he can minister in and through that name as though he were the Father; and thus, so far

---
[36]John 10:11-18.   [37]Mosiah 5:7; 15:10-13; *D. & C.* 39:1-3; 45:7-8.

as power and authority are concerned, his words and acts become and are those of the Father.

FATHER AS CREATOR. Our Lord is also called the Father in the sense that he is the Father or Creator of the heavens and the earth and all things.[38]

CHRIST ONLY HATH POWER OF IMMORTALITY

"SOUL-SLEEPERS" DENY IMMORTALITY. Perhaps the most important passage that the "soul-sleepers," as they are called, rely upon in their contention that the body is the soul of man (divested of life, save for a "short, average tenure of three score years and ten"), is Paul's reference to our Savior as "the King of kings, and Lord of lords; Who only hath immortality, dwelling in the light which no man can approach unto."[39] Basing their claims upon this passage, they argue that this is conclusive proof that man in no sense has the gift of immortality, and shall cease to exist when mortal death overtakes him.

SAINTS RESURRECTED WITH CHRIST. It is strange they will hold so tenaciously to this expression, interpreting it to mean that the Savior is the only one who has received the resurrection from the dead, and therefore the only one "who hath immortality," and overlook the fact recorded by Matthew that "the graves were opened; and many bodies of the saints which slept arose, And came out of the graves after his resurrection, and went into the holy city, and appeared unto many."[40] If these had also partaken of the resurrection, as we are assured by an eye witness, had they not also received the blessing of immortality and eternal life as well as the Son of God? It is recorded in the *Book of Mormon* that after the resurrection of Jesus Christ, the faithful dead on this continent also arose in the resurrection.[41]

---

[38]Pers. Corresp.; Mosiah 15:4; Alma 11:38-39; Ether 4:7.
[39]1 Tim. 6:15-16.
[40]Matt. 27:52-53.
[41]3 Ne. 23:9-10.

THE SON OF GOD

CHRIST HAD POWER OVER DEATH. This being true, what then did Paul mean by saying to Timothy, according to the King James *Bible*, that the Son of God "only hath immortality"? Simply this: That of all who have dwelt upon this earth, *the Son of God stands out alone as the only one who possessed life in himself and power over death inherently*. Christ was never subject unto death, even on the cross, but death was ever subject unto him. "As the Father hath life in himself," the Savior said, "so hath he given to the Son to have *life in himself*."[42] Again, he said: "Therefore doth my Father love me, because I lay down my life, *that I might take it again*. No man taketh it from me, but I lay it down of myself. I have power to lay it down, *and I have power to take it again*. This commandment have I received of my Father."[43]

Can any man say this? Is there anyone else who could truthfully say that he had life in himself, by which he could lay down his body and take it again? We are all subject to the mortal death, and none of us has power over death. The Savior, however, because he was the Only Begotten Son of the Father in the flesh, was endowed with life in himself from his birth, even as his Father had life in himself—which is immortality.[44]

THE LIGHT AND HOPE OF IMMORTALITY. With this understanding we can use this passage in Timothy effectively as it now reads. But the further fact is that this same controversial passage has not come down to us in the King James *Bible* with the same clarity it had when Paul wrote it. As corrected by the Prophet in the *Inspired Version* it declares that Christ is "the King of kings, and Lord of lords, to whom be honor and power everlasting; Whom no man hath seen, nor can see, unto whom no man can approach, only he who hath the light and the hope of immortality dwelling in him."[45]

---

[42]John 5:26.
[43]John 10:17-18.
[44]*Era*, vol. 19, pp. 198-199.
[45]*Inspired Version*, 1 Tim. 6:15-16.

CHRIST WORKED OUT HIS OWN SALVATION

CHRIST BEGAN MORTALITY AS MEN DO. Our Savior was a God before he was born into this world, and he brought with him that same status when he came here. He was as much a God when he was born into the world as he was before. But as far as this life is concerned it appears that he had to start just as all other children do and gain his knowledge line upon line. Luke says he "increased in wisdom and stature, and in favour with God and man."[46] John records that "he received not of the fulness at the first," but had to progress "from grace to grace, until he received a fulness."[47] Paul wrote, "Though he were a Son, yet learned he obedience by the things which he suffered."[48]

HOW HE GAINED LIGHT AND TRUTH. Evidently, before he was 12 years old—for then he astonished the doctors and wise men in the temple—he had learned a great deal about his Father's business.[49] This knowledge could come to him by revelation, by the visitation of angels, or in some other way. But his knowledge, so far as this life was concerned, had to come line upon line and precept upon precept. Without question he was in communication, from time to time, with his Heavenly Father.

The *Inspired Version* tells us: "Jesus grew up with his brethren, and waxed strong, and waited upon the Lord for the time of his ministry to come. And he served under his father, and he spake not as other men, neither could he be taught; for he needed not that any man should teach him. And after many years, the hour of his ministry drew nigh."[50]

HOW HE DID WHAT HE HAD SEEN THE FATHER DO. The statement of our Lord that he could do nothing but what he had seen the Father do,[51] means simply that

---
[46]Luke 2:52.
[47]*D. & C.* 93:6-16.
[48]Heb. 5:8.
[49]Luke 2:42-50.
[50]*Inspired Version*, Matt. 3:24-26.
[51]John 5:19-20.

it had been revealed to him what his Father had done. Without doubt, Jesus came into the world subject to the same condition as was required of each of us—he forgot everything, and he had to grow from grace to grace. His forgetting, or having his former knowledge taken away, would be requisite just as it is in the case of each of us, to complete the present temporal existence.

CHRIST GAINED FULNESS AFTER RESURRECTION. The Savior did not have a fulness at first, but after he received his body and the resurrection all power was given unto him both in heaven and in earth.[52] Although he was a God, even the Son of God, with power and authority to create this earth and other earths, yet there were some things lacking which he did not receive until after his resurrection. In other words he had not received the fulness until he got a resurrected body, and the same is true with those who through faithfulness become sons of God. Our bodies are essential to the fulness and the continuation of the seeds forever.[53]

TEACH THAT CHRIST WAS MORE THAN A MAN

EVENTUAL SORROW OF FALSE TEACHERS. If the worth of souls is great and our joy shall be great in heaven with those we may be able to bring unto the strait and narrow way, what will be our feelings if, through any teachings of ours, one soul is barred from the celestial kingdom? If that which we have taught and practiced shall destroy the faith of one individual so that he does not accept the truth, and that fact is made known unto us when we stand before the judgment seat, then, let me ask, how great will be our sorrow? How great will be the condemnation which we will merit in that we have barred, through our influence and through our teachings, one of the children of our Father from entering into eternal exaltation?

SEVERE PUNISHMENT FOR FALSE TEACHERS. I tell

---

[52]D. & C. 93:16-17; Matt. 28:18.   [53]Pers. Corresp.

you that these men who stand up and say that Jesus is not the Christ, that he was a great teacher, but not the Son of God, the Only Begotten of the Father, and thus lead many to deny the power of the resurrection and the divinity of Christ, are taking upon themselves a most terrible responsibility that should cause them to fear and tremble. I could not stand it to know that I had taught an untruth that would lead people to destruction. And when these men realize what they have done and that, not only their own souls have not been saved, but they have been the means of destroying the souls of other men, leading them away from truth and righteousness, I tell you that it shall be hard with them, and their punishment shall be most severe in eternity.[54]

HISTORICITY OF JESUS

ENEMIES OF CHRIST ADMIT HE LIVED. Many who deny the divinity of Jesus Christ are convinced of his historicity. One of the most persistent and determined foes of Jesus Christ in modern times admits that the evidence is beyond reasonable dispute and that Jesus Christ lived and taught the people of Judea. Moreover, he declares that Paul, the chief writer of epistles and advocate for Jesus Christ, was a real personality who came in contact with the Christians within the first decade after the death of Christ.

"Paul . . . habitually speaks of Cephas and others who were actual companions of Jesus. We have to deny the genuineness of all the epistles to doubt this. . . . He joined the Christian body and mingled with them in Jerusalem, within less than ten years of the execution of Jesus. No Jew there seems to have told him that Jesus was a mere myth. In all the bitter strife of Jew and Christian the idea seems to have occurred to nobody. Setting aside the gospels entirely, ignoring all the Latin writers are supposed to have said in the second century, we have a

---
[54]Conf. Rep., Apr., 1923, pp. 138-139; 2 Ne. 28:15.

THE SON OF GOD

large and roughly organized body of Christians at the time when men were still alive who remembered events of the fourth decade of the century.

"I conclude that it is more reasonable to believe in the historicity of Jesus. There is no parallel in history to the sudden growth of a myth and its conversion into a human personage in one generation. . . . From the earliest moment that we catch sight of Christians in history the essence of their belief is that Jesus was an incarnation, in Judea, of the great God of the universe. . . . So it seems to me far more reasonable, far more scientific, far more consonant with the facts of religious history which we know, to conclude that Jesus was a man who was gradually turned into a God."[55]

BOOK OF MORMON PROVES CHRIST LIVED. We have "a more sure word of prophecy," as Peter might put it, "whereunto ye do well that ye take heed,"[56] by which we may know that Jesus Christ lives and is indeed the Only Begotten Son of God.

The *Book of Mormon*, while an ancient record, has come to light within the knowledge of this generation. We all know how it was revealed and how it was translated, and that the Lord raised up witnesses, "as seemeth him good," who testified "to the truth of the book and the things therein." Moreover, the *Book of Mormon* was preserved, as it is recorded, to come forth in the latter days to bear witness of the truth of the record of the Jews (*Bible*), and to bear witness, "to the convincing of the Jew and Gentile that JESUS is the CHRIST, the ETERNAL GOD, manifesting himself unto all nations."[57] The *Book of Mormon* bears record of the personality and reality of Jesus Christ, both by prophecy uttered hundreds of years before he was born and by recording his personal appearance among the ancient people on this American continent. In this sacred volume we have his words recorded and the testimony of wit-

---

[55]Joseph McCabe, *The Story of Religious Controversy*, p. 228.
[56]2 Pet. 1:19.
[57]*Book of Mormon*, Title page.

nesses who saw him and unto whom he ministered after his resurrection.

CHRIST SEEN BY MODERN PROPHETS. However, we are not dependent upon the writings and the testimony of men who lived and wrote in ancient times. Although we accept their sayings, we have the testimony of witnesses of our own time. Joseph Smith, Oliver Cowdery, Sidney Rigdon, and others, have borne witness to the world—as they were commanded to do—that they saw Jesus Christ, conversed with him, were ministered to by him, and received from him instruction. These facts are recorded as they were written at the time. This testimony has gone forth into all the world and has been before the world for more than 100 years.

Joseph Smith and Oliver Cowdery were in the presence of the Lord Jesus Christ in the Kirtland Temple, April 3, 1836, and heard his voice.[58] Joseph Smith and Sidney Rigdon were in his presence February 16, 1832, and have given their testimony as follows: "And now, after the many testimonies which have been given of him, this is the testimony, last of all, which we give of him: *That he lives!* For we saw him, even on the right hand of God; and we heard the voice bearing record that he is the Only Begotten of the Father—That by him, and through him, and of him, the worlds are and were created, and the inhabitants thereof are begotten sons and daughters unto God."[59]

RIGHTEOUS MAY STILL SEE CHRIST. This testimony has gone forth into all the world. There are thousands who know it is true for they too have had witness borne in upon their souls. There are thousands who believe in the promise of the Lord, "that every soul who forsaketh his sins and cometh unto me, and calleth on my name, and obeyeth my voice, and keepeth my commandments, shall see my face and know that I am."[60] And

---
[58]*D. & C.* 110:1-10.
[59]*D. & C.* 76:22-24.
[60]*D. & C.* 93:1.

this promise is unto all men everywhere so that all may know if they will.[61]

APPEARANCE OF THE LORD TO BROTHER OF JARED

Christ Revealed Himself Partially to Some.

I have always considered Ether 3:15 to mean that the Savior stood before the Brother of Jared plainly, distinctly, and showed him his whole body and explained to him that he was a spirit. In his appearance to Adam and Enoch, he had not made himself manifest in such a familiar way. His appearances to earlier prophets had not been with that same fulness.

The scriptural accounts of talking face to face and of walking with God should not be interpreted in the sense that the Savior stood before those prophets and revealed his whole person. That he may have done so at later periods in the cases of Abraham and Moses is possible, but he had not done so in that fulness in the antediluvian days. For the Brother of Jared he removed the veil completely. He had never showed himself to man before in the manner and way he did to that prophet.[62]

---
[61]*Era*, vol. 33, pp. 725-726.   [62]Pers. Corresp.

CHAPTER 3

THE HOLY GHOST, LIGHT OF CHRIST, AND SECOND COMFORTER

THE HOLY GHOST

A PERSONAGE OF SPIRIT. The Holy Ghost is the third member of the Godhead. *He is a Spirit, in the form of a man.* The Father and the Son are personages of tabernacle; they have bodies of flesh and bones. The Holy Ghost is a personage of Spirit, and has a spirit body only.[1] His mission is to bear witness of the Father and the Son and of all truth.[2]

As a Spirit personage *the Holy Ghost has size and dimensions. He does not fill the immensity of space,* and cannot be everywhere present in person at the same time. He is also called the Holy Spirit, the Spirit of God, the Spirit of the Lord, the Spirit of Truth, and the Comforter.[3]

HOLY GHOST A REVELATOR. His mission is to teach us all truth. He partakes of the things of the Father and the Son and reveals them to those who serve the Lord in faithfulness. It was through the teachings of the Comforter, or Holy Ghost, that the teachings of Jesus Christ were recalled by the apostles.[4] It is through the teachings of the Holy Spirit that prophecy comes.[5]

GIFT OF HOLY GHOST COMES BY LAYING ON OF HANDS. The promise was made in the days of the primitive Church of Jesus Christ that all who would repent, be baptized for the remission of sins and would be faithful, should receive the gift of the Holy Ghost by the

---
[1] *D. & C.* 130:22-23.
[2] 2 Ne. 31:18; Moro. 10:5.
[3] Pers. Corresp.
[4] John 14:26.
[5] 2 Pet. 1:21.

laying on of hands. That same promise has been made to all who will accept the gospel in this dispensation, for the Lord says: "And whoso having faith you shall confirm in my church, by the laying on of the hands, and I will bestow the gift of the Holy Ghost upon them."[6]

It is the duty of the elders in the Church "to confirm those who are baptized into the church, by the laying on of hands for the baptism of fire and the Holy Ghost, according to the scriptures."[7]

AVOID SPECULATING ON DESTINY OF THE SPIRIT. The Holy Ghost is not a personage with a body of flesh and bones, and in this respect differs from the Father and the Son. The Holy Ghost is not a woman, as some have declared, and therefore is not the mother of Jesus Christ.

It is a waste of time to speculate in relation to his jurisdiction. We know what has been revealed and that the Holy Ghost, sometimes spoken of as the Holy Spirit, and Comforter, is the third member of the Godhead, and that he, being in perfect harmony with the Father and the Son, reveals to man by the spirit of revelation and prophecy the truths of the gospel of Jesus Christ. Our great duty is so to live that we may be led constantly in light and truth by this Comforter so that we may not be deceived by the many false spirits that are in the world.[8]

I have never troubled myself about the Holy Ghost whether he will sometime have a body or not because it is not in any way essential to my salvation. He is a member of the Godhead, with great power and authority, with a most wonderful mission which must be performed by a spirit. This has satisfied me without delving into mysteries that would be of no particular benefit.[9]

GIFT OF THE HOLY GHOST

BESTOWING THE HOLY GHOST. The Holy Ghost is given permanently only to those who have come to a

[7]D. & C. 20:41.
[6]D. & C. 33:15.
[8]Era, vol. 37, p. 866.
[9]Pers. Corresp.

knowledge of the truth, through hearkening to the Spirit of Christ, and who have been baptized and confirmed members of the Church. That brings us to the difference between the Holy Ghost and the gift of the Holy Ghost, which some of us get confused in our minds.

It is a mistake, when we are called upon to confirm someone a member of the Church, to say, "Receive ye the gift of the Holy Ghost." We should say, "Receive the Holy Ghost." (I do not say "ye" because that is a plural pronoun.) That covers everything, and they get the gift.

GIFT OF HOLY GHOST DEFINED. What is the gift of the Holy Ghost? Nothing more nor less than the right to the companionship of the Holy Ghost. As President Joseph F. Smith says: "He does not have to dwell with one constantly." This man here, another one over there, and a man over in England, are confirmed members of the Church. The question arises, "How can the Holy Ghost be with them all at the same time?" He does not have to be, but the power of the Holy Ghost is such that it can be manifest in every place at the same moment of time.

President Joseph F. Smith has expressed it thus: *"The Holy Ghost as a personage of Spirit can no more be omnipresent in person than can the Father or the Son, but by his intelligence, his knowledge, his power and influence, over and through the laws of nature, he is and can be omnipresent throughout all the works of God."*[10] Thus when it becomes necessary to speak to us, he is able to do so by acting through the other Spirit, that is, through the Light of Christ.

Joseph Smith said: "There are certain key words and signs belonging to the priesthood which must be observed in order to obtain the blessing. The sign of Peter was to repent and be baptized for the remission

---
[10]Pres. Joseph F. Smith, *Gospel Doctrine*, 4th ed., pp. 73-75.

of sins, with the promise of the gift of the Holy Ghost; and in no other way is the gift of the Holy Ghost obtained."

HOLY GHOST RETURNS MAN TO PRESENCE OF GOD. You cannot get the gift of the Holy Ghost by praying for it, by paying your tithing, by keeping the Word of Wisdom—not even by being baptized in water for the remission of sins. You must complete that baptism with the laying on of hands for the gift of the Holy Ghost. The Prophet said on one occasion that you might as well baptize a bag of sand as not confirm a man and give him the gift of the Holy Ghost, by the laying on of hands. You cannot get it any other way. The man who is confirmed receives, in addition to this Spirit of Christ, the companionship of the third member of the Godhead. Therefore, he is back again in the presence of God, through the gift of the Holy Ghost.

HOLY GHOST AND THE GIFT COMPARED. The Prophet continued: "*There is a difference between the Holy Ghost and the gift of the Holy Ghost.* Cornelius received the Holy Ghost before he was baptized, which was the convincing power of God unto him of the truth of the gospel, but he could not receive the gift of the Holy Ghost until after he was baptized. Had he not taken this sign or ordinance upon him, the Holy Ghost which convinced him of the truth of God, would have left him. Until he obeyed these ordinances and received the gift of the Holy Ghost, by the laying on of hands, according to the order of God, he could not have healed the sick or commanded an evil spirit to come out of a man, and it obey him; for the spirits might say unto him, as they did to the sons of Sceva: 'Paul we know and Jesus we know, but who are ye?' It mattereth not whether we live long or short on the earth after we come to a knowledge of these principles and obey them unto the end. I know that all men will be damned if they do not come in the way which he hath opened, and this is the way marked out by the word of the Lord."[11]

HOLY GHOST CAN TESTIFY TO A NON-CHURCH MEMBER. The question often arises: "How is it you say a man cannot receive the gift of the Holy Ghost except by the laying on of hands, when Cornelius received the Holy Ghost before he was baptized, before he had gone to Peter to find out what he should do to be saved?" The Holy Ghost will manifest himself to any individual who asks for the truth, just as he did to Cornelius. Moroni said this: "And when ye shall receive these things, I would exhort you that ye who would ask God, the Eternal Father, in the name of Christ, if these things are not true; and if ye shall ask with sincere heart, with real intent, having faith in Christ, he will manifest the truth of it unto you, by the power of the Holy Ghost."[12]

Every man can receive a manifestation of the Holy Ghost, even when he is out of the Church, if he is earnestly seeking for the light and for the truth. The Holy Ghost will come and give the man the testimony he is seeking, and then withdraw; and the man does not have a claim upon another visit or constant visits and manifestations from him. He may have the constant guidance of that other Spirit, the Spirit of Christ. Every man may receive such a manifestation from the Holy Ghost when he is seeking for the truth, but not the power to call upon the Holy Ghost whenever he feels he needs the help, as a man does who is a member of the Church.[13]

GIFT OF HOLY GHOST FOR CHURCH MEMBERS ONLY. We may after baptism and confirmation become companions of the Holy Ghost who will teach us the ways of the Lord, quicken our minds and help us to understand the truth. The people of the world do not receive the gift of the Holy Ghost.

Joseph Smith did not have the gift of the Holy Ghost

---

[11]Joseph Fielding Smith, *Teachings of the Prophet Joseph Smith,* p. 199.
[12]Moro. 10:4.
[13]*Church News.,* Apr. 27, 1935, p. 7.

at the time of the First Vision, but he was overshadowed by the Holy Ghost; otherwise, he could not have beheld the Father and the Son.[14]

OUR RIGHT TO GUIDANCE FROM HOLY GHOST. We have the right to the guidance of the Holy Ghost, but we cannot have that guidance, if we wilfully refuse to consider the revelations that have been given to help us to understand and to guide us in the light and truth of the everlasting gospel. We cannot hope to have that guidance when we refuse to consider these great revelations which mean so much to us both temporally and spiritually.

Now if we find ourselves in this condition of unbelief or unwillingness to seek for the light and the knowledge which the Lord has placed within our reach, then we are liable or in danger of being deceived by evil spirits, the doctrines of devils, and the teachings of men. And when these false influences are presented before us, we will not have the distinguishing understanding by which we can segregate them and know that they are not of the Lord. And so we may become prey unto the ungodly, to the vicious, to the cunning, to the craftiness of men.[15]

HOLY GHOST A SURE WITNESS OF TRUTH

THOSE GUIDED BY THE SPIRIT NOT DECEIVED. If we are humble, if we are diligent in the service of the Lord, if we seek to serve him with an eye single to the glory of our Father in heaven (keeping in mind that he has asked for that service with a full heart, with all our might, with all our mind, and with all our strength), we will not go astray. We will not be seduced by evil spirits nor by the spirits of men, but we will be led and directed by the Spirit of God.

Every member of the Church has had hands laid upon his head for the gift of the Holy Ghost. He has a

---
[14]Pers. Corresp.; John 14:16-17, 26; 15:26. [15]Conf. Rep., Oct., 1952, pp. 59-60.

right to receive the revelations that are expedient and necessary for his guidance individually; not for the Church, but for himself. He has a right through his obedience, through his humility, to receive light and truth as it shall be revealed through the Spirit of Truth, and he who will hearken to that Spirit and seek for the gift of the Spirit in humility and faith shall not be deceived.

Now there are some of our people who are being deceived. Why? Because they lack knowledge, because they lack understanding, and because they are not in tune with the Holy Spirit, which they have a right to receive through their faithfulness and obedience.[16]

TESTIMONY COMES FROM HOLY GHOST. Christ is the second person in the Godhead. But Christ has himself declared that the manifestations we might have of the Spirit of Christ, or from a visitation of an angel, a tangible resurrected being, would not leave the impression and would not convince us and place within us that something which we cannot get away from which we receive through a manifestation of the Holy Ghost.[17] Personal visitations might become dim as time goes on, but this guidance of the Holy Ghost is renewed and continued, day after day, year after year, if we live to be worthy of it.

A man may receive manifestations of the Holy Spirit, and then he may sin and the Spirit withdraws. He is left to himself, and he will forget, to a very large extent, the things he learned before. But when a man has known the power of God, and partakes of it and then turns away, knowingly defying the truth, there is no forgiveness for him.[18]

I have in mind certain missionaries whom I have heard testify when they returned home, and also some whom I have heard in the mission field get up and speak by the power of the Spirit, bearing witness of the truth;

---
[16]Conf. Rep., Apr., 1940, p. 96; D. & C. 46:7-8.
[17]Luke 16:27-31; D. & C. 5:7-10.
[18]D. & C. 76:30-49; 132:27; Matt. 12:31-32; Heb. 6:4-8.

THE HOLY GHOST AND LIGHT OF CHRIST

yet years later they have lost that testimony; it has departed from them.

I have in mind now a prominent schoolteacher who filled a good mission and the Spirit of the Lord was upon him. Today he is not a member of the Church. His mind has become clouded. His testimonies have become dimmed. I do not know that he will ever get away from them, for if he received them in the clearness and the power in which we are capable of receiving them, he could not altogether forget. A man through denying the truth and leaving the Church does not become a son of perdition, unless he has had enough light to become a son of perdition.[19]

THE HOLY SPIRIT OF PROMISE

ORDINANCES SEALED BY SPIRIT. *The Holy Spirit of Promise is the Holy Ghost* who places the stamp of approval upon every ordinance: baptism, confirmation, ordination, marriage. *The promise is that the blessings will be received through faithfulness.*

If a person violates a covenant, whether it be of baptism, ordination, marriage or anything else, the Spirit withdraws the stamp of approval, and the blessings will not be received.

Every ordinance is sealed with a promise of a reward based upon faithfulness. The Holy Spirit withdraws the stamp of approval where covenants are broken.[20]

THE HOLY GHOST LED ALL THE PROPHETS

THE HOLY GHOST DURING CHRIST'S MINISTRY. While Christ was here in his ministry, his disciples did not have the constant companionship of the Holy Ghost. He told them they could not have that Spirit while he was with them, but when he went, he would send the Comforter to be their guide.[21] He was one of the Godhead,

---
[19]*Church News*, Apr. 27, 1935, p. 7. [21]John 16:7, 13.
[20]D. & C. 76:52-53; 132:7.

and while he was there in their presence, they did not have the companionship of the Holy Ghost.

It is true that the Holy Ghost came to them *on occasions* while Christ was yet with them. But they were in the same condition as Cornelius. They had special manifestations of the power of the Holy Ghost, but did not enjoy the gift itself, that is, they did not have the right to the constant companionship of that member of the Godhead.[22] The Holy Ghost did speak to Peter, right in the presence of the Savior, but the gift or power to have it with him constantly while he was there, the Savior clearly told them, was unnecessary.[23]

THE HOLY GHOST IN A FUTURE ETERNITY. This does not mean that when we come into the presence of God after the resurrection or in the millennium, we will not have the gift of the Holy Ghost, although Christ is there. When things come to that perfect state, and especially after the resurrection, I think we will be in the presence of all three—Father, Son, and Holy Ghost.

ANCIENT PROPHETS HAD THE HOLY GHOST. There is another point which often arises from the fact that the Savior said the Holy Ghost could not come while he was here. Many people say that the ancients never had the Holy Ghost, that he could not come until after Christ had come and died and been raised in the resurrection. You do not find the term Holy Ghost in the Old Testament, as we now have it, but you do find the Spirit of God.[24]

The fact is *all the prophets had the Holy Ghost*. They were led and directed by him. And without this power they would not have been prophets. Peter said that prophecy itself "came not in old time by the will of man: but holy men of God spake as they were moved by the Holy Ghost."[25] The Book of Moses, which is

---

[22] Acts 10:34-38.
[23] Matt. 16:13-17; John 7:39; Luke 24:49; Acts 2:1-13.
[24] Gen. 41:38; Ex. 31:3; 35:31; Nu. 24:2; 1 Sam. 10:10; 11:6 19:20, 23; 2 Chron. 15:1 Ezek. 11:24.
[25] 2 Pet. 1:21.

the original and perfect record of a part of Genesis, speaks of the Holy Ghost;[26] so do the Nephite prophets, including those who lived in the era before Christ.[27]

THE SIN AGAINST THE HOLY GHOST

BLASPHEMY AGAINST HOLY GHOST. When the Pharisees in their wickedness declared that Jesus cast out devils by the power of Beelzebub, the prince of devils, Jesus said to them:

"Wherefore I say unto you, All manner of sin and blasphemy shall be forgiven unto men *who receive me and repent;* but the blasphemy against the Holy Ghost, it shall not be forgiven unto men. And whosoever shall speak a word against the Son of Man, it shall be forgiven him; but whosoever speaketh against the Holy Ghost, it shall not be forgiven him; neither in this world; neither in the world to come."[28]

HOLY GHOST WILL GUIDE INTO ALL TRUTH. The mission of the Holy Ghost is to lead those who are entitled to the gift, which is conferred by the laying on of hands, in all truth and righteousness. The Savior told his apostles that the Comforter would dwell in them and testify of the Father and the Son; would guide them in all truth, and show them things to come.[29] In the revelations given to the Church in this day, these same promises are made, and the mission of the Holy Ghost is declared to be exactly what it was in the former dispensations.[30] Therefore, a person who will walk in the light as that light is revealed by the third member of the Godhead, will know with a positive and unerring understanding that Jesus is the Christ and the Redeemer of the world, and the plan of salvation will be plainly comprehended.

SPIRIT SPEAKING TO SPIRIT. The Spirit of God speaking to the spirit of man has power to impart truth

---

[26]Moses 1:24; 5:58; 6:52, 65-66; 8:24.
[27]Pers. Corresp.; 1 Ne. 10:17-19; 2 Ne. 31:13-21.
[28]*Inspired Version,* Matt. 12:26-27.
[29]John 14:16-17, 26; 15:26; 16:13-15.
[30]D. & C. 8:1-3; 14:8; 18:18; 33:15.

with greater effect and understanding than the truth can be imparted by personal contact even with heavenly beings. Through the Holy Ghost the truth is woven into the very fibre and sinews of the body so that it cannot be forgotten. So positive and powerful are the teachings of the Spirit that when a man receives this knowledge and partakes of this power of God, which can only come after receiving the covenants and obligations belonging to the new and everlasting covenant, and he then turns away from this knowledge and these covenants, he sins knowingly.

SONS OF PERDITION. It is for this reason that the Lord has said: "Thus saith the Lord concerning all those who know my power, and have been partakers thereof, and suffered themselves through the power of the devil to be overcome, and to deny the truth and defy my power—They are they who are the sons of perdition, of whom I say that it had been better for them never to have been born; For they are vessels of wrath, doomed to suffer the wrath of God, with the devil and his angels in eternity; Concerning whom I have said there is no forgiveness in this world nor in the world to come—Having denied the Holy Spirit after having received it, and having denied the Only Begotten Son of the Father, having crucified him unto themselves and put him to an open shame."[31]

In harmony with this, the writer to the Hebrews said: "For it is impossible for those who were once enlightened, and have tasted of the heavenly gift, and were made partakers of the Holy Ghost, And have tasted the good word of God, and the powers of the world to come, If they shall fall away, to renew them again unto repentance; seeing they crucify to themselves the Son of God afresh, and put him to an open shame."[32]

A SIN UNTO DEATH. Peter said, "It had been better for them not to have known the way of righteousness, than, after they have known it, to turn from the

---

[31]D. & C. 76:31-35.   [32]Heb. 6:4-6.

holy commandment delivered unto them,"[33] and John called it a sin unto death.[34] It is a sin unto death, for it brings a spiritual banishment—the second death—by which those who partake of it are denied the presence of God and are consigned to dwell with the devil and his angels throughout eternity.

All who partake of this, the greatest of sins, sell themselves as did Cain to Lucifer. They learn to hate the truth with an eternal hatred, and they learn to love wickedness. They reach a condition where they will not and cannot repent. The spirit of murder fills their hearts and they would, if they had the power, crucify our Lord again, which they virtually do by fighting his work and seeking to destroy it and his prophets.

PUTTING CHRIST TO OPEN SHAME. Before a man can sink to this bitterness of soul, he must first know and understand the truth with a clearness of vision wherein there is no doubt. *The change of heart does not come all at once,* but is due to transgression in some form, which continues to lurk in the soul without repentance, until the Holy Ghost withdraws, and then that man is left to spiritual darkness. Sin begets sin; the darkness grows until the love of truth turns to hatred, and the love of God is overcome by the wicked desire to destroy all that is just and true. In this way Christ is put to open shame, and blasphemy exalted.

How fortunate it is that in the mercy of God there will be comparatively few who will partake of this awful misery and eternal darkness.[35]

THE LIGHT OF CHRIST

THE OMNIPRESENT HOLY SPIRIT. The Holy Ghost should not be confused with the Spirit which fills the immensity of space and which is everywhere present. This other Spirit is impersonal and has no size, nor dimension; it proceeds forth from the presence of the

---
[33] 2 Pet. 2:20-21.
[34] 1 John 5:16.
[35] *Millennial Star,* vol. 97, pp. 722-723.

Father and the Son and is in all things. We should speak of the Holy Ghost as a personage as "he" and this other Spirit as "it," although when we speak of the power or gift of the Holy Ghost we may properly say "it."[36]

THE SPIRIT OF JESUS CHRIST. The Holy Ghost, as we are taught in our modern revelation, is the third member in the Godhead and a personage of Spirit. These terms are used synonymously: Spirit of God, Spirit of the Lord, Spirit of Truth, Holy Spirit, Comforter; all having reference to the Holy Ghost. The same terms largely are used in relation to the Spirit of Jesus Christ, also called the Light of Truth, Light of Christ, Spirit of God, and Spirit of the Lord; and yet they are separate and distinct things. We have a great deal of confusion because we have not kept that clearly in our minds. The Lord revealed this to Joseph Smith:

"For the word of the Lord is truth, and whatsoever is truth is light, and whatsoever is light is Spirit, even the Spirit of Jesus Christ. And the Spirit giveth light to every man that cometh into the world; and the Spirit enlighteneth every man through the world, that hearkeneth to the voice of the Spirit. And everyone that hearkeneth to the voice of the Spirit cometh unto God, even the Father. And the Father teacheth him of the covenant which he has renewed and confirmed upon you, which is confirmed upon you for your sakes, and not for your sakes only, but for the sake of the whole world.

"And the whole world lieth in sin, and groaneth under darkness and under the bondage of sin. And by this you may know they are under the bondage of sin, because they come not unto me. For whoso cometh not unto me is under the bondage of sin. And whoso receiveth not my voice is not acquainted with my voice, and is not of me."[37]

Moroni tells us the same thing: "For behold, the

---

[36]Pers. Corresp.   [37]*D. & C.* 84:45-52.

Spirit of Christ is given to every man, that he may know good from evil; wherefore, I show unto you the way to judge; for everything which inviteth to do good, and to persuade to believe in Christ, is sent forth by the power and gift of Christ; wherefore ye may know with a perfect knowledge it is of God."[38]

EVERY MAN RECEIVES THE LIGHT OF CHRIST. We do not find this doctrine so clearly defined in the *New Testament* as in the *Doctrine and Covenants* and the *Book of Mormon*. But we discover this: The Lord has not left men (when they are born into this world) helpless, groping to find the light and truth, but every man that is born into the world is born with the right to receive the guidance, the instruction, the counsel of the Spirit of Christ, or Light of Truth, sometimes called the Spirit of the Lord in our writings.

THE LIGHT OF CHRIST ACTS AS OUR CONSCIENCE. If a man who has never heard the gospel will hearken to the teachings and manifestations of the Spirit of Christ, or the Light of Truth, which come to him, often spoken of as conscience—every man has a conscience and knows more or less when he does wrong, and the Spirit guides him if he will hearken to its whisperings—it will lead him eventually to the fulness of the gospel. That is, he is guided by the Light, and when the gospel comes he will be ready to receive it. This is what the Lord tells us in section 84 of the *Doctrine and Covenants*.

This Spirit of Truth, or Light of Christ, also has other functions. We read this in the revelation: "This ... glory is that of the church of the Firstborn, even of God, the holiest of all, through Jesus Christ, his Son— He that ascended up on high, as also he descended below all things, in that he comprehended all things, that he might be in all and through all things, the light of truth; Which truth shineth. This is the light of Christ. As also he is in the sun, and the light of the sun, and the

---
[38]Moro. 7:16, 18.

power thereof by which it was made. As also he is in the moon, and is the light of the moon, and the power thereof by which it was made; As also the light of the stars, and the power thereof by which they were made; And the earth also, and the power thereof, even the earth upon which you stand. And the light which shineth, which giveth you light, is through him who enlighteneth your eyes, which is the same light that quickeneth your understandings; *Which light proceedeth forth from the presence of God to fill the immensity of space.*"

LIGHT OF CHRIST IS THE POWER OF GOD. This Light of Christ is not a personage. It has no body. I do not know what it is as far as substance is concerned; but it fills the immensity of space and emanates from God. It is the light by which the worlds are controlled, by which they are made. It is the light of the sun and all other bodies. It is the light which gives life to vegetation. It quickens the understanding of men, and has these various functions as set forth in these verses.

It is: "The light which is in all things, which giveth life to all things, which is the law by which all things are governed, even the power of God who sitteth upon his throne, who is in the bosom of eternity, who is in the midst of all things."[39]

This is our explanation in regard to the Spirit of Christ, or Light of Truth, which every man receives and is guided by. Unless a man had the blessings that come from this Spirit, his mind would not be quickened; there would be no vegetation grow; the worlds would not stay in their orbits; because it is through this Spirit of Truth, this Light of Truth, according to this revelation, that all these things are done.[40]

INVESTIGATORS LED BY LIGHT OF CHRIST. The Lord has given to "every man that cometh into the world," the guidance of the Light of Truth, or Spirit of Jesus Christ, and if a man will hearken to this Spirit he will

---
[39]D. & C. 88:4-13, 41.   [40]*Church News,* Apr. 20, 1935, p. 6.

be led to the truth and will recognize it and will accept it when he hears it. We have seen this demonstrated thousands of times, where men were led to investigate and have had the desire to investigate in spite of the prejudices and traditions which they were taught in the world.

If they refuse to come unto him, then he calls them wicked and they are under the bondage of sin. It seems to me that when a person declares that he is satisfied with his religion and therefore does not care to investigate, it is evidence that he has not hearkened to the Light of Truth which was given him; else he would not have been satisfied with the false religion which he has and would be seeking the truth.

THE SPIRIT POURED OUT ON ALL FLESH. The inspiration which was promised to all flesh by the Lord through the prophecy of Joel, is not the promise of the Holy Ghost, but the promise of the guidance of the Light of Christ, or Spirit of Truth, which is given to every man who comes into the world.[41] It is through this Spirit that the inspiration comes to those who are not members of the Church. This Spirit has been poured out and is the active agency by which the great discoveries in these modern times have been accomplished. It is this Spirit which the Lord declares he will withdraw from the world,[42] and which he said to Noah would not always "strive with man," and not the Holy Ghost which they never had.[43] It is this Spirit which led Columbus in his discoveries.[44]

It is this Spirit which the Savior speaks of in the revelations which is given to guide men.[45] When he speaks of the Holy Ghost being their guide, and that this gift will come to the Gentiles, the necessary implication is that the Gentiles will have been cleansed and baptized so that they can receive these blessings.[46]

---
[41]Joel 2:28-29; Joseph Smith 2:41.
[42]D. & C. 63:32.
[43]Moses 8:17; Gen. 6:3; D. & C. 1:33.
[44]1 Ne. 13:10-11.
[45]D. & C. 11:12; 20:37.
[46]Acts 10:44-48; 3 Ne. 15:23.

THE TRUE GUARDIAN ANGEL. We have often heard of guardian angels attending us and many patriarchs have spoken of such protection. There are times no doubt when some unseen power directs us and leads us from harm. However, the true guardian angel given to every man who comes into the world is the Light of Truth or Spirit of Christ.

The Holy Ghost is given to faithful members of the Church to guard and direct them; theirs is the privilege, through their faithfulness, to have such guidance and protection.

There is no angel following us about like a stenographer taking notes and making a record of our lives. The Lord has a more perfect way by which the acts of our lives are recorded.[47]

THE HOLY GHOST WORKS THROUGH THE LIGHT OF CHRIST. The person of the Holy Ghost can work through the Spirit of Christ that permeates everything, or he can work by personal contacts. The Holy Ghost can act through some other influence or force. This may be a crude illustration, and yet I think it answers our purpose. We have in this building a young lady sitting down at the switchboard. Someone on this floor wants to get in touch with someone on the second floor; somebody else in another part of the building wants to talk with someone in another building; and so on. They are all connected with the parties they want to talk to. In a similar way the Holy Ghost could speak to someone here, someone over there, and someone way off in some other part of the country, even in a foreign land, and each receive the message intended for him. That is not hard to understand when we think ͟ ͟legraphy. They send several messages over a wire at the same time. Radio stations send messages of different wave lengths all over the earth.[48]

---

[47]Pers. Corresp.   [48]*Church News*, Apr. 27, 1935, p. 7.

THE SECOND COMFORTER

Two Comforters. Joseph Smith speaks of two Comforters: the first is the Holy Ghost, the second is the Son of God himself. He uses the 14th chapter of John as the basis for his discourse.[49] Verses 16, 17, and 26 definitely refer to the Holy Ghost. They speak of the Spirit of Truth which "dwelleth with you, and shall be *in* you." Verses 18, 21, and 23 clearly refer to the Lord himself and his coming to man.

Second Comforter Not Holy Spirit of Promise. The Holy Spirit of Promise is not the Second Comforter. The Holy Spirit of Promise is the Holy Ghost who places the stamp of approval upon every ordinance that is done righteously;[50] and when covenants are broken he removes the seal.

Denying the Second Comforter. There is no forgiveness for denying the First Comforter. But if a man received honor enough to have the presence of the Son, he would also have the knowledge of the First Comforter and should he turn away, his sin would be unpardonable. A man could not deny the Second Comforter any more than he could the first.

If a man gets knowledge enough to have the companionship of the Son of God, the chances are his call and election would be sure.[51]

---

[49]Smith, *op. cit.,* pp. 149-151.
[50]*D. & C.* 132:7.
[51]Pers. Corresp.; 2 Pet. 1:1-21; *D. & C.* 131:5; 132:49.

Chapter 4

OUR FIRST AND SECOND ESTATES

PRE-EXISTENCE OF MAN

SAINTS HAVE KNOWLEDGE OF SPIRIT LIFE. The Latter-day Saints are the only people in the world, as far as my knowledge goes, who have a clear, distinct doctrine in regard to the questions: Where did we come from? Why are we here? and, Where are we going? I believe we are the only people in the world who believe in the pre-existence of the human family. There are many who believe in the pre-existence of Jesus Christ,[1] but they do not believe that we, individually, lived before we came into this life.[2]

One of the strange things to me is the fact that so many people believe that there is a spirit in man and when he dies that spirit continues to live as an immortal thing, yet that it had no existence until man was born in this mortal life.[3]

WE LIVED AS SPIRIT BEINGS. We lived in the presence of God in the spirit before we came here. We desired to be like him, we saw him, we were in his presence. There is not a soul who has not seen both the Father and the Son, and in the spirit world we were in their presence;[4] but it became necessary for us to gain experiences which could not be obtained in that world of spirits, and so we were accorded the privilege of coming down here upon this earth.[5]

WE HAVE SEEN GOD. When we lived in the presence of our Father, we were not like him; we were just

---

[1]John 1:1-5, 14; 3:13, 31; 6:32-38, 50-51, 62; 16:28; 17:5.
[2]D. & C. 93:21-23.
[3]*Church News*, May 31, 1947, p. 1.
[4]D. & C. 88:47-50; Abra. 3:22-28.
[5]*Rel. Soc. Mag.*, vol. 28, p. 4.

spirits. We did not have bodies of flesh and bones, but he did. He was a glorious personage with a body of flesh and bones, his spirit and body being inseparably connected, and his body shining with a brightness beyond the brightness of the sun. *We saw him in his majesty;* and when the plan of salvation was presented to us, it was made known to us that if we would pass through this mortal existence, and be true and faithful to all the commandments our Father would give unto us—thus keeping the second estate as we had kept the first—we, too, eventually would have the privilege of coming back into his presence with bodies of flesh and bones which would also shine with the brightness of the sun, to share in all the fulness of his kingdom.[6]

COUNCILS WERE HELD IN PRE-EXISTENCE. In the pre-existence we dwelt in the presence of God our Father. When the time arrived for us to be advanced in the scale of our existence and pass through this mundane probation, councils were held and the spirit children were instructed in matters pertaining to conditions in mortal life, and the reason for such an existence. In the former life we were spirits. In order that we should advance and eventually gain the goal of perfection, it was made known that we would receive tabernacles of flesh and bones and have to pass through mortality where we would be tried and proved to see if we, by trial, would prepare ourselves for exaltation. We were made to realize, in the presence of our glorious Father, who had a tangible body of flesh and bones which shone like the sun, that we were, as spirits, far inferior in our station to him.

SPIRITS WERE TAUGHT ABOUT MORTALITY. We were instructed that by faithfulness in the mortal life which was promised us, we also should, after passing through trials and tribulation, obtain bodies that would also be glorious, just like our Father's. We were duly informed that in this mortal life we would have to walk

---
[6]*Church News,* May 31, 1947, pp. 1, 8.

by faith. Previously we had walked by sight, but now was to come a period of trial to see if by faith we would be true to every covenant and commandment our Father required at our hands. We were informed that many would fail. Those who rebelled against the light which would be revealed to them should be deprived of exaltation. They could not come back to dwell in the presence of God, but would have to take a place in some other sphere where they would be blessed according to their works, and likewise restricted in their privileges.[7]

PLAN OF SALVATION PRESENTED IN PRE-EXISTENCE. There was a council held in heaven, when the Lord called before him his spirit children and presented to them a plan by which they should come down on this earth; partake of mortal life and physical bodies; pass through a probation of mortality, and then go on to a higher exaltation through the resurrection which should be brought about through the atonement of his Only Begotten Son Jesus Christ.[8] The thought of passing through mortality and partaking of all the vicissitudes of earth life in which they would gain experiences through suffering, pain, sorrow, temptation and affliction, as well as the pleasures of life in this mundane existence, and then, if faithful, passing on through the resurrection to eternal life in the kingdom of God, to be like him,[9] filled them with the spirit of rejoicing, and they "shouted for joy."[10] The experience and knowledge obtained in this mortal life they could not get in any other way, and the receiving of a physical body was essential to their exaltation.

AGENCY AND PROGRESSION IN PRE-EXISTENCE. God gave his children their free agency even in the spirit world, by which the individual spirits had the privilege, just as men have here, of choosing the good and rejecting the evil, or partaking of the evil to suffer the consequences of their sins. Because of this, some even there were more

---

[7]*Church News*, June 12, 1949, p. 21.
[8]Moses 4:1-3; Abra. 3:22-28.
[9]1 John 3:1-3.
[10]Job. 38:1-7; Isa. 49:1-5.

faithful than others in keeping the commandments of the Lord. Some were of greater intelligence than others, as we find it here, and were honored accordingly. . . .

SOME SPIRITS GREATER THAN OTHERS. The spirits of men had their free agency, some were greater than others, and from among them the Father called and foreordained his prophets and rulers. Jeremiah and Abraham were two of them.[11] . . . *The spirits of men were not equal. They may have had an equal start,*[12] and we know they were all innocent in the beginning;[13] but the right of free agency which was given to them enabled some to outstrip others, and thus, through the eons of immortal existence, to become more intelligent, more faithful, for they were free to act for themselves, to think for themselves, to receive the truth or rebel against it.[14]

CHILDREN OF ISRAEL FOREKNOWN. The Lord declared through Moses the following:

"Remember the days of old, consider the years of many generations: . . . When the Most High divided to the nations their inheritance, when he separated the sons of Adam, he set the bounds of the people according to the number of the children of Israel."[15]

A similar passage to this occurs in Acts where Paul declares to the Athenians that the Lord "hath made of one blood all nations of men for to dwell on all the face of the earth, and hath determined the times before appointed, and the bounds of their habitation."[16]

These passages clearly indicate that the numbers of the children of Israel were known and the bounds of their habitation fixed, in the days of old when the Lord divided to the nations their inheritance. We conclude, therefore, that there must have been a division of the spirits of men in the spiritual world, and those who were appointed to be the children of Israel were separated and prepared for a special inheritance.

---

[11]Jer. 1:5; Abra. 3:23.
[12]Alma 13:5-7.
[13]D. & C. 93:38.
[14]*Era,* vol. 19, pp. 318-319.
[15]Deut. 32:7-8.
[16]Acts. 17:26.

WHY NO REMEMBRANCE OF FIRST ESTATE. This mortal existence is conclusive evidence that all who receive it kept their first estate. In our former, or spirit existence, we walked by sight. We were in the presence of both the Father and the Son, and were instructed by them and under their personal presence. In this mortal life, or second estate, the Lord willed that we should walk by faith and not by sight, that we might, with the great gift of free agency, be proved to see if we would do all things whatsoever the Lord our God commanded us.[17] Therefore, he took away from us all knowledge of our spiritual existence and started us out afresh in the form of helpless infants, to grow and learn day by day. In consequence of this we received no former knowledge and wisdom at birth, and, as it is written of the Son of God, who in the beginning made all things, we "received not of the fulness at the first, but received grace for grace."[18]

PRE-EXISTENT LIFE AFFECTS MORTALITY. Notwithstanding this fact that our recollection of former things was taken away, the character of our lives in the spirit world has much to do with our disposition, desires and mentality here in mortal life. *The spirit influences the body to a great extent, just as the body in its desires and cravings has an influence on the spirit.* The Lord has caused it to be so. Therefore, those who were the noble and great ones in that former world, the Lord foreordained to be his prophets and rulers here, for he knew them before they were born, and through *the action of the spirit on the body,* he knows they will be likely to serve him here. Environment and many other causes, however, have great influence on the progress and destiny of man, but we must not lose sight of the fact that the characteristics of the spirit, which were developed through many ages of a former existence, play a very important part in our progression through mortal life.[19]

[17]Abra. 3:25.
[18]D. & C. 93:12; Luke 2:52.
[19]*Era,* vol. 19, pp. 315-316, 425-426.

WHY MEN ARE BORN TO DIFFERENT RACES. We are the children of God. He is our Father and he loves us. He loves all men whether they be white or black. No matter what their color, no matter what the conditions under which they were born and reared, the Lord looks upon all his children in mercy and will do for them just the best that he can. . . .

There is a reason why one man is born black and with other disadvantages, while *another is born white* with great advantages. The reason is that we once had an estate before we came here, and were obedient, more or less, to the laws that were given us there. *Those who were faithful in all things there received greater blessings here, and those who were not faithful received less.*[20]

MEN NOT FOREORDAINED TO DO EVIL. Every soul coming into this world came here with the promise that through obedience he would receive the blessings of salvation.[21] No person was foreordained or appointed to sin or to perform a mission of evil. No person is ever predestined to salvation or damnation. Every person has free agency. Cain was promised by the Lord that if he would do well, he would be accepted.[22] Judas had his agency and acted upon it; no pressure was brought to bear on him to cause him to betray the Lord, but he was led by Lucifer.[23] If men were appointed to sin and betray their brethren, then justice could not demand that they be punished for sin and betrayal when they are guilty.[24]

LORD HAS CREATED MANY EARTHS. The Lord never created anything for nothing, nor out of nothing. Everything has a place and was created for a purpose. Man was not created to be destroyed. This work has been going on forever. There never was a time when there was not an earth; never a time when there were not people on it, for that is the work of the Lord, and the heavens are innumerable, and so are the earths that have

[20]*Gen. & Hist. Mag.,* vol. 17, p. 154.
[21]Third Article of Faith; 2 Ne. 26:33; 3 Ne. 27:20; Mark 16:15.
[22]Moses 5:22-23; Gen. 4:6-7.
[23]Luke 22:3.
[24]Pers. Corresp.

passed away to their exaltation and glory. As they pass away others take their places. This is not the only world.[25]

MANY EARTHS INHABITED BY OUR BROTHERS AND SISTERS. We are not the only people that the Lord has created. *We have brothers and sisters on other earths. They look like us because they, too, are the children of God* and were created in his image, for they are also his offspring.[26] His great work is to create earths and people them with his children who are called upon to pass through the mortal probation like unto this we are now in, suffering pain, sorrow and the ills of the flesh, coming face to face with sin, with temptation; and having the right within themselves, God-given, to reject the evil and receive the good or reject the good and receive the evil, if they will, with the understanding, of course, that they shall be judged before his bar for their deeds and receive their reward accordingly. Every man has his agency to choose good or evil, to be rewarded or debased, and of course each will be rewarded.[27]

PRE-EXISTENCE OF ALL CREATURES

ALL LIFE CREATED IN THE SPIRIT. *Every creature had a spiritual existence. The spirits of men, beasts, and all animal life, existed before the foundations of the earth were laid, and are living entities.*[28] *As death, through the fall, has passed upon all, so the resurrection, through the mission of Jesus Christ, comes to all.*[29]

ANIMALS CREATED FOR MAN. I want to give you a little explanation of man's relationship to the animals upon the earth, as the Lord has given it to us by revelation—not as it is taught by man in the world—but the true relationship which exists between man and beast. Man is the greatest of all the creations of God. He is

---
[25]Moses 1:29-35; 7:29; *D. & C.* 76:22-25; Heb. 1:1-2.
[26]Moses 7:29-31, 36.
[27]*Rel. Soc. Mag.*, vol. 7, pp. 7-9.
[28]Moses 3:5-9.
[29]*Church News*, Feb. 15, 1941, pp. 1, 7; *D. & C.* 29:22-25.

OUR FIRST AND SECOND ESTATES

his offspring. We are all his children. It was made known through the Prophet Joseph Smith and Sidney Rigdon, who saw it in vision, that the inhabitants of this earth and other worlds are begotten sons and daughters unto God.[30] That ought to put an end—so far as Latter-day Saints are concerned—to all this nonsense prevailing in the world regarding the origin of man.

Man, I say, as the offspring of God, is the greatest of all his creations. He is greater than the moon, the sun, and the stars, which are the work of the fingers of God, and are made for the benefit of man. *It is man's place to rule, and stand at the head of all other dominions, powers, creations, and beings, which the Lord our God has created.*[31]

ANIMALS HAVE SOULS. The idea prevails in general, I believe, in the religious world where the gospel truth is misunderstood, that man is the only being on the earth that has what is called a soul or a spirit. We know this is not the case, for the Lord has said that not only has man a spirit, and is thereby a living soul, but likewise the beasts of the field, the fowl of the air, and the fish of the sea have spirits, and hence are living souls. But this does *not* make them *kinsmen* to the sons and daughters of God. They are *our Father's creations, not his offspring,* and that is the great difference between man and beast.

It would be a very strange world where animals were not found. If, after the resurrection of the dead, we discovered that man was the only living creature with immortality, we would certainly consider it a very strange world. Yet the idea does prevail that man has a spirit and the animals have not. Some people think this is the great thing that distinguishes man from all other beings.

FORM OF ANIMAL SPIRITS. The fish, the fowl, the beasts of the field, lived before they were placed naturally in this earth, and so did the plants that are upon the face

---
[30]D. & C. 76:24.   [31]Ps. 8:1-9.

of the earth. *The spirits that possess the bodies of the animals are in the similitude of their bodies.* In other words, the bodies of animals conform to the spirits which possess them, and which existed before they were placed on the earth; "that which is spiritual being in the likeness of that which is temporal; and that which is temporal in the likeness of that which is spiritual; the spirit of man in the likeness of his person, as also the spirit of the beast, and every other creature which God has created."[32]

THE WAR IN HEAVEN

REBELLIOUS SPIRITS CAST OUT. When the plan of redemption was presented and Jesus was chosen to be the Redeemer of the world, some rebelled. They were not willing to accept him as "the Lamb slain from the foundation of the world."[33] . . . In this great rebellion in heaven, Lucifer, or Satan, a son of the morning, and one-third of the hosts thereof were cast out into the earth because Lucifer sought to destroy the free agency of man and the one-third of the spirits sided with him. He sought the throne of God, and put forth his plan in boldness in that great council, declaring that he would save all, that not one soul should be lost, provided God would give him the glory and the honor.[34] When his plan was rejected for a better one, he rebelled and said, as Isaiah states the case: "I will ascend into heaven, I will exalt my throne above the stars of God, . . . I will be like the Most High."[35]

FREE AGENCY IN PRE-EXISTENCE. If there had been no free agency, there could have been no rebellion in heaven; but what would man amount to without this free agency? He would be no better than a mechanical contrivance. He could not have acted for himself, but in all things would have been acted upon, and hence

---

[32]*Gen. & Hist. Mag.*, vol. 17, pp. 152-154; *D. & C.* 77:2.
[33]Rev. 13:8.
[34]*D. & C.* 29:36-39; 76:25-29; Rev. 12:7-10; Moses 4:1-4; Abra. 3:27-28; Luke 10:18; Jude 6; 2 Pet. 2:4; 2 Ne. 2:17-18; 9:8-9.
[35]Isa. 14:12-20.

OUR FIRST AND SECOND ESTATES

unable to have received a reward for meritorious conduct. He would have been an automaton; could have had no happiness nor misery, "neither sense nor insensibility,"[36] and such could hardly be called existence. Under such conditions there could have been no purpose in our creation.

DEVILS DENIED MORTAL BODIES. The punishment of Satan and the third of the host of heaven who followed him, was that they were denied the privilege of being born into this world and receiving mortal bodies. They did not keep their first estate and were denied the opportunity of eternal progression. The Lord cast them out into the earth, where they became the tempters of mankind—the devil and his angels. "And it must needs be," the Lord has said, "that the devil should tempt the children of men, or they could not be agents unto themselves; for if they never should have bitter they could not know the sweet."[37]

DEVILS STEAL BODIES. At times these fallen spirits steal possession of the bodies of men and women, overpowering the spirit who has rightful ownership. They realize what they have lost and are willing, when opportunity is given them, of possessing bodies of lower animals, so anxious are they to be clothed with flesh even for a season. On one occasion a legion of these evil spirits, when cast out by the Lord, asked the privilege of entering the bodies of a herd of swine.[38] Out of Mary Magdalene the Lord cast seven devils.[39] These evil spirits know the Lord from the knowledge and experience they obtained in the heavens before their banishment for rebellion. They called him by name when he disturbed them in their stolen habitations, saying: "Thou art Christ the Son of God, . . . for they knew that he was Christ."[40]

NO NEUTRALS IN HEAVEN. There were no neutrals

---

[36]2 Ne. 2:11-16.
[37]D. & C. 29:39.
[38]Matt. 8:31.
[39]Luke 8:2.
[40]Era, vol. 19, pp. 319, 321, 425; Luke 4:41; Mark 1:24; Acts 19:15.

in the war in heaven. *All took sides either with Christ or with Satan.*⁴¹ Every man had his agency there, and men receive rewards here based upon their actions there, just as they will receive rewards hereafter for deeds done in the body. The Negro, evidently, is receiving the reward he merits.

ALL SPIRITS INNOCENT IN THE BEGINNING. The Lord has said, "Every spirit of man was innocent in the beginning; and God having redeemed man from the fall, men became again, in their infant state, innocent before God."⁴²

This is speaking of the spirits of men when they were created, or born in the spirit, not when they were dwelling in the spirit world, for one-third of them rebelled and were not innocent. When a child comes into this world he is innocent as far as this mortal life is concerned, but children soon lose their innocence as they grow and come in contact with the world.⁴³

MORTALITY

TWO PURPOSES OF EARTH LIFE. *We came into this world to die.* That was understood before we came here. It is part of the plan, all discussed and arranged long before men were placed upon the earth. When Adam was sent into this world, it was with the understanding that he would violate a law, transgress a law, in order to bring to pass this mortal condition which we find ourselves in today. There are two purposes for life—*one to gain experience* that could not be obtained in any other way, and *the other to obtain these tabernacles* of flesh and bones. Both of these purposes are vital to the existence of man.

In the spirit world we saw our Father. We dwelt in his presence. He tells us in one of these revelations that we saw him, and if we are faithful, we will have the privilege of seeing him again; but we beheld a vast differ-

---

⁴¹Matt. 12:30; Mark 9:40; Luke 9:50; 11:23. ⁴²D. & C. 93:38.
⁴³Pers. Corresp.

ence between him and us. We were spirits. He was a spirit clothed with a glorious body—an immortal body. He had become a soul according to the definition which he himself has given, that is, a soul is the spirit and body united.[44] We noted the difference, and naturally wanted to become like him.

We were informed that the earth would be prepared where we might have the privilege of going and sojourning for a season, there to obtain bodies, tangible bodies of flesh and bones, but in obtaining these bodies we would have to pass through all the vicissitudes of mortality. We would have to come in contact with pain, with sorrow, with suffering, with sin, as well as with pleasures which we find in the mortal life.[45] The whole plan was laid before us, and we shouted for joy because this opportunity, this great opportunity, was going to be presented to us, of receiving tabernacles.

MORTALITY A STATE OF CORRUPTION. The tabernacles we were to receive were to be *tabernacles of corruption*. Do not misunderstand me in the use of that word, for I mean bodies that are changeable, subject to change as we see change in mortality. Our bodies are constantly changing, throwing off the waste and taking on the new to replace the waste. And so in the scriptures they are spoken of as being corruptible bodies.

Notwithstanding that, we rejoiced in the opportunity to receive bodies of that kind, for a season, with the understanding that eventually we would pass through death and then the resurrection, and then we would take up those bodies incorruptible. The spirit and the body in that resurrection would be again united, inseparably, never again to die, never again to receive corruption in the sense in which I am using that term, but to exist forever.[46] Is there any wonder that the sons of God shouted for joy?

---
[44]*D. & C.* 88:15.   [46]1 Cor. 15:42-54; Alma 11:45; 12:18.
[45]Alma 12:24; 34:32-35; 42:4, 13; *D. & C.* 29:42-43.

GLORIOUS BODIES FOR THE FAITHFUL. And our Father taught us that if we were faithful in the keeping of the commandments that should be given to us, that we would be like him, and would have *glorious bodies shining like the sun,* as his glorious body shines, and we should be called his sons and his daughters, and should be clothed with the fulness of all the blessings of his kingdom.[47]

So we were ready and willing to make that journey from the presence of God in the spirit world to the mortal world, here to suffer all that pertains to this life, its pleasures and its sorrows, and to die; and *death is just as essential as birth.* Who would want to live in this world, in this mortal condition, forever, with all the pain and the suffering and the anguish of soul that come? None of us would wish it, and especially if we understood that this is only a temporary probation and that by passing on we should come to a glorious condition of eternal life. We would not want to stay here. And so we have before us the plan of salvation.[48]

PURPOSE OF WEALTH OF WORLD. We are here for a great purpose. That purpose is not to live 100 years, or less, and plant our fields, reap our crops, gather fruit, live in houses, and surround ourselves with the necessities of mortal life. That is not the purpose of life. These things are necessary to our existence here, and that is the reason why we should be industrious. But how many men spend their time thinking that all there is in life is to accumulate the things of this world, to live in comfort, and surround themselves with all the luxuries, and privileges, and pleasures it is possible for mortal life to bestow, and never give a thought to anything beyond?

Why, all these things are but temporary blessings. We eat to live. We clothe ourselves to keep warm and covered. We have houses to live in for our comfort and convenience, but we ought to look upon all these blessings

---

[47] 1 John 3:1-3; D. & C. 93:20; 3 Ne. 28:10. [48] *Gen. & Hist. Mag.,* vol. 29, pp. 10-11.

OUR FIRST AND SECOND ESTATES

as temporary blessings needful while we journey through this life. And that is all the good they are to us. We cannot take any of them with us when we depart. Gold, silver, and precious stones, which are called wealth, are of no use to man, only as they enable him to take care of himself, and to meet his necessities here.[49]

IMPORTANCE OF THIS MORTAL PROBATION. This mortal probation was to be a brief period, just a short span linking the eternity past with the eternity future. Yet it was to be a period of tremendous importance. It would either give to those who received it the blessing of eternal life, which is the greatest gift of God, and thus qualify them for godhood as sons and daughters of our Eternal Father, or, if they rebelled and refused to comply with the laws and ordinances which were provided for their salvation, it would deny them the great gift and they would be assigned, after the resurrection, to some inferior sphere according to their works. *This life is the most vital period in our eternal existence.* It is filled with awful responsibilities and dangers. Here we are face to face with innumerable temptations. Lucifer, formerly a son of the morning, now Satan, the deceiver, is here with his rebellious hosts to tempt us and lead us astray.

We have to pass through pain and sorrow and are constantly in need of protection against sin and error. This is given us through the Spirit of God if we will but heed it. All of this was made known to us in the preexistence, and yet we were glad to take the risk.[50]

THE STRAITNESS OF THE WAY. *Mortality is the testing or proving ground for exaltation* to find out who among the children of God are worthy to become Gods themselves, and the Lord has informed us that *"few there be that find it."*[51] The way is strait and narrow, but the great difficulty with most of us is that we think it is broad and not restricted. *When we are informed that there*

---

[49]*Ibid.,* vol. 17, p. 154; *D. & C.* 6:7; 117:4-8; Rev. 3:17-18. [50]*Church News,* June 12, 1949, p. 21. [51]*D. & C.* 132-20-25.

are *straitened commandments and exacting covenants which must in this life be obeyed, we become rebellious and immediately commence arguing about the justice of God and his great mercy, thus losing our sense of correct vision and understanding.*[52]

FREE AGENCY IN BOTH ESTATES

AGENCY ESSENTIAL TO SALVATION. The Lord has given to man his agency. That is a divine principle—it is inherent, born with us. We have it because the Lord gave it to us in the spirit world. It is the only principle upon which exaltation can come. It is the only principle upon which rewards can be given in righteousness. Satan's plan in the beginning was to compel. He said he would save all men and not one soul should be lost. He would do it if the Father would give him the honor and the glory.[53] But who wants salvation when it comes through compulsion, if we have not the power within ourselves to choose and to act according to the dictates of conscience? What would salvation mean to you if you were compelled?[54] And so, that great gift of agency has been given to us. By it we may climb to the heights, we may enter the kingdom of God to sit on the throne and be exalted as sons and daughters of God, but we must be obedient.

AGENCY TO PREACH GOSPEL. I am willing to defend any man in the privilege which is his by his agency. If he wants to worship a cat or a dog; the sun or the moon; a crocodile or a bull—and men have done all these things —that is his privilege. But it is also my privilege and right to try to teach him to do better and to accept a better worship. I will defend him in his rights, and at the same time endeavor to teach him that he may see more clearly and walk in the light of truth.[55]

---

[52]Pers. Corresp.
[53]Moses 4:1-4; Abra. 3:26-28; D. & C. 29:36-40.
[54]2 Ne. 2:10-17, 26-30.
[55]Conf. Rep., Oct. 3, 1936, pp. 60-61.

UNRIGHTEOUS USE OF AGENCY. We Latter-day Saints hold that every man is entitled to his religious views, and should have the privilege of worshiping according to the dictates of his conscience, let him worship how, where, or what he may. And we will protect him in this right. But we are opposed to the custom adopted by certain men who travel through the settlements of our people abusing the authorities of the Church, distorting our doctrines and defaming the dead, for the purpose of destroying the faith and confidence of the Latter-day Saints.[56]

---
[56]*Origin of the "Reorganized" Church,* p. 5.

Chapter 5

THE EARTH: ITS CREATION AND DESTINY

MANY EARTHS AND THEIR SALVATION

EARTHS CREATED FOR MAN. The Lord declared to Moses that his great work and glory is "to bring to pass the immortality and eternal life of man." For this purpose earths have been and are now being built; and *the Lord's purpose is to provide for his children immortality and eternal life, not only on this earth, but on the countless earths throughout the universe.* They are numberless to man, yet our Father knows them all and they are numbered unto him. The Lord has said: "And as one *earth shall pass away,* and the heavens thereof even so shall another come; and there is no end to my works, neither to my words."[1]

HOW EARTHS PASS AWAY. This passing away does *not* mean that earths grow old and die, becoming cold, lifeless bodies, wandering through space, perhaps to disintegrate, be broken up and in some unknown manner be recreated, by some natural force working on the energy in the universe. We have every reason to believe that *the passing away of an earth simply means that it will undergo, or has undergone, the same definite course which is destined for our earth,* and the Lord has made that perfectly clear. *This earth is a living body.* It is true to the law given it. It was created to become a celestial body and the abode for celestial beings.[2]

Other earths, no doubt, are being *prepared as habitations for terrestrial and telestial beings,* for there must be places prepared for those who fail to obtain celestial glory, who receive immortality but not eternal life. More-

---
[1]Moses 1:27-40.   [2]D. & C. 88:17-26; Isa. 51:6-7; Ps. 102:25-26.

THE EARTH: ITS CREATION AND DESTINY

over, since the Lord has never created anything to be destroyed,[3] every earth, whether created for celestial glory, or for terrestrial or telestial, will have to pass through the condition of death and the resurrection, just the same as our earth will have to do. *The "passing away," therefore, means that after they have finished their "probationary state" in mortality, they will die and be raised again to receive the "glory" for which they were designed, and to become the eternal abodes of man.*[4]

LIFE, DEATH, AND RESURRECTION OF THE EARTH. In one of the revelations to Joseph Smith the Lord said to the Church and to all who are willing to receive it: "And again, verily, verily, I say unto you that when the thousand years are ended, and men again begin to deny their God, then will *I spare the earth but for a little season."* The Lord here is speaking of his second coming, of the millennial reign which shall be followed by a short period of wickedness and then the end.

The revelation continues: *"And the end shall come, and the heaven and the earth shall be consumed and pass away, and there shall be a new heaven and a new earth."* This does not mean that this earth shall pass away and another take its place, and the heaven thereof shall pass away, and another heaven take its place; but that *the earth and its heaven shall, after passing away through death, be renewed again in immortality.*

This earth is living and must die, but since it keeps the law it shall be restored through the resurrection by which it shall became celestialized and the abode of celestial beings. The next verse of this revelation explains this as follows: "For *all* old things shall pass away, and *all* things shall become new, *even the heaven and the earth, and all the fulness thereof,* both men and beasts, the fowls of the air, and the fishes of the sea; And not one hair, neither mote, shall be lost, for it is the workmanship of mine hand."[5]

---

[3]Eccl. 3:14-15; *D. & C.* 132:13-14.   [5]*D. & C.* 29:22-25.
[4]Pers. Corresp.

ATONEMENT FOR EARTH AND ALL LIFE. So we see that the Lord intends to save not only the earth and the heavens, not only man who dwells upon the earth, but all things which he has created. The animals, the fishes of the sea, the fowls of the air, as well as man, are to be re-created, or renewed, through the resurrection, for they too are living souls.[6] *The earth, as a living body, will have to die and be resurrected, for it, too, has been redeemed by the blood of Jesus Christ.*[7]

THE LORD'S BLUEPRINT OF CREATION

CHRIST CREATED MANY WORLDS. Under the direction of his Father, *Jesus Christ created this earth.* No doubt *others helped him,* but it was Jesus Christ, our Redeemer, who, under the direction of his Father, came down and organized matter and made this planet, so that it might be inhabited by the children of God.[8]

Jesus Christ is the light and the life of men; he was a Creator before this world was made. But we are not concerned so much just now with the works he then performed, nor are we concerned just now with these other worlds and their inhabitants.

This we know, and that will suffice until all things are revealed, the inhabitants of these worlds created by Jesus Christ, are begotten sons and daughters unto God. *Life did not originate here. Man did not first come into existence here.* We are told by our Father in heaven that *man is eternal;* that he has always existed, and that *all life on this earth came from elsewhere.* We may not be able to comprehend all this now, but the time will come in the providence of the Lord, when all these things shall be made known and we shall have knowledge in the fulness.[9]

ADAM AND OTHERS HELPED IN CREATION. It is true

---

[6]Conf. Rep., Oct., 1928, pp. 99-100.
[7]Pers. Corresp.
[8]*Millennial Star,* vol. 93, p. 241; D. & C. 38:1-3; John 1:1-5; 1 Cor. 8:6; Col. 1:16; Eph. 3:9.
[9]Conf. Rep., Oct., 1925, p. 113; Moses 1:32-33; D. & C. 76:24; 93:10; Heb. 1:2.

THE EARTH: ITS CREATION AND DESTINY

that Adam helped to form this earth. He labored with our Savior Jesus Christ. I have a strong view or conviction that there were others also who assisted them. Perhaps Noah and Enoch; and *why not Joseph Smith,* and those who were appointed to be rulers before the earth was formed? We know that Jesus our Savior was a Spirit when this great work was done. He did all of these mighty works before he tabernacled in the flesh.[10]

THE CREATORS PLAN THE CREATION. The account of the creation in the Book of Abraham is "The Lord's Blueprint of Creation." By this I mean Abraham gives an account of the *planning* in heaven for this earth and its inhabitants, *before* the work of building was done. I do not say that this planning contemplated the creation of the sun or other heavenly bodies, but rather the placing of the earth in the position which it was to occupy in relation to these orbs.[11]

PHYSICAL CREATION OF ALL THINGS

ACCOUNT OF PHYSICAL CREATION. While it is true that all things were created spiritually, or as spirits, before they were naturally upon the face of the earth, this creation, we are informed, was in heaven. This applies to animals of all descriptions and also to plant life, before there was flesh upon the earth, or in the water, or in the air.[12] *The account of the creation of the earth as given in Genesis, and the Book of Moses, and as given in the temple, is the creation of the physical earth, and of physical animals and plants.*[13] I think the temple account, which was given by revelation, is the clearest of all of these. *These physical creations were made out of the natural elements.*

NO REVEALED ACCOUNT OF SPIRIT CREATION. There is *no account* of the creation of man or other forms of life when they were created as spirits. There is just

---
[10]Abra. 3:24.
[11]Abra. 4:1-31; 5:1-21.
[12]Moses 3:5, 9; Gen. 2:5, 9.
[13]Moses 1, 2, 3; Gen. 1, 2.

the simple statement that they were so created *before* the physical creation. The statements in Moses 3:5 and Genesis 2:5 are *interpolations* thrown into the account of the physical creation, explaining that all things were first created in the spirit existence in heaven before they were placed upon this earth.

We were all created untold ages before we were placed on this earth. We discover from Abraham 3:22-28, that it was before the earth was formed that the plan of salvation was presented to the spirits, or "intelligences." This being true, then *man, animals and plants were not created in the spirit at the time of the creation of the earth, but long before.*

SPIRITUAL OR PHYSICAL, AND SPIRIT CREATIONS. The account of creation in Genesis was not *a spirit* creation, but it was in a particular sense, a *spiritual creation.* This, of course, needs some explanation. *The account in Genesis, chapters one and two, is the account of the creation of the physical earth.* The account of the placing of all life upon the earth, up and until the fall of Adam, is an account, in a sense, of the spiritual creation of all of these, but it was also a physical creation. *When the Lord said he would create Adam, he had no reference to the creation of his spirit for that had taken place ages and ages before when he was in the world of spirits and known as Michael.*[14]

Adam's body was created from the dust of the earth, but at that time it was a spiritual earth. Adam had a spiritual body until mortality came upon him through the violation of the law under which he was living, but he also had *a physical body of flesh and bones.*

NATURE OF A SPIRITUAL BODY. Now what is a *spiritual body? It is one that is quickened by spirit and not by blood.* Our Father in heaven and our Savior and all those who have passed through the resurrection have physical bodies of flesh and bones, but their bodies are

---
[14]Moses 2:26-28; Gen. 1:26-28.

quickened by spirit and not by blood, hence they are *spiritual bodies* and not *blood bodies*. *The immortal body is quickened by spirit, but the mortal body is quickened by blood.* The Lord said to Noah, that blood is the life of the body in this mortal sphere.[15] In latter-day revelation we have the following:

"For notwithstanding they die, they also shall rise again, a spiritual body. They who are of a celestial spirit shall receive the same body which was a natural body [i.e. a mortal body]; even ye shall receive your bodies, and your glory shall be that glory by which your bodies are quickened."[16]

From this we have the Lord's endorsement of a spiritual body being the body which has ceased to be a blood body. Now when Adam was in the Garden of Eden, he was not subject to death. There was no blood in his body and he could have remained there forever. *This is true of all the other creations.*[17] This statement may not be very pleasing to our evolutionists, but it is true.

ADAM: FIRST MAN AND FIRST FLESH. After the fall, which came by a transgression of the law under which Adam was living, the forbidden fruit had the power to create blood and change his nature and mortality took the place of immortality, and all things, partaking of the change, became mortal. Now I repeat, *the account in Genesis one and two, is the account of the physical creation of the earth and all upon it, but the creation was not subject to mortal law until after the fall. It was, therefore, a spiritual creation and so remained until the fall when it became temporal, or mortal.*[18]

There was no living thing upon the earth until it was prepared for living life. The *Pearl of Great Price* does *not* say that man was the first living thing on the earth, but that he was the first flesh and the first man also. *He became the first mortal flesh when he fell.* By flesh is meant

---
[15]Gen. 9:4; Lev. 17:11, 14. [17]2 Ne. 2:22.
[16]*D. & C.* 88:27-28; 1 Cor. 15:44-54. [18]*D. & C.* 77:6.

mortality, and Adam was the first mortal on the earth; but *animals and other forms of life were placed on earth first*, and he was not on the earth until everything was prepared for him. Since Adam was the first man on the earth, that does away with *the false notion that there were pre-Adamites*.[19]

AGE OF THE EARTH

TIME ELEMENT IN THE CREATION. *This earth was created on the Lord's time, which is celestial time.* By revelation we know exactly the nature of that time, and just how many days of celestial time were required to create this earth. Moreover, we know how long this earth has endured, approximately, and how long it will endure according to our present rate of reckoning. The Lord revealed to Abraham:

"And the Lord said unto me, by the Urim and Thummim, that Kolob was after the manner of the Lord, according to its times and seasons in the revolutions thereof; that *one revolution was a day unto the Lord,* after his manner of reckoning, it being *one thousand years* according to the time appointed unto that whereon thou standest. *This is the reckoning of the Lord's time,* according to the reckoning of Kolob. . . .

"And thus there shall be the reckoning of the time of one planet above another, until thou come nigh unto Kolob, which Kolob is after the reckoning of the Lord's time; which Kolob is set nigh unto the throne of God, to govern all those planets which belong to the same order as that upon which thou standest."[20]

CELESTIAL TIME USED IN CREATION. Also: "Fig. 1. Kolob, signifying the first creation, nearest to the celestial, or the residence of God. First in government, the last pertaining to the measurement of time. The measurement according to *celestial time,* which celestial time

---

[19]Joseph Fielding Smith, *Man: His Origin and Destiny,* chapters 15, 16, 17.   [20]Abra. 3:4, 9.

THE EARTH: ITS CREATION AND DESTINY

signifies one day to a cubit. *One day in Kolob is equal to a thousand years according to the measurement of this earth, which is called by the Egyptians Jah-oh-eh.*"[21]

When this earth was created, it was not according to our present time, but it was created *according to Kolob's time,* for the Lord has said it was created on celestial time which is Kolob's time. Then he revealed to Abraham that *Adam was subject to Kolob's time before his transgression.* "Now I, Abraham, saw that it was after the Lord's time, which was after the time of Kolob; *for as yet the Gods had not appointed unto Adam his reckoning.*"[22]

AGE OF THE EARTH SINCE ADAM. We have evidence beyond dispute that *Adam was driven out of the Garden of Eden about 6,000 years ago,* or perhaps a short time less. It is possible for us, by using the *Bible* chronology and that given by the Lord in the *Book of Mormon* and *Doctrine and Covenants* to figure this almost accurately.

In the Book of Revelation, chapters five to 10, we have the story of the opening of the seven seals by the Lamb, each seal representing 1,000 years of the temporal existence of this earth. In the *Doctrine and Covenants,* section 88:92-116, we have the confirmation of this with other detail in regard to the opening of the seals. In section 77:6-15, we have more information in relation to the opening of these seals, with the following significant detail:

Verse 6: "Q. What are we to understand by the book which John saw, which was sealed on the back with seven seals?

"A. We are to understand that it contains the revealed will, mysteries, and works of God; *the hidden things* of his economy concerning *this earth during the seven thousand years of its continuance, or its temporal existence.*"

---

[21] Book of Abraham, p. 35, figure 1.   [22] Abra. 5:13.

TEMPORAL EXISTENCE OF EARTH. Here is a definite statement by revelation to us that this earth will go through 7,000 years of *temporal* existence. Temporal, by all interpretations, *means passing, temporary or mortal.* This, then, has reference to the earth in its fallen state, for the earth was cursed when Adam, who was given dominion over it, transgressed the law. *Before that time this earth was not mortal any more than Adam was.* This we learn from other scriptures; for instance, see 2 Nephi 2:22.

In verse 12 of section 77, the Prophet by inspiration from the Lord, sets days of a thousand years off against years of our measurement, in these words:

"We are to understand that as *God made the world in six days,* and on the seventh day he finished his work, and sanctified it, and also formed man out of the dust of the earth, even so, *in the beginning of the seventh thousand years will the Lord God sanctify the earth,* and complete the salvation of man, and judge all things, and shall redeem all things, except that which he hath not put into his power, when he shall have sealed all things, unto the end of all things; and the sounding of the trumpets of the seven angels are the preparing and finishing of his work, *in the beginning of the seventh thousand years—* the preparing of the way before the time of his coming."

CREATION DID NOT TAKE MILLIONS OF YEARS. Here we have the Prophet comparing the days of creation with seven periods of 1,000 years each, corresponding to days, according to the Lord's time, in harmony with the teaching of Abraham and the other scriptures. The earth's temporal existence, according to this, is to endure for just one week, or seven days of 1,000 years each. Moreover, since the earth was built according to the celestial time, which is the Lord's days, which he clearly defined to Abraham, we can hardly be justified in trying to harmonize the days of creation with the extended periods of millions of years according to the reckoning of the so-called scientists.

THE EARTH: ITS CREATION AND DESTINY

Both from the *Bible* and from the Book of *Doctrine and Covenants,* we know that the flood came in the year 1600 from the driving of Adam out of the Garden of Eden. We know that Abraham was living in the days of Shem, son of Noah, if not in the days of Noah himself. Profane history corroborates the history of Israel and Abraham. So a man is wilfully blind who would push these days back tens of thousands, much less, hundreds of thousands of years.

MEANING OF THE MERIDIAN OF TIME. Moreover, our Savior came in the meridian of time. That dispensation is called the dispensation of the meridian of time. This means that it was about half way from the *beginning of "time" to the end of "time."* Anyone who desires can figure it for himself that our Lord came about 4,000 years from the time of the fall. The millennium is to come some time following the 2,000 years after his coming. Then there is to be the millennium for 1,000 years, and following that a *"little season,"* the length of which is not revealed, but which may *bring "time" to its end* about 8,000 years from the beginning.

We have seen that the Lord had not given to this earth its *present time* until after the fall. Before that time it was subject to *Kolob's time, which is eternal time. After the temporal existence of the earth is finished, it will again go back on celestial time, and there shall be "time no longer."*[23] This does not mean that the inhabitants of the earth, who will be celestial beings, will not reckon by time, but by a different time—Kolob's time which the Lord says is his time.

If men prefer to believe the strong delusions taught by evolutionists, rather than what the Lord has revealed, we cannot help it, but it certainly shows in them a lack of faith, which is not to their credit.

---
[23]*D. & C.* 88:110-111.

THE TELESTIAL EARTH

FOUR STAGES OF EARTH'S EXISTENCE. This earth is passing through four grand degrees or stages: 1. The *creation* and the condition antedating the fall. 2. The *telestial condition* which has prevailed since the fall of Adam. 3. The *terrestrial condition* that will prevail when the Savior comes and ushers in the millennial era. 4. The *celestial or final state* of the earth when it has obtained its exaltation. There is, also, what the Lord has called a *"little season,"* following the millennium when Satan will be loosed and the last great battle will be fought.[24]

TELESTIAL STATUS RESULT OF ADAM'S FALL. When the earth was created, the Lord pronounced it good. *Everything on its face was created without the seeds of death and could have endured forever.* This is taught, among other places, in 2 Nephi 2:22. Death had not entered the world, and *Adam was immortal in the sense that he was not subject to death.* However, *he had not passed through the resurrection, and, therefore, he was in a condition by which he could fall so that his body would become subject to death or mortality. This happened and this condition then passed upon the earth and all creatures living upon it.*

From the time Adam was driven out of the Garden until now this earth and its inhabitants, man, beast, fowl, fish, and every creature has been subject to death. The earth itself must die and receive its resurrection. This present condition, which we refer to as a telestial condition, will endure until Christ comes. We are informed that this temporal existence will endure for 6,000 years.[25]

TELESTIAL STATUS SOON TO END. The days of this earth's present condition in its scenes of wickedness, of crime, of greed, when Satan rules, are drawing to their close. Before many days shall pass, Satan shall be bound, that he shall have no place in the hearts of the

---
[24]*D. & C.* 29:22-23; 43:30-31; 88:101-115; Rev. 20:3-9.   [25]Pers. Corresp.

children of men. Christ shall come to take possession of the earth, since it belongs to him, and he is the rightful ruler. We are promised that he shall reign upon the earth for 1,000 years, but when that time comes, only the righteous, the God-fearing, the humble, the meek, shall inherit the earth.

TELESTIAL WORLD RULED BY SATAN. This earth, since its fall, must pass through three distinct stages. We are in one of those stages now. In this mortal condition, which has continued since the days of Adam until now, wickedness has prevailed on the earth. Satan has had sway. He has usurped authority and found favor with men. Through his power, his cunning and craftiness, he has won mankind very largely over to his side.

But this condition, as I have said, is drawing to its close. The day is near at hand when this earth itself shall be changed, when righteousness shall prevail, and wickedness cease upon its face. Then, for 1,000 years, the earth shall rest; and that will be the second stage in the history of this planet since man was placed upon it.[26]

END OF WORLD IS NOT END OF EARTH. The world is not the earth. The end of the world does not mean the destruction of the earth and everything upon it.

The disciples came to Christ shortly before his crucifixion seeking further light concerning certain statements he had made pertaining to the destruction of Jerusalem and the end of the world. In the translation which has come to us we do not get the clearest understanding, but from the inspired rendering which has been given to us in modern days, through Joseph Smith, the Prophet, certain matters which were not clear to the world are made clear to the Latter-day Saints, and I shall read one or two paragraphs from the revision of the 24th chapter of Matthew.

"And Jesus left them, and went upon the Mount of Olives. And as he sat upon the Mount of Olives, the

---

[26]*Millennial Star*, vol. 93, pp. 241-242.

disciples came unto him privately, saying: Tell us when shall these things be which thou hast said concerning the destruction of the temple, and the Jews; and what is the sign of thy coming, and of *the end of the world, or the destruction of the wicked, which is the end of the world?*

"And Jesus answered, and said unto them: . . . And again, this Gospel of the Kingdom shall be preached in all the world, for a witness unto all nations, and then shall the end come, or the destruction of the wicked."[27]

The Lord was not speaking of the end of the earth. The disciples were not asking concerning the end of the earth; they were asking concerning Christ's second coming, which would bring to pass the *end of wickedness, or the end of the world as it is now constituted,* and the Lord gave them the answer.[28]

THE TERRESTRIAL EARTH

EARTH TO BE RENEWED. When our Savior comes, the earth will be changed to a terrestrial condition and will then be made the fit abode for terrestrial beings, and this condition will last until after the close of the millennium when the earth will die and be raised again in a resurrection to receive its glory as a celestial body, which is its final state.

We are living in the great day of restoration. The Lord has declared that all things are to be restored to their primitive condition. Our tenth Article of Faith says, "We believe . . . that Christ will reign personally upon the earth; and, that *the earth will be renewed and receive its paradisiacal glory."* Too many have the idea that this has reference to the celestialized earth, but this is *not* the case. It refers to the *restored earth* as it will be when Christ comes to reign. This is taught in Isaiah 65:17-25, and in the *Doctrine and Covenants,* section 101:23-31.

RESTORATION OF THE EARTH. Joseph Smith gave

---
[27]Joseph Smith 1:4-5, 31. [28]*Church News,* Nov. 3, 1934, p. 4.

THE EARTH: ITS CREATION AND DESTINY

this inspired summary of latter-day events: "There shall be famine, and pestilence, and earthquake in divers places; and the prophets have declared that the valleys should rise; that the mountains should be laid low; that a great earthquake should be, in which the sun should become black as sack-cloth of hair, and the moon turn into blood; yea, the Eternal God hath declared that *the great deep shall roll back into the north countries and that the land of Zion and the land of Jerusalem shall be joined together, as they were before they were divided* in the days of Peleg. No wonder the mind starts at the sound of the last days!"[29]

Here the Prophet tells us that the dividing of the earth was in the days of Peleg.[30] When Christ comes, it will be brought back again as it was before it was divided.

EARTH TO BE RESTORED TO PARADISIACAL GLORY. Now in time past this earth had a paradisiacal glory, and then came the fall, bringing a change, and that change has been upon the earth in the neighborhood of 6,000 years.

What is meant by the restoration of the earth? *This earth is to be renewed and brought back to the condition in which it was before it was cursed through the fall of Adam.* When Adam passed out of the Garden of Eden, then the earth became a telestial world, and it is of that order today. I do not mean a telestial glory such as will be found in telestial worlds after their resurrection, but a telestial condition which has been from the days of Adam until now and will continue until Christ comes.

WICKED WILL BURN AS STUBBLE. When Christ comes, the earth will be changed and so will all upon its face. It will become a terrestrial world then and will so remain for 1,000 years; and all those who have lived a telestial law will be eliminated. They will be as stubble

---

[29]*Evening and Morning Star*, Feb., 1835; *D. & C.* 49:23; 109:74; 133:17-25, 44; Isa. 40:4; 54:10; Ezek. 38:20; Rev. 16:15-20. [30]Gen. 10:25.

and be consumed. The earth will be cleansed from its wickedness and pass into the terrestrial order. This will necessitate a change in the very elements of the earth, and also of its inhabitants; yet they will still be mortal. Those who belong to the terrestrial order will dwell upon the earth during this period.[31]

TIME OF FIRST RESURRECTION. The Lord tells us that in that day the heathen nations shall be redeemed and they who knew no law shall have part in the resurrection which to us is known as the first. "At his coming," apparently meaning after he has established his government and holy order, those will come forth who have kept the terrestrial law. Those who have kept the celestial law will come forth to meet him in the clouds preceding the resurrection of the terrestrial inhabitants.[32]

NON-MEMBERS OF CHURCH DURING MILLENNIUM. Some members of the Church have an erroneous idea that when the millennium comes all of the people are going to be swept off the earth except righteous members of the Church. That is not so. There will be millions of people, Catholics, Protestants, agnostics, Mohammedans, people of all classes, and of all beliefs, still permitted to remain upon the face of the earth, but they will be those who have lived clean lives, those who have been free from wickedness and corruption. All who belong, by virtue of their good lives, to the terrestrial order, as well as those who have kept the celestial law, will remain upon the face of the earth during the millennium.[33]

Eventually, however, the knowledge of the Lord will cover the earth as the waters do the sea. But there will be need for the preaching of the gospel, after the millennium is brought in, until all men are either converted or pass away. In the course of the thousand years all men will either come into the Church, or kingdom of God, or they will die and pass away. In that day there will be

---

[31]*D. & C.* 63:20-21; 101:23-31; Malachi 3:2-3; 4:1-6; Joseph Smith 2:36-40; 3 Ne. 20:23.

[32]Pers. Corresp.; *D. & C.* 45:54-55; 88:96-99.

[33]*Church News,* Nov. 3, 1934, p. 8.

no death until men are old. Children will not die but will live to the age of a tree. Isaiah says this is 100 years. When the time comes for men to die, they will be changed in the twinkling of an eye, and there will be no graves.[34]

EARTH AFTER THE MILLENNIUM. Will the earth go back to the telestial order after the millennium? No, but the people on the face of the earth, many of them, will be like the Nephites who lived 200 years after the coming of Christ. They will rebel against the Lord knowingly, and the great last struggle will come, and the devil and his forces will be defeated; then the earth will die and receive its resurrection and become a celestial body. The resurrection of the wicked will take place as one of the last events before the earth dies.[35]

THE CELESTIAL EARTH

"THE BATTLE OF THE GREAT GOD." After the thousand years Satan will be loosed again and will go forth again to deceive the nations. Because men are still mortal, Satan will go out to deceive them. Men will again deny the Lord, but in doing so they will act with their eyes open and because they love darkness rather than light, and so *they become sons of perdition*. Satan will gather his hosts, both those on the earth and the wicked dead who will eventually also be brought forth in the resurrection. Michael, the Prince, will gather his forces and the last great battle will be fought. Satan will be defeated with his hosts. Then will come the end. Satan and those who follow him will be banished into outer darkness.

CELESTIAL DESTINY OF THE EARTH. The earth will be cleansed again. It was once baptized in water. When Christ comes, it will be baptized with fire and the power of the Holy Ghost. At the end of the world *the earth will die; it will be dissolved, pass away, and then it will be renewed, or raised with a resurrection*. It will receive

---

[34]*D. & C.* 101:23-31; Isa. 65:17-25.   [35]*D. & C.* 88:25-26, 100-116.

its resurrection to become a celestial body, so that they of the celestial order may possess it forever and ever. Then *it will shine forth as the sun and take its place among the worlds that are redeemed.* When this time comes the terrestrial inhabitants will also be taken away and be consigned to another sphere suited to their condition. Then the words of the Savior will be fulfilled, for the meek shall inherit the earth.[36]

WHEN THE MEEK SHALL INHERIT THE EARTH. The Lord gave the promise to Abraham that he should have Palestine, or the land of Canaan, as an everlasting possession.[37] Yet, as Stephen said at the time of his martyrdom, Abraham never received as much as a foot of it as a possession while he lived.[38]

Then what did the Lord mean in making a promise to Abraham of that kind, giving him that portion of the earth as an everlasting possession for himself and his posterity, the righteous part of it, forever? Simply this, that the time would eventually come, after the resurrection from the dead, when Abraham and his children who have been faithful in the keeping of the commandments of the Lord, should possess that land, and they shall also spread forth as far as it is necessary for them to receive an inheritance.

The Lord gave this land upon which we dwell, America, as an everlasting possession to Joseph, the son of Jacob. His posterity, *when cleansed from sin,* and when they come forth in the resurrection, shall inherit this part of the earth. This land shall be theirs forever.[39]

The Lord gave this land also to others at an earlier date, the Jaredites, and they, too, who are righteous among them, shall possess it forever.[40]

EARTH TO BE A CELESTIAL SUN. It is my opinion that *the great stars that we see, including our sun, are*

---

[36]Pers. Corresp.; *D. & C.* 29:22-30; 88:14-33, 95-116; Rev. 4:6; 15:1-4; 20:1-15; 21:1-27; 22:1-5.
[37]Gen. 17:1-8.
[38]Acts. 7:5.
[39]Gen. 49:22-26.
[40]*Millennial Star,* vol. 93, pp. 243-244; Ether 1:41-43.

celestial worlds; at least worlds that have passed on to their exaltation or other final resurrected status. This is in conflict, of course, with the teachings of scientific men, who declare that the sun is losing its energy and gradually cooling off and will eventually be a dead world. I do not believe the Lord has any such thing in his plan. The Lord lives in "everlasting burnings" we are informed. President Brigham Young has said that *this earth when it is celestialized will shine like the sun,* and why not?

"If the people could fully understand this matter," he said, "they would perceive that it is perfectly reasonable and *has been the law of all worlds.* And this world, so benighted at present, and so lightly esteemed by infidels, as observed by Brother Clements, when it becomes celestialized, it will be like the sun, and be prepared for the habitation of the saints, and be brought back into the presence of the Father and the Son. It will not then be an opaque body as it now is, but it will be like the stars of the firmament, full of light and glory; it will be a body of light. John compared it, in its celestialized state, to a sea of glass."[41]

Orson Pratt has given us the following: "Who, in looking upon *the earth* as it *ascends in the scale of the universe,* does not desire to keep pace with it? that when it shall be *classed in its turn, among the dazzling orbs of the blue vault of heaven, shining forth in all the splendor of celestial glory,* he may find himself proportionally advanced in the scale of intellectual and moral excellence? Who, but the most abandoned, does not desire to be counted worthy to associate with those *higher orders of beings who have been redeemed, exalted, and glorified together with the worlds they inhabit,* ages before the foundations of our earth were laid? O man, remember the future destiny and the glory of the earth, and secure thine everlasting inheritance upon the same, that when it shall be glorious, thou shalt be glorious also."[42]

---

[41]*Journal of Discourses,* vol. 7, p. 163. [42]Pers. Corresp.; *Millennial Star,* vol. 12, p. 72.

CHAPTER 6

MICHAEL OUR PRINCE

CREATION OF ADAM

STATUS OF ADAM IN PRE-EXISTENCE. *The first man placed upon the earth was a perfect being, a son of God.* He was Michael, the Archangel, who had reached great distinction and power before he ever came to this earth; and who *helped to frame this earth while he was yet a spirit,* just as our Lord and Savior Jesus Christ was a spirit before he was born in Bethlehem.[1]

Michael, after being placed upon this earth, is known as Adam. He received his tabernacle of flesh from the dust of *this* earth. He belongs to it, but *he was one of the greatest of the intelligences,* and was sent here to this earth to stand at the head of his posterity, to rule over them through the ages of eternity. We are indebted to him for more than we think. Through him we get these tabernacles of flesh and bones, tabernacles for our spirits. Our spirits are the begotten sons and daughters of God; so is Adam's, but he was sent here for the purpose of peopling this earth with bodies of flesh and bones.[2]

ADAM CREATED FROM DUST OF THIS EARTH. The *Book of Mormon,* the *Bible,* the *Doctrine and Covenants,* and the *Pearl of Great Price* all declare that Adam's body was created from the dust of the ground,[3] that is, from the dust of *this ground, this earth.* Moreover the Lord said to Adam, that if he partook of the fruit of the tree of the knowledge of good and evil, he should surely die. "By the sweat of thy face shalt thou eat bread, until thou shalt *return* unto the ground—for thou shalt

---
[1]Abra. 3:22-25; 5:4-8; Moses 3:7; Rev. 12:7-9.
[2]*Rel. Soc. Mag.,* vol. 39. pp. 4-5.
[3]Alma 42:2; Gen. 2:7; D. & C. 77:12; Moses 3:7.

surely die—for out of *it* [i.e. *the ground*] wast thou taken: for *dust thou wast,* and unto dust shalt thou return."⁴ Now how could he return to the dust of the earth, if his body was not taken from it?⁵

ADAM CREATED IN IMMORTALITY. When Adam came into this world, he was not subject to death. He was immortal. He could have lived forever. Had he remained in the Garden of Eden and not transgressed the law that had been given to him, he and Eve would have been there yet.⁶

Now Adam's immortality, when he was in the Garden of Eden, was *different* from the immortality which will come eventually to every creature; for after the resurrection from the dead, spirit and body become inseparably connected, that man may receive a fulness of joy, provided he has kept the commandments of God. In a state of resurrected immortality the spirit and body become inseparably connected, welded together, that they may never be divided again.

ADAM NOT RESURRECTED IN EDEN. We hear a lot of people talk about Adam passing through mortality and the resurrection on another earth and then coming here to live and die again. Well, that is a contradiction of the word of the Lord, for a resurrected being does not die, whether that resurrected being enters the celestial kingdom, the terrestrial kingdom, or the telestial kingdom, or whether he becomes a son of perdition and is cast out into hell, because the spirit and the body become inseparably connected in the resurrection. *Adam had not passed through a resurrection when he was in the Garden of Eden,* and having not passed through a resurrection, spirit and body could be separated by the violation of the law. And the Lord provided the law so it could happen, because the mortal estate in which we find ourselves is absolutely necessary to our exaltation.⁷

---

⁴Moses 4:25; Gen. 3:19.
⁵Pers. Corresp.
⁶2 Ne. 2:22; Moses 6:58-59.
⁷*Church News,* Apr. 15, 1939, pp. 3, 6; Alma 11:45; 12:18; *D. & C.* 63:49; 88:16, 116; 93:33-34.

ADAM: FIRST MAN AND FIRST FLESH

ADAM QUICKENED BY SPIRIT, NOT BY BLOOD. Man became a living spirit clothed with a physical, flesh and bones body, but the body was *not* quickened by blood, but by spirit, for *there was no blood in Adam's body before the fall. He was not then "flesh" as we know it, that is in the sense of mortality.* In that state Adam could have remained in the Garden of Eden forever and all things that were created would have remained in that same condition forever.[8]

MEANING OF "FIRST FLESH." But Adam was the *first* flesh on the earth and the *first* man also.[9] *By flesh is meant mortality.* There are numerous passages in the scriptures in which mortality and flesh are used synonymously.[10] Adam was placed on the earth *after* all other creatures were here. He came when the earth was prepared for him.[11] The Lord speaks of his becoming *the first "flesh," or mortal, because of his fall.* He was, of course, the first man on the earth, contrary to the teachings of our evolutionists. His name means "many," in reference to the greatness of his posterity as the human father of mankind.

ADAM BROUGHT MORTALITY TO ALL THINGS. After Adam's fall, the Lord declared that he placed a "curse" upon the earth, and this mortal condition then passed upon the earth and all upon its face. President Brigham Young in speaking of this said: "It is very true, *had not sin entered into the world, and opposition been introduced, death would not have entered.* From that time to this death, opposition, selfishness, malice, anger, pride, darkness and wickedness of every description that could be invented by the children of men, as they have multiplied and spread abroad on the earth, have increased."[12]

And again: "How did Adam and Eve sin? Did

---

[8] 2 Ne. 2:22; Gen. 9:2-6; Lev. 17:10-14.
[9] Moses 3:7.
[10] *D. & C.* 1:19; 67:11; 76:73-74; 84:21; John 8:15; Rom. 8:12-13; Jer. 17:5.
[11] Gen. 1:11-30; Moses 2:11-30.
[12] *Journal of Discourses*, vol. 1, p. 235.

they come out in direct opposition to God and to his government? No, but they transgressed a command of the Lord, and through that transgression sin came into the world. . . . *Then came the curse upon the fruit, upon the vegetables, and upon our mother earth; and it came upon the creeping things, upon the grain in the field, the fish in the sea, and upon all things pertaining to this earth, through man's transgression.*"[13]

"THE FIRST MAN OF ALL MEN." Many revelations attest the truth that Adam was the first man.[14] The Prophet corrected the genealogy of Christ as given in Luke so that it includes this statement: "Adam who was formed of God, and the first man upon the earth."[15]

The First Presidency has given the *doctrine of the Church* in these words: "It is held by some that Adam was not the first man upon this earth, and that the original human was a development from lower orders of the animal creation. These, however, are the theories of men. The word of the Lord declares that Adam was 'the first man of all men,' and we are therefore in duty bound to regard him as *the primal parent of the race.*"[16]

Joseph Smith has given us this statement: "Commencing with Adam, who was the first man, who is spoken of in Daniel as the 'Ancient of Days,' or in other words, *the first and oldest of all, the great, grand progenitor* of whom it is said in another place he is Michael, because *he was the first and father of all, not only by progeny, but the first to hold the spiritual blessings,* to whom was made known the plan of ordinances for the salvation of his posterity unto the end."[17]

ADAM COMMANDED TO REPLENISH THE EARTH

MEANING OF REPLENISH. Adam was commanded to multiply and replenish the earth. Some have sup-

---

[13]*Journal of Discourses,* vol. 10, p. 312.
[14]*D. & C.* 84:16; Moses 1:34; 3:7; 6:45; Abra. 1:3; 1 Ne. 5:11.
[15]*Inspired Version,* Luke 3:45.
[16]*Era,* vol. 13, p. 75; Joseph Fielding Smith, *Man: His Origin and Destiny,* pp. 348-355.
[17]Joseph Fielding Smith, *Teachings of the Prophet Joseph Smith,* p. 167.

posed this meant to fill up the earth again, but this is not so. The original Hebrew word appears many times in the Old Testament; only once is it translated "replenish."

It is a translation from the Hebrew word "male" pronounced malay. It is the same Hebrew word which is translated "fill" in the first chapter of Genesis, verse 22, in reference to the multiplying of fish of the sea and fowl of the air and the beasts of the field. This same Hebrew word is translated more than a score of times in other parts of the Bible and always as "fill," or "make full," never as replenish.

The Hebrew Lexicon defines the word as follows: "male intrans, *to be or become full, to be fulfilled or completed.*" Why this word was translated "replenish" in the one case, but "fill" or "make full" in reference to fish, fowl and beasts and in a score of other places, I do not know.

In the Catholic Bible, it is translated, "fill." And God said to them, "Be fruitful and multiply so as to fill the earth and subdue it."

In the Smith and Goodspeed translation it reads: "Be fruitful, multiply, fill the earth, and subdue it."

In Farrer Fenton's (English) translation, it reads: "God then gave them his blessing; and God said to them, Be fruitful and multiply so as to fill the earth, and subdue it."

Even in the English unabridged dictionary, *one meaning of replenish is "to make full."*

ADAM: INTELLIGENT AND CIVILIZED

ADAM NOT END PRODUCT OF EVOLUTION. *Adam was placed here, not a wild, half-civilized savage, but a perfectly-developed man, with wonderful intelligence, for he helped to create this earth. He was chosen in pre-existence to be the first man upon the earth and the father of the human race, and he will preside over his posterity forever.*

Now, the Lord did not choose a being that had just developed from the lower forms of life, to be a prince, an archangel, to preside over the human race forever! Adam, as Michael, was one of the greatest intelligences in the spirit world and he stands next to Jesus Christ. When he came upon the earth, the Lord gave him a perfect form of government.[18]

ADAM SPOKE CELESTIAL LANGUAGE. The first man placed upon this earth was an intelligent being, created in the image of God, possessed of wisdom and knowledge, with power to communicate his thoughts in a language, both oral and written, which was superior to anything to be found on the earth today. This may sound very sweeping and dogmatic to those who hold to the other view, but it is not any more so than their statements to the contrary. Moreover, I do not say it of myself, but merely repeat what the Lord has said; and surely the Creator, above all others, ought to know!

ADAM TAUGHT BY GOD. The first man was instructed by the best teacher man ever had, for he was taught of God, and spoke the language of the Most High, in which angels conversed. This language he taught to his children. It is true that he was left to work out, through the use of his faculties, many of nature's great secrets; but the Lord did not leave him helpless, but instructed him, and he was inspired by the Spirit of the Lord.[19]

GOSPEL REVEALED TO ADAM. The Lord gave him commandments after he was driven out of the Garden of Eden, revealed to him the plan of salvation, and he taught his children, and he set up a government. It was a perfect government, for Adam listened to the counsels of the Almighty, his Father, and our Father. He taught his children principles of divine truth and endeavored

---

[18]Pers. Corresp.   [19]*Era*, vol. 22, p. 466; Moses 2:26-27; 5:58; 6:5-6, 46.

to establish them in the knowledge and understanding of the things of the kingdom of God.[20]

ADAM HAD THE TEN COMMANDMENTS. Some people have the idea that the Ten Commandments were first given by Moses when he directed the children of Israel and formulated their code of laws. This is not the case. These great commandments are from the beginning and were understood in righteous communities in the days of Adam. They are, in fact, fundamental parts of the gospel of Jesus Christ, and the gospel in its fulness was first given to Adam.[21]

THE ADAM-GOD THEORY

SOURCE OF ADAM-GOD THEORY. President Brigham Young is quoted—in all probability the sermon was erroneously transcribed!—as having said: "Now hear it, O inhabitants of the earth, Jew and Gentile, saint and sinner! When our father Adam came into the Garden of Eden, he came into it with a celestial body, and brought Eve, one of his wives, with him. He *helped* to make and organize this world. He is *Michael, the Archangel, the Ancient of Days,* about whom holy men have written and spoken—He is our father and our God, and the only God with whom we have to do."[22]

RELATIONSHIP OF ELOHIM, JEHOVAH, AND MICHAEL. If the enemies of the Church who quote this wished to be honest, they could not help seeing that President Brigham Young definitely declares that Adam is Michael, the Archangel, the Ancient of Days, which indicates definitely that Adam is *not* Elohim, or the God whom we worship, who is the Father of Jesus Christ.

Further, they could see that President Young declared that Adam *helped* to make the earth. If he helped then he was *subordinate* to someone who was superior. In another paragraph in that same discourse, President

---

[20]*Rel. Soc. Mag.,* vol. 39, pp. 4-5; Moses 5:2-15, 57-59; 6:51-68; 7:1.
[21]*Era,* vol. 44, p. 525.
[22]*Journal of Discourses,* vol. 1, p. 50.

Young said: "It is true that *the earth was organized by three distinct characters,* namely, *Elohim, Jehovah, and Michael.*" Here he places Adam, or Michael, third in the list, and hence the least important of the three mentioned, and this President Young understood perfectly. We believe that Adam, known as Michael, had authority in the heavens before the world was framed. *He dwelt in the presence of the Father and the Son and was subject to their direction* as the scriptures plainly indicate.[23]

NATURE OF ADAM'S CELESTIAL BODY. When President Young says that Adam came here with a celestial body, he speaks the truth. We teach that Adam or Michael had authority in heaven. He dwelt in the presence of the Father and the Son, hence *he came from a celestial world.* If so, then did he not have a celestial body? I think the same can be said of all of us, if we accept the teachings of the Lord—for we all came from the presence of God, hence had *celestial bodies,* even if they were *spirit bodies,* as was Adam's.

Again in this discourse President Young said: "Then the Lord by his power and wisdom *organized the mortal tabernacle of man.* We were made first spiritual [i.e. in heaven] and afterwards temporal [i.e. on this earth.]" Now what man was organized *first* by the Lord? Naturally, it was Adam, and so President Young taught in this very same discourse. There are Gods *above* Adam, even the Father and the Son.

ALL EXALTED MEN BECOME GODS. To believe that Adam is a god should not be strange to any person who accepts the *Bible.* When Jesus was accused of blasphemy because he claimed to be the Son of God, he answered the Jews: "Is it not written in your law, I said, Ye are gods? If he called them gods, unto whom the word of God came, and the scripture cannot be broken; Say ye of him, whom the Father hath sanctified, and sent into the

---
[23]Moses 2:26-30; 3:4-25; 4:5-31; 5:1-12.

world, Thou blasphemest; because I said, I am the Son of God?"[24]

Paul said, writing to the members of the Church in Rome: "For as many as are led by the Spirit of God, they are the sons of God."[25] And to the Galatians he said: "And because ye are sons, God hath sent forth the Spirit of his Son into your hearts, crying, Abba, Father."[26]

Joseph Smith taught a plurality of gods, and that man by obeying the commandments of God and keeping the whole law will eventually reach the power and exaltation by which he also will become a god.[27]

How ADAM IS OUR GOD. The expression that Adam is the only God with whom we have to do, has caused great discussion and the question naturally arises, do we not have to do with Jesus Christ and his Father? Certainly we do, and we are taught to pray to the Father in the name of Jesus Christ, the Son, and all that we do is to be done in the name of the Son. To make clear what President Young had in mind, I will give this illustration:

The army is composed of a great number of privates and officers of various ranks. The private in the army is, of course, under the captain, and the captain is under the colonel who receives instructions from his superior officers. In other words the only person with whom the private has to do is his captain. This illustration may seem rather crude, but I think it will convey the thought.

President Brigham Young was thoroughly acquainted with the doctrine of the Church. He studied the *Doctrine and Covenants* and many times quoted from it the particular passages concerning the relationship of Adam to Jesus Christ. He knew perfectly that Adam was subordinate and obedient to Jesus Christ. He knew perfectly that Adam had been placed at the head of the

---
[24]John 10:34-36.
[25]Rom. 8-14.
[26]Gal. 4:6.
[27]D. & C. 132:17, 19-25, 29-32, 37, 49.

MICHAEL OUR PRINCE 99

human family by commandment of the Father, and this doctrine he taught during the many years of his ministry. When he said Adam was the only god with whom we have to do, he evidently had in mind this passage given by revelation through Joseph Smith:

"That you may come up unto the crown prepared for you, and be made rulers over many kingdoms, saith the Lord God, the Holy One of Zion [i.e. Jesus Christ], who hath established the foundations of Adam-ondi-Ahman; Who hath *appointed Michael [Adam] your prince, and established his feet, and set him upon high, and given him the keys of salvation under the counsel and direction of the Holy One,* who is without beginning of days and end of life."[28]

ADAM HOLDS KEYS OF SALVATION UNDER CHRIST. This doctrine was also taught by Joseph Smith, who said: "The Priesthood was first given to Adam. . . . He obtained it in the creation, before the world was formed. . . . He had dominion given him over every living creature. He is Michael the Archangel, spoken of in the scriptures. . . . The Priesthood is an everlasting principle, and existed with God from eternity, and will to eternity, without beginning of days or end of years. The keys have to be brought from heaven whenever the gospel is sent. When they are revealed from heaven, it is *by Adam's authority.* . . . *Christ is the Great High Priest, Adam next.*"[29]

If the keys of salvation have been committed to the hands of Adam, *under the direction of Jesus Christ,* then is there anything out of place for President Brigham Young to declare that it is Adam with whom we have to do? And yet here is the acknowledgment of the *superiority* of Jesus Christ. This being true, then *the human family is immediately subject to Adam and he to the Redeemer of the world.*

Again, to illustrate this point: In the Church we have

---

[28]*D. & C.* 78:15-16.   [29]Smith, *Teachings of the Prophet Joseph Smith,* pp. 157-158.

a presiding officer whom we call the bishop. He has full charge in the ward over which he presides. This bishop is subject to the direction of the stake president, and he in turn to the Presidency of the Church. The *only* one, *in the same sense,* with whom the members have to do is the bishop, but he is not the superior officer by any means.

STATUS OF ADAM REVEALED TO JOSEPH SMITH. In another revelation which President Young taught many times, we find the following: "Wherefore, verily I say unto you that all things unto me are spiritual, and not at any time have I given unto you a law which was temporal; neither any man, nor the children of men; neither Adam, your father, *whom I created.*"[30]

The doctrine taught by the Church in relation to Adam is clearly defined in the following revelation: "Three years previous to the death of Adam, he called Seth, Enos, Cainan, Mahalaleel, Jared, Enoch, and Methuselah, who were all high priests, with the residue of his posterity who were righteous, into the valley of Adam-ondi-Ahman, and there bestowed upon them his last blessing.

"*And the Lord appeared unto them,* and they rose up and blessed Adam, and called him Michael, the prince, the archangel. *And the Lord administered comfort unto Adam, and said unto him: I have set thee to be at the head;* a multitude of nations shall come of thee, and thou art a prince over them forever. And Adam stood up in the midst of the congregation; and, notwithstanding he was bowed down with age, being full of the Holy Ghost, predicted whatsoever should befall his posterity unto the latest generation."[31]

STATUS OF ADAM KNOWN BY BRIGHAM YOUNG. From these passages President Brigham Young could very properly say that *we are subject to Adam;* that *he rules over his posterity,* and he *gives* us commandments, even as he *receives* commandments from Jesus Christ,

---
[30]*D. & C.* 29:34. [31]*D. & C.* 107:53-56.

who *directs* him in his ministry and will do so to the latest day of time. And this does not detract anything from the power, greatness, and glory of God the Father and his Son Jesus Christ.

Men who harp upon this saying in the discourse of President Brigham Young should know just as well as they know anything—for it has come to their attention hundreds of times—that *Brigham Young did not confuse Adam with Jesus Christ or the Father whom he worshipped.*

There is a volume published containing the saying of President Brigham Young in which his doctrine concerning the Father and the Son, and Adam's relationship to them is clearly declared in many pages. But when men desire to malign and misrepresent, such things count for nothing.

This is from one of the discourses of Brigham Young: "We are all the children of *Adam and Eve,* and they *are the offspring of Him who dwells in the heavens,* the Highest Intelligence that dwells anywhere that we have any knowledge of." Now, if he believed what some people like to interpret him as saying, then he could not say such a thing as that!

Again he said: "The greatest desire in the bosom of our *Father Adam,* or of *his faithful children who are co-workers with God, our Father in Heaven,* is to save the inhabitants of the earth"[32] This certainly does not sound like the interpretations, erroneously credited to him, give his views in relation to the Father and the Son and *Adam whom God created!*

PRESIDENT YOUNG TEACHES PATERNITY OF CHRIST. Another ambiguous statement from President Brigham Young—also, quite likely, not recorded exactly as he said it—is torn from its context and used by enemies of the truth to make it appear that he believed something

---
[32]*Discourses of Brigham Young,* 2nd ed., p. 94.

entirely different from the whole burden of all his other teachings. It is:

"When the Virgin Mary conceived the child Jesus, the Father had begotten him in his own likeness. He was *not* begotten by the Holy Ghost. And *who* is the Father? He is the *first* of the human family; and when *he [Christ]* took a tabernacle, it was begotten by *his* Father in heaven, after the same manner as the tabernacles of Cain, Abel, and the rest of the sons and daughters of Adam and Eve. . . .

"Jesus, our elder brother, was begotten in the flesh by the same character that was in the Garden of Eden, and who is our Father in Heaven. . . .

"Now, remember from this time forth, and forever, that Jesus Christ was not begotten by the Holy Ghost."[33]

The statement by President Brigham Young that the Father is the *first* of the human family is easily explained. But the expression that he was the same character that was in the Garden of Eden has led to misunderstanding because of the implication which our enemies place upon it that it had reference to Adam. Unfortunately President Brigham Young is not here to make his meaning in this regard perfectly clear. Under the circumstances we must refer to other expressions by President Brigham Young in order to ascertain exactly what his views really were in relation to God, Adam, and Jesus Christ.

GOD: FIRST OF THE HUMAN FAMILY. Let me comment first upon the expression that God is the "first of the human family." This same doctrine was taught by Joseph Smith. It is a fundamental doctrine of the Church of Jesus Christ of Latter-day Saints. According to the teachings of Joseph Smith, he beheld the Father and the Son in his glorious vision, and he taught that each had a body of flesh and bones. He has expressed it in these words:

---
[33]*Journal of Discourses,* vol. 1, pp. 50-51.

"The Father has a body of flesh and bones as tangible as man's; the Son also; but the Holy Ghost has not a body of flesh and bones, but is a personage of Spirit. Were it not so, the Holy Ghost could not dwell in us."[34]

He also taught that, literally, God is our Father; that men are of the *same race—the race called humans; and that God, the Progenitor, or Creator, is the Father of the human race.* "In the image of his own body, male and female, created he them, and blessed them, and called their name Adam, in the day when they were created and became living souls in the land upon the footstool of God."[35]

It is a doctrine common to the Latter-day Saints, that *God, the Great Elohim, is the First, or Creator, of the human family.*

THE FATHER WAS WITH ADAM IN EDEN. In discussing the statement by President Brigham Young that the Father of Jesus Christ is the same character who was in the Garden of Eden, it should be perfectly clear that President Young was *not* referring to Adam, *but to God the Father, who created Adam, for he was in the Garden of Eden;* and according to Mormon doctrine *Adam was in his presence constantly, walked with him, talked with him, and the Father taught Adam his language.* It was not until the fall, that the Father departed from Adam and no longer visited him in the Garden of Eden.

Surely we must give President Brigham Young credit for at least ordinary intelligence, and in stating this I place it mildly. If he meant to convey the thought that the character who was in the Garden of Eden, "*and who is our Father in Heaven,*" was Adam, then it would mean that this expression was in conflict with all else that he taught concerning God the Father, and I am bold to say that President Brigham Young was not inconsistent in his teaching of this doctrine. The very expression in question, "the same character that was in

---

[34]*D. & C.* 130:22.   [35]Moses 6:9.

the Garden of Eden, and *who is our Father in Heaven,"* contradicts the thought that he meant Adam.

BRIGHAM YOUNG'S TEACHINGS ABOUT ADAM. Now let me present one or two expressions in other discourses by President Young—of course, the critics never think of referring to these:

"How has it transpired that theological truth is thus so widely disseminated? It is because God was once known on the earth among his children of mankind, as we know one another. *Adam was as conversant with his Father who placed him upon this earth* as we are conversant with our earthly parents. *The Father frequently came to visit his son Adam,* and talked and walked with him; and the children of Adam were more or less acquainted with him, and the things that pertain to God and to heaven were as familiar among mankind in the first ages of their existence on the earth, as these mountains are to our mountain boys."[36]

"How did Adam and Eve sin? Did they come out in direct opposition to God and to his government? No. But *they transgressed a command of the Lord,* and through that transgression sin came into the world."[37]

"The human family are formed after the image of our Father and God. After the earth was organized *the Lord placed his children* upon it, gave them possession of it, and told them that it was their home. . . . Then Satan steps in and overcomes them through the weakness there was in *the children of the Father when they were sent to the earth,* and sin was brought in, and thus we are subject to sin."

"Our Lord Jesus Christ—the Savior, who has redeemed the world and all things pertaining to it, is the Only Begotten of the Father pertaining to the flesh. He is our Elder Brother, and the Heir of the family, and as such we worship him. *He has tasted death for every*

---

[36]*Discourses of Brigham Young,* 2nd ed., p. 159.   [37]*Ibid.,* p. 157.

man, and has paid the debt contracted by our first parents [that is Adam and Eve]."³⁸

"The Latter-day Saints believe in Jesus Christ, the Only Begotten Son of the Father, who came in the meridian of time, performed his work, suffered the penalty and paid the debt of man's original sin by offering up himself, [they believe he] was resurrected from the dead, and ascended to his Father; and as Jesus descended below all things, so he will ascend above all things."³⁹

It is very clear from these expressions that *President Brigham Young did not believe and did not teach, that Jesus Christ was begotten by Adam. He taught that Adam died and that Jesus Christ redeemed him. He taught that Adam disobeyed the commandment of the Father, or God, and was driven from the Garden of Eden. He said that Adam was conversant with his Father in the Garden of Eden.* This is believed by all members of the Church, and also that the Father *was* in the Garden of Eden until Adam was driven out for his transgression.

ADAM NOT FATHER OF CHRIST. The statement, "And when he took a tabernacle it was begotten by his Father in heaven, after the same manner as the tabernacles of Cain, Abel, and the rest of the sons and daughters of Adam and Eve," has reference to the body of Jesus Christ.

*Adam died as the Father said he would through partaking of the fruit of the tree of the knowledge of good and evil.*⁴⁰ *Adam's spirit and body were separated, and he did not get the resurrection until after the resurrection of Jesus Christ.*⁴¹ *Adam, when a spirit without the body, could not beget a body of flesh and bones, therefore, he could not be the Father of Jesus Christ in the flesh.*

*Again, Adam was as dependent on Jesus Christ as we are for the resurrection which came through the fact that Jesus had life in himself as his Father did.*⁴² There-

---
³⁸*Ibid.*, p. 40.
³⁹*Ibid.*, p. 39.
⁴⁰Moses 3:16-17; 4:9, 17; 6:10-12.
⁴¹Acts 26:23; 1 Cor. 15:20-23; Col. 1:18; Rev. 1:5.
⁴²John 10:14-18.

fore, he had to have a Father who had a body of flesh and bones who was immortal, not a father who was a spirit with a body in the grave, whose body had turned to dust.

WORSHIP ELOHIM: NOT ADAM. We worship Elohim, the Father of Jesus Christ. We do not worship Adam and we do not pray to him. We are all his children through the flesh, but Elohim, the God we worship, is the Father of our spirits; and Jesus Christ, his first Begotten Son in the spirit creation and his Only Begotten Son in the flesh, is our Eldest Brother.

THE ANCIENT OF DAYS. Daniel speaks of Adam as the Ancient of Days. In this dispensation the Ancient of Days will sit in the valley of Adam-ondi-Ahman; and the judgment will be set; Christ will come; and the kingdom will be turned over to Christ; and he will be sustained in his calling as King of Kings and Lord of Lords.[43]

---
[43]Pers. Corresp.; Dan. 7:9-14; *D. & C.* 116; Smith, *Teachings of the Prophet Joseph Smith,* p. 157.

Chapter 7

THE FALL OF ADAM

STATUS OF ADAM BEFORE THE FALL

BLESSINGS OF MORTALITY UNKNOWN IN EDEN. We find Adam in the Garden of Eden with the promise that he can live there, he can stay there, he can enjoy himself as far as is possible under the conditions, as long as he wants to, as long as he does not do something he is told not to do, and that is to partake of the fruit of the tree of knowledge of good and evil. He was told that in the day that he should eat of that fruit he should surely die.[1]

We find, then, Adam's status before the fall was:

1. *He was not subject to death.*[2]
2. *He was in the presence of God.*[3] He saw him just as you see your fathers; was in his presence, and learned his language. Now if any of you are professors from our schools of language, and have an idea that language came as these theorists say, I am going to tell you that Adam had a perfect language, for he was taught the language of God. That was the first language upon this earth. So much for those theories.
3. *He had no posterity.*
4. *He was without knowledge of good and evil.*[4] He had knowledge, of course. He could speak. He could converse. There were many things he could be taught and was taught; but under the conditions in which he was living at that time it was impossible for him to visualize or understand the power of good and evil. He did not know what pain was. He did not know what sorrow was; and a thousand other things that have come

---

[1]Moses 3:8-9, 16-17; Abra. 5:8-13; Gen. 2:8-9, 15-17.
[2]2 Ne. 2:22.
[3]2 Ne. 9:6; Al. 42:7-23; Hela. 14:16-17; Moses 5:10.
[4]2 Ne. 2:23; Moses 5:11.

to us in this life that Adam did not know in the Garden of Eden and could not understand and would not have known had he remained there. That was his status before the fall.[5]

No Death on Earth Before Fall. The Lord pronounced the earth *good* when it was finished. Everything upon its face was called good. *There was no death in the earth before the fall of Adam.* I do not care what the scientists say in regard to dinosaurs and other creatures upon the earth millions of years ago, that lived and died and fought and struggled for existence. When the earth was created and was declared *good*, peace was upon its face among all its creatures. Strife and wickedness were not found here, neither was there any corruption. . . .

All life in the sea, the air, on the earth, was without death. Animals were not dying. Things were not changing as we find them changing in this mortal existence, for mortality had not come. Today we are living in a world of change because we are living under very different conditions from those which prevailed in the beginning and before the fall of man.

Book of Mormon Teaches Truth About Fall. We Latter-day Saints accept the *Book of Mormon* as the word of God. We have the assurance that the Lord placed the stamp of approval upon it at the time of the translation, and spoke with his own voice to the witnesses, and commanded them to bear record of it in all the world. The word of the Lord means more to me than anything else. I place it before the teachings of men. The truth is the thing which will last. All the theory, philosophy and wisdom of the wise that is not in harmony with revealed truth from God will perish. They must change and pass away, and they are changing and passing away constantly, but when the Lord speaks that is eternal truth on which we may rely.

[5]*Church News*, Apr. 15, 1939, p. 6.

THE FALL OF ADAM

The gospel teaches us that if Adam and Eve had not partaken of that fruit of the tree of the knowledge of good and evil, they would have remained in the Garden of Eden in that same condition prevailing before the fall. Under those conditions they would have had no seed. *"Adam fell that men might be"* as it was decreed in the heavens before the world was. Lehi has given us a very clear and comprehensive view of the mission of Adam and of the atonement of Jesus Christ, and the *Book of Mormon* is very explicit in teaching these fundamental doctrines. In regard to the pre-mortal condition of Adam and the entire earth, Lehi has stated the following:

"And now, behold, if Adam had not transgressed he would not have fallen, but he would have remained in the garden of Eden. And *all things which were created must have remained in the same state in which they were after they were created; and they must have remained forever, and had no end."*[6]

Is not this statement plain enough? Whom are you going to believe, the Lord, or men?

ADAM FOREORDAINED TO FALL. The Lord did not intend the earth to stay in that condition. Lehi further says: "But behold, *all things have been done in the wisdom of him who knoweth all things."* This earth was prepared for the advancement of the children of God. We came from the pre-existence to receive tabernacles of flesh and bones and to pass through mortality. It was decreed in the heavens that men should die after coming into this probation and learning the pains and tribulations of mortality as well as its joys and happiness. Jesus Christ is spoken of in the scriptures as the Lamb slain from the foundation of the world.[7] Peter says we were not redeemed with corruptible things, as silver and gold, but with the precious blood of Christ, as of a lamb without blemish, "Who verily was foreordained before the foundation of the world, but was manifest in these last

---
[6] 2 Ne. 2:19-26.   [7] Rev. 13:8.

times for you."⁸ So the plan of salvation was all understood in the world of spirits, and we were taught the purpose of mortal life which Adam should bring into the earth.

ADAM HAD POWER TO BRING DEATH INTO WORLD. By revelation we are well informed that *Adam was not subject to death when he was placed in the Garden of Eden, nor was there any death upon the earth.* The Lord has not seen fit to tell us definitely just how Adam came for we are not ready to receive that truth. He did not come here a resurrected being to die again for we are taught most clearly that those who pass through the resurrection receive immortality, and can die no more.

It is sufficient for us to know, until the Lord reveals more about it, that Adam was not subject to death but had the power, through transgressing the law, to become subject to death and to cause the same curse to come upon the earth and all life upon it. For this earth, once pronounced good, was cursed after the fall. It is passing through its mortal probation as well as the life which is upon it, and will eventually receive the resurrection and a place of exaltation which is decreed in the heavens for it.

TRUTHS ABOUT FALL YET TO BE REVEALED. The time will come when we shall be informed all about Adam and the manner of creation, for the Lord has promised that when he comes he will make all these things known. These are his words:

"Yea, verily I say unto you, in that day when the Lord shall come, he shall reveal all things—Things which have passed, and hidden things which no man knew, things of the earth, by which it was made, and the purpose and the end thereof—Things most precious, things that are above, and things that are beneath, things that are in the earth, and upon the earth, and in heaven."⁹

For my part, I am willing to wait until this time to learn the truth of these things. This information was

---
⁸1 Pet. 1:20.   ⁹*D. & C.* 101:32-34.

THE FALL OF ADAM

given to the saints at one time in a former dispensation, but the Lord has said we may not have it in the days of wickedness. When the Gentiles "shall repent of their iniquity, and become clean before the Lord," then it shall be revealed again.[10]

STATUS OF ADAM AFTER THE FALL

BLESSINGS OF MORTALITY CAME WITH FALL. Adam's status after the fall was:

1. *He was banished from the presence of God and partook of the spiritual death.* Now that was a terrible calamity. At least, as we read in the 9th chapter of 2nd Nephi, it would have been a most terrible thing, that banishment from the presence of God, if there had been no remedy.[11]

2. *He also partook of the temporal or physical death,* and that would have been also a terrible calamity if there had been no remedy for it.[12]

3. *He gained knowledge and experience—knowledge of good and evil.*

4. *He obtained the great gift of posterity.*[13]

ADAM BROUGHT SPIRITUAL AND TEMPORAL DEATH. Because of Adam's transgression, a spiritual death—banishment from the presence of the Lord—as well as the temporal death, were pronounced upon him. The spiritual death came at the time of the fall and banishment; and the seeds of the temporal death were also sown at that same time; that is, a physical change came over Adam and Eve, who became mortal, and were thus subject to the ills of the flesh which resulted in their gradual decline to old age and finally the separation of the spirit from the body.

Before this temporal death took place the Lord, by his own voice and the visitation and ministration of

---
[10]*Gen. & Hist. Mag.,* vol. 21, pp. 148-150; Ether 4:6-7.
[11]2 Ne. 2:5; 9:8-9; Mosiah 16:1-15; Alma 42:6-11.
[12]2 Ne. 9:6-8; Mosiah 16:4-11; Alma 12:26; Hela. 14:16-17; Mormon 9:13.
[13]*Church News,* Apr. 15, 1939, p. 6; 2 Ne. 2:23; Moses 5:10-11.

angels, taught Adam the principles of the gospel and administered unto him the saving ordinances, through which he was again restored to the favor of the Lord and to his presence. Also, through the atonement, not only Adam, but all his posterity were redeemed from the temporal effects of the fall, and shall come forth in the resurrection to receive immortality.[14]

ADAM'S TRANSGRESSION BROUGHT DEATH. That death came by the transgression of Adam, we are taught in the scriptures. For instance, the Lord has revealed, "That by reason of transgression cometh the fall, which *fall bringeth death,* and inasmuch as ye were born into the world by water, and blood, and the spirit, which I have made, and so became of dust a living soul, even so ye must be born again."[15]

I cannot think that the Lord created death in any creature, plant, animal, or even the earth on which we dwell, at the time of its creation. *Death came through the violation of a law, and it passed upon all things by the judgment of the Almighty,* through the transgression of Adam, he being the lord who had been given dominion over all of these things.

DEATH FOR ALL LIFE CAME BY FALL. President Brigham Young has said: "Some may regret that our first parents sinned. This is nonsense. If we had been there, and they had not sinned, we would have sinned. I will not blame Adam or Eve. Why? Because it was necessary that sin should enter into the world; no man could ever understand the principle of exaltation without its opposite; no one could ever receive an exaltation without being acquainted with its opposite. How did Adam and Eve sin? Did they come out in direct opposition to God and to his government? No. But they transgressed a command of the Lord, and through that transgression sin came into the world. The Lord knew they would

---

[14]*Era,* vol. 21, p. 192; *D. & C.* 29:41-43. [15]Moses 6:59; 2 Ne. 9:6.

THE FALL OF ADAM

do this, and he had designed that they should. *Then came the curse upon the fruit, upon the vegetables, and upon our mother earth; and it came upon the creeping things, upon the grain in the field, the fish in the sea, and upon all things pertaining to this earth, through man's transgression.*"[16]

Elder Parley P. Pratt and President John Taylor have left us this teaching: *"First, man fell from his standing before God, by giving heed to temptation; and this fall affected the whole creation, as well as man, and caused various changes to take place; he was banished from the presence of his Creator, and a veil was drawn between them, and he was driven from the Garden of Eden, to till the earth, which was then cursed for man's sake, and should begin to bring forth thorns and thistles; and in the sweat of his face should earn his bread, and in sorrow eat of it, all the days of his life, and finally return to dust."*[17]

FALL OF ADAM A BLESSING

NO IMMORTALITY OR ETERNAL LIFE WITHOUT FALL. When Adam was driven out of the Garden of Eden, the Lord passed a sentence upon him. Some people have looked upon that sentence as being a dreadful thing. It was not; it was a blessing. I do not know that it can truthfully be considered even as a punishment in disguise.[18]

In order for mankind to obtain salvation and exaltation it is necessary for them to obtain bodies in this world, and pass through the experiences and schooling that are found only in mortality. The Lord has said that his great work and glory is, "to bring to pass the immortality and eternal life of man."[19] Without mortality this great blessing could not be accomplished. Therefore, worlds

---

[16]*Discourses of Brigham Young*, 2nd ed., pp. 157-158.
[17]Pers. Corresp.; John Taylor, *The Government of God*, pp. 106-115, quoting Parley P. Pratt, *The Voice of Warning*.
[18]Conf. Rep., Apr. 6, 1945, p. 48.
[19]Moses 1:39.

are created and peopled with the children of God, and they are granted the privilege to pass through the mortal existence, with the great gift of agency in their possession. Through this gift they choose good or choose evil, and thus receive a reward of merit in the eternities to come. Because of Adam's transgression we are here in mortal life....

The fall of man came as a blessing in disguise, and was the means of furthering the purposes of the Lord in the progress of man, rather than a means of hindering them.[20]

"TRANSGRESSION" NOT "SIN" OF ADAM. I never speak of the part Eve took in this fall as a sin, nor do I accuse Adam of a sin. One may say, "Well did they not break a commandment?" Yes. But let us examine the nature of that commandment and the results which came out of it.

In no other commandment the Lord ever gave to man, did he say: "But of the tree of the knowledge of good and evil, thou shalt not eat of it, *nevertheless, thou mayest choose for thyself.*"[21]

It is true, the Lord warned Adam and Eve that to partake of the fruit they would transgress a law, and this happened. But it is not always a sin to transgress a law. I will try to illustrate this. The chemist in his laboratory takes different elements and combines them, and the result is that something very different results. He has *changed* the law. As an example in point: hydrogen, two parts, and oxygen, one part, passing through an electric spark will combine and form water. Hydrogen will burn, so will oxygen, but water will put out a fire. This may be subject to some disagreement by the critics who will say it is not transgressing a law. Well, *Adam's transgression was of a similar nature, that is, his transgression was in accordance with law.*

The transgression of Adam did *not* involve sex sin

---

[20]*Church News*, Feb. 15, 1941, p. 1.   [21]Moses 3:17.

THE FALL OF ADAM 115

as some falsely believe and teach. Adam and Eve were married by the Lord while they were yet immortal beings in the Garden of Eden and before death entered the world.

ADAM AND EVE REJOICED IN FALL. Before partaking of the fruit Adam could have lived forever; therefore, his status was one of immortality. When he ate, he became subject to death, and therefore he became mortal. This was a transgression of the law, but not a sin in the strict sense, for it was something that Adam and Eve had to do!

I am sure that neither Adam nor Eve looked upon it as a sin, when they learned the consequences, and this is discovered in their words after they learned the consequences.

Adam said: *"Blessed be the name of God, for because of my transgression my eyes are opened, and in this life I shall have joy, and again in the flesh I shall see God."*

Eve said: *"Were it not for our transgression we never should have had seed, and never should have known good and evil, and the joy of our redemption, and the eternal life which God giveth unto all the obedient."*[22]

We can hardly look upon anything resulting in such benefits as being a sin, in the sense in which we consider sin.[23]

DEATH FULFILLS MERCIFUL PLAN OF GOD. We have partaken of the benefits, and of the things that are not called benefits—if there are any such—coming out of the fall of Adam. The fall of Adam brought to pass all of the vicissitudes of mortality. It brought pain. It brought sorrow. It brought death; but we must not lose sight of the fact that it brought blessings also, as spoken of in these scriptures. It brought the blessing of knowledge and understanding and mortal life.

Now if we had been left in that condition, without

---
[22]Moses 5:10-11.   [23]Pers. Corresp.

any hope of redemption from the fall, then that fall would have been a most dreadful calamity. I want to read to you some of the words that Jacob taught the people, as recorded in the 9th chapter of 2nd Nephi:
"For as death hath passed upon all men, to fulfil the *merciful plan* of the great Creator"—I pause now after reading that. That is a very peculiar expression. It is not customary among men to look upon the transgression of Adam, which brought death, in that light—that it came in order to bring to pass "the merciful plan of the great Creator."

DEATH AS IMPORTANT AS BIRTH. In other words, death is just as important in the welfare of man as is birth. There is no greater blessing that can come than the blessing of birth. One third of the hosts of heaven, because of rebellion, were denied that privilege, and hence they have no bodies of flesh and bones, that great gift of God.

But who would like to live forever in this mundane world, filled with pain, decay, sorrow, and tribulation, and grow old and infirm and yet have to remain with all the vicissitudes of mortality? I think all of us would come to the conclusion, if that proposition were placed before us, that we would not like to have it. We would reject it. We would not want life of that nature. Life here in this world is short of necessity, and yet all that is required may be accomplished, but death is just as important in the plan of salvation as birth is. We have to die—it is essential—and death comes into the world "to fulfil the merciful plan of the great Creator."[24]

"NO ADAM, NO FALL: NO FALL, NO ATONEMENT"

IS OUR DOCTRINE ABOUT ADAM TRUE? *Did Adam bring death into the world? Are we laboring under a misapprehension? Are we wrong? Is it true that millions of years before Adam came into this world death was*

---
[24]*Church News,* Apr. 22, 1939, p. 3,
2 Ne. 9:6.

THE FALL OF ADAM

here? If so, I want to know who brought it. Who was the transgressor? And who atoned for the beings who died before Adam's fall?[25]

Adam cannot be held responsible for death before he came here. Now is it true or isn't it true that Adam brought death into the world? Are these scriptures true? Are these brethren true—and I have quoted three of the Presidents of the Church, including the Prophet himself? Are they true, or are we to discard their teachings and the teachings of the scriptures because the philosophies of men today declare a contrary doctrine?

EVOLUTIONISTS DENY FALL. And where does that doctrine lead you? I am going to tell you. John Fisk was considered to be a great man. Let us hear what he says: "Theology has much to say about original sin. This original sin is neither more nor less than the brute-inheritance which every man carries with him."[26] That is what one great editor and historian has to say.

Here is what Dr. E. W. McBride said at a religious conference—the Oxford Conference of Modern Churchmen—and he is a minister: "If mankind have been slowly developing out of ape-like ancestors, then what is called sin consists of nothing but the tendencies which they have inherited from these ancestors: there never was a state of primeval innocence, and all the nations of the world have developed out of primitive man by processes as natural as those which gave rise to the Jews."[27]

I have been teaching you here from these revelations that the fall of Adam brought sin into the world, and there wasn't any sin until he brought it. Now this is what the other doctrine teaches.

Here is what Dr. H. D. A. Major said at the same conference: "Science has shown us that what is popularly called 'original sin' ... consists of man's inheritance from his brute ancestry."[28]

---

[25]Mosiah 3:11; 4:7.
[26]John Fisk, *The Destiny of Man*, p. 103.
[27]*The Modern Churchman*, Sept. 1924, p. 232.
[28]*Ibid.*, p. 206.

EVOLUTIONISTS DENY ATONEMENT. Here is what Sir Oliver Lodge has to say. Now these are distinguished men that I am quoting. "As a matter of fact, the higher man of today is not worrying about his sins at all, still less about their punishment. His mission, if he is good for anything, is to be up and doing; and insofar as he acts wrongly or unwisely he expects to suffer. He may unconsciously plead for mitigation on the ground of good intentions, but never either consciously or unconsciously will anyone but a cur ask for the punishment to fall on someone else, nor rejoice if told that it already has so fallen."[29]

In other words, because I believe in the redemption that has come to men through Jesus Christ, that he is the Redeemer of the world, that he gave his life that men might live and be redeemed from the original transgression, I am a cur, according to the teaching of Sir Oliver Lodge. Well, let me be classed among the curs, for goodness knows I do not want to sink to the level that this man has reached who ridicules the atonement of Jesus Christ.

Here is another one, from a Christian minister—so-called—Durant Drake. He says: "What sort of justice is it that could be satisfied with the punishment of one innocent man and the free pardon of myriads of guilty men? The theory seems a remnant of the ancient idea that the Gods need to be placated; but by the side of the pagan gods, who were content with humble offerings of flesh and fruit, the Christian God, demanding the suffering and death of his own Son, appears a monster of cruelty."[30]

EVOLUTIONISTS RIDICULE GOD AND RELIGION. Now, my good brethren and sisters, this *damnable doctrine* that is so prevalent in the world today, that is taught in the colleges throughout our country, and has swept over the face of the earth like a destructive flood of evil, *is striking*

---

[29]*Man and the Universe*, p. 204.   [30]*Problems of Religion*, p. 176.

THE FALL OF ADAM 119

at the fundamentals of your faith—that is the doctrine so circulated ridiculing the Son of God, making light of his Father as a cruel monster (I was going to say inhuman but I cannot say that) because he would permit his Son to suffer for you and for me.

Is it any wonder that the world is ridiculing the prophets and making light of the holy scriptures when the leading men who are setting the pace for education, who are controlling the thought of the world are teaching such terrible, soul-destroying doctrines as these I have read to you? And these are only a few. Thousands of books have been published with similar thoughts.

BELIEF IN ADAM AND CHRIST GO TOGETHER. In contrast to this I am going to quote to you from another great man. He was great. He was mistaken in many things, of course, but he did the best he could under the circumstances, and I think the Spirit of the Lord was leading him in many things. John Wesley said: *"The fall of man is the very foundation of revealed religion. If this be taken away, the Christian system is subverted, nor will it deserve so honorable an appellation as that of a cunningly devised fable."*[31]

Then he adds: "All who deny this—call it original sin, or by any other title—are but heathens still in the fundamental point which differentiates heathenism from Christianity."[32] Now that has a better ring, doesn't it?

And here is another truth stated by another great thinker, Robert Blatchford. He says: *"But—no Adam, no Fall; no Fall, no Atonement; no Atonement, no Savior. Accepting Evolution, how can we believe in a Fall? When did man fall; was it before he ceased to be a monkey, or after? Was it when he was a tree man, or later? Was it in the Stone Age, or the Bronze Age, or in the Age of Iron? . . . And if there never was a Fall, why should there be any Atonement?"*[33]

Those are pertinent questions that Mr. Blatchford

---

[31]*The Works of John Wesley*, vol 1, p. 176.
[32]*Ibid.*, vol. 5, p. 195.
[33]*God and My Neighbor*, p. 159.

asks. "No Adam, no Fall; no Fall, no Atonement." That is just as true as it is that we are here. If death was always here, then Adam did not bring it, and he could not be punished for it. *If Adam did not fall, there was no Christ, because the atonement of Jesus Christ is based on the fall of Adam.* And so we face these problems.

SALVATION RESTS ON FALL AND ATONEMENT. If there is anybody here that believes that death has always been going on, and that sin was always here, he will have a difficult time to explain Adam and the fall, or the atonement. You see from these writings what a dreadful state these men get in when they do not believe in the fall and the introduction of sin into the world.

Of course, if I put my hand upon a hot stove it will get burned—that is natural, that would not be a sin; and that is the way they look upon everything. *Man cannot sin, according to this doctrine. Do you know of anything that is more damnable than that?* And that is what it leads to.

If death was always here, then there could be no atonement, and if there is no atonement there is no salvation. Now that is just as plain as anything can be. *If things did not occur as the Lord has said they did occur, in these revelations, then we are still in a hopeless condition, and when we die we do not exist, because if all this is true there is no existence after this life—that is the end.* I want to tell you that forces are at work in this world to destroy Jesus Christ and his mission.[34]

[34]*Church News*, Apr. 15, 1939, p. 8.

Chapter 8

THE ATONEMENT OF CHRIST

ATONEMENT BASED ON THE FALL

FALL AND ATONEMENT FOREORDAINED. The plan of salvation, or code of laws, which is known as the gospel of Jesus Christ, was adopted in the heavens, before the foundation of the world was laid. It was appointed there that Adam, our father, should come to this earth and stand at the head of the whole human family. It was a part of this great plan, that he should partake of the forbidden fruit and fall, thus bringing suffering and death into the world, even for the ultimate good of his children.

By many he has been severely criticized because of his fall, but Latter-day Saints, through modern revelation, have learned that such was necessary in order that man should have his agency and, through the various vicissitudes he has to pass, receive a knowledge of both good and evil, without which it would be impossible for him to gain the exaltation prepared for him.

It was also necessary because of Adam's transgression for the Only Begotten Son of the Father to come to redeem the world from Adam's fall. This also was a part of the plan chosen before the earth was made, for Jesus is called the Lamb that was slain from the foundation of the world. He came and redeemed us from the fall—even all the inhabitants of the earth. Not only did he redeem us from Adam's transgression, but he also redeemed us from our own sins, on condition that we obey the laws and ordinances of the gospel.[1]

---
[1]*Salvation Universal,* pp. 3-4; Rev. 13:8; Heb. 5:8-11; Matt. 7:21; 2 Ne. 2:22-27.

122   DOCTRINES OF SALVATION

TWOFOLD NATURE OF FALL. Adam's transgression brought these two deaths: spiritual and temporal—man being banished from the presence of God, and also becoming mortal and subject to all the ills of the flesh. In order that he should be brought back again, there had to be *a reparation of the broken law.* Justice demanded it.

The fall brought death. That is not a desirable condition. We do not want to be banished from the presence of God. We do not want to be subject forever to mortal conditions. We do not want to die and have our bodies turn to dust, and the spirits that possess these bodies by right, turned over to the realm of Satan and become subject to him.

JUSTICE DEMANDS ATONEMENT FOR FALL. But that was the condition; and if Christ had not come as the atoning sacrifice, in demand of the law of justice, to *repair* or to *atone* or to *redeem* us from the condition that Adam found himself in, and that we find ourselves in; then mortal death would have come; the body would have gone back to the dust from where it came; the spirit would have gone into the realms of Satan's domain, and have been subject to him forever. Justice demanded that the law which was broken be repaired. Justice demanded that by the giving of life Adam and his posterity will be brought back into the presence of God.[2]

To *amend* the broken law and redeem us from the power which death held over us through the fall, it was necessary that we be redeemed by an infinite sacrifice by the shedding of blood. For this purpose Jesus Christ came into the world, for he had volunteered in the preexistence to come and die that we might live.[3]

CHRIST SATISFIES DEMANDS OF JUSTICE. There was never a sin committed in this world for which reparation has not been, or will not have to be made. If I sin, there must be a reparation or penalty required to pay the

---
[2]*Church News,* Mar. 2, 1935, p. 7; D. & C. 29:40-45; 2 Ne. 9:6-9.   [3]*Church News,* June 12, 1949, p. 21; Moses 4:1-2; Abra. 3:27.

THE ATONEMENT OF CHRIST

debt. If you sin, it is the same. There never was any sin committed, big or small, that has not been atoned for, or that will not have to be atoned for. . . .

Justice made certain demands, and Adam could not pay the price, so mercy steps in. The Son of God says: "I will go down and pay the price. I will be the Redeemer and redeem men from Adam's transgression. I will take upon me the sins of the world and redeem or save every soul from his own sins who will repent." That is the only condition. The Savior does not save anybody from his individual sins only on condition of his repentance. So *the effect of Adam's transgression was to place all of us in the pit with him. Then the Savior comes along, not subject to that pit, and lowers the ladder.* He comes down into the pit and makes it possible for us to use the ladder to escape.[4]

ATONEMENT RANSOMS US FROM THE FALL

TWOFOLD NATURE OF ATONEMENT. The atonement of Jesus Christ is of a twofold nature. Because of it, all men are redeemed from mortal death and the grave, and will rise in the resurrection to immortality of the soul. Then again, by obedience to the laws and ordinances of the gospel, man will receive remission of individual sins, through the blood of Christ, and will inherit exaltation in the kingdom of God, which is eternal life.

ATONEMENT BRINGS RESURRECTION TO ALL. The resurrection of the dead must of necessity be just as broad as was the curse that brought death into the world. Paul said, "For as in Adam all die, even so in Christ shall all be made alive. But every man in his own order: Christ the first fruits; afterwards they that are Christ's at his coming. Then cometh the end, when he shall have delivered up the kingdom to God, even the Father; when he shall have put down all rule and all authority

---
[4]*Church News*, Apr. 22, 1939, p. 5;
2 Ne. 2:6-29; 9:6-27; Alma 42:2-30.

and power. For he must reign, till he hath put all enemies under his feet. The last enemy that shall be destroyed is death."[5]

From this we learn that the atonement reaches out and embraces every living creature in the resurrection. Just as long as one soul remains unredeemed from mortal death and the grave, death has not been destroyed; therefore, *every soul shall be ferreted out and receive the resurrection. Death shall be destroyed and immortality gain the victory.*[6]

CHRIST PAID THE RANSOM. We were in bondage, through Adam's transgression. He and his posterity after him became subject to death. Death had dominion over us, and if that had continued, hell would have had dominion over us. What did Christ do? He ransomed us. He restored us. He brought us back through his atonement, through the shedding of his blood. He paid the price, as Paul says.[7] He rescued us from captivity and bondage. That is what ransomed means. He liberated us from death. He paid the price that death required; and we, through his redemption, were recovered by the payment of the shedding of his blood.

CHRIST TOOK CAPTIVITY CAPTIVE.[8] That is the gospel of Jesus Christ. That is what is taught in our scriptures; and it was a very surprising thing to me to run across this kind of doctrine falsely taught by some, that Christ could not be a ransom for us, that he could not redeem us, because that involved the paying of something which nobody could receive, so somebody was cheated.

Nobody was cheated. Death was paid. Hell was robbed, but hell had no right or claim, only that which it had assumed. Death had the claim, and death was forced to give it up because Christ, the Son of God, who was never subject to death, who always had the power

---

[5] 1 Cor. 15:22-26.
[6] *Era*, vol. 19, p. 427; Acts 24:15; John 5:28-29.
[7] 1 Cor. 6:20; 7:23; 15:54-55; Gal. 3:13; 4:5; Eph. 1:7.
[8] Ps. 68:18.

THE ATONEMENT OF CHRIST 125

over death, came and destroyed death through the shedding of his blood. So we are redeemed.

FEW TO GAIN "AT-ONE-MENT" WITH GOD. We often hear the word *atonement* defined as being "at-one-ment" with God. That is a very small part of it. In fact, *the great majority of mankind never becomes one with God, although they receive the atonement.* "Because strait is the gate, and narrow is the way, which leadeth unto life, and few there be that find it."[9] We do not all become "at one" with God, if we mean that we are brought back again and given the fulness of life which is promised to those who keep the commandments of God and become sons and daughters of God.[10]

MANKIND BOUGHT WITH A PRICE. I am sorry to say that I have heard of some members of the Church saying that Christ did not *buy* us with his blood. One of them has said: "That people of the world owed a debt and Jesus paid the debt for all: This thought does violence to justice, for the suffering of the good to pay the debt of the bad is contrary to the law of life." Another says: "That Jesus *was a ransom* for a captive world: In this case Jesus must have been paid to someone who held the world captive; but in the very nature of his mission or ransom he could not be held captive and God must have deceived the captor."

Well, such thoughts as these might do honor to an infidel, but not to a member of the Church. Those who speak this way need to repent. They should read the scriptures and especially the *Book of Mormon*. *Jesus did come into the world to ransom it. Through his atonement we were bought from death and hell. Death and hell were paid—paid in full—and Christ was the only one who could pay that debt.* What did Paul mean when he said we were "bought with a price?"[11] What does Jesus mean when he calls himself our "Redeemer?"[12] If

---
[9]Matt. 7:14.
[10]*Church News*, Mar. 9, 1935, p. 6.
[11]1 Cor. 6:20; 7:23.
[12]Isa. 41:14; D. & C. 8:1; Rev. 5:9-10.

we were not bought, if we were not ransomed by Jesus Christ, then we are still in our sins and still subject to death and hell. These men, ignorant of the plan of salvation, should read intensively the scriptures.[13]

ATONEMENT A VICARIOUS SACRIFICE. The whole plan of redemption is based on vicarious sacrifice, One without sin standing for the whole human family, all of whom were under the curse. It is most natural and just that he who commits the wrong should pay the penalty —atone for his wrongdoing. Therefore, when Adam was the transgressor of the law, justice demanded that he, and none else, should answer for the sin and pay the penalty with his life.

But Adam, in breaking the law, himself became subject to the curse, and being under the curse could not atone for or undo, what he had done. Neither could his children, for they also were under the curse, and it required one who was not subject to the curse to atone for that original sin. Moreover, since we were all under the curse, we were also powerless to atone for our individual sins.

It, therefore, became necessary for the Father to send his Only Begotten Son, who was free from sin, to atone for our sins as well as for Adam's transgression, which justice demanded should be done. He accordingly offered himself a sacrifice for sins, and through his death upon the cross took upon himself both Adam's transgression and our individual sins, thereby redeeming us from the fall, and from our sins, on condition of repentance.

ATONEMENT RANSOMS FROM A PIT. Let us illustrate: A man walking along the road happens to fall into a pit so deep and dark that he cannot climb to the surface and regain his freedom. How can he save himself from his predicament? Not by any exertions on his part, for there is no means of escape in the pit. He calls

---
[13]*Gen. & Hist. Mag.*, vol. 21, p. 155.

for help and some kindly disposed soul, hearing his cries for relief, hastens to his assistance and by lowering a ladder, gives to him the means by which he may climb again to the surface of the earth.

This was precisely the condition that Adam placed himself and his posterity in, when he partook of the forbidden fruit. All being together in the pit, none could gain the surface and relieve the others. The pit was banishment from the presence of the Lord and temporal death, the dissolution of the body. And all being subject to death, none could provide the means of escape.

Therefore, in his infinite mercy, the Father heard the cries of his children and sent his Only Begotten Son, who was not subject to death nor to sin, to provide the means of escape. This he did through his infinite atonement and the everlasting gospel.

CHRIST HAD LIFE IN HIMSELF

ATONEMENT A VOLUNTARY ACT. The Savior *voluntarily* laid down his life and took it up again to satisfy the demands of justice, which required this infinite atonement. His Father accepted this offering *in the stead* of the blood of all those who were under the curse, and consequently helpless. The Savior said, "I lay down my life for the sheep. . . . Therefore doth my Father love me, because I lay down my life, that I might take it up again. *No man taketh it from me, but I lay it down of myself.* I have power to lay it down, and I have power to take it again. This commandment have I received of my Father."[14]

WHY CHRIST COULD WORK OUT ATONEMENT. From this we see that *he had life in himself*, which he received from the Father, being his Only Begotten Son in the flesh. And it was this principle that gave him power to atone for the sins of the world, both for Adam's transgression and for our individual sins, from which we could not of ourselves get free. Therefore, Christ died

---
[14]John 10:10-18.

in our stead, because to punish us would not relieve the situation, for we would still be subject to the curse, even if our blood had been shed, and through his death we receive life and "have it more abundantly."[15]

WHY CHRIST COULD CHOOSE TO LIVE OR DIE. Every man born into this world inherited death from Adam except Jesus Christ. He always was master of death. He had the power to die. He got that from his mother, because she was mortal. He had blood in his body, and blood is the life of the mortal body. When his heart beat, blood circulated through his body just as it does through ours, but there was something else in him far different from us. *He did not have a mortal father. Joseph was not his Father. The Father of his body is the Father of our spirits. And he gave to Jesus Christ, his Son, life in himself. Death had no power over him.* . . .

HOW CHRIST GAINED KEYS OF RESURRECTION. Now, we have not power to lay down our lives and take them again. But Jesus had power to lay down his life, and he had power to take it up again, and when he was put to death on the cross, he yielded to those wicked Jews. When he was nailed to the cross, he meekly submitted, but he had power within himself, and he could have resisted. *He came into the world to die that we might live, and his atonement for sin and death is the force by which we are raised to immortality and eternal life.*

So Jesus Christ did for us something that we could not do for ourselves, through his infinite atonement. On the third day after the crucifixion he took up his body and gained the *keys of the resurrection*, and thus has *power to open the graves for all men*, but this he could not do until he had first passed through death himself and conquered.

---
[15]*Salvation Universal*, pp. 10-12; Alma 34:7-16.

THE ATONEMENT OF CHRIST

Now it is not a hard thing to understand how Jesus Christ, as the Son of God, had this power within himself, because *he inherited life from his Father who is eternal and immortal.* We may not fully understand how it was that he was required to perform the work for us vicariously through the shedding of his blood, but this is the case, and we owe all to him for he bought us through the shedding of his blood.[16]

THE PRICE CHRIST PAID FOR US

CHRIST SUFFERED FOR ALL WHO REPENT. He came into this world and took upon him our individual sins on condition of our repentance. Christ does not redeem any man from his individual sins who will not repent and who will not accept him. All those who refuse to accept him as the Redeemer and refuse to turn from their sins will have to pay the price of their own sinning.

"For behold, *I, God, have suffered these things for all, that they might not suffer if they would repent; But if they would not repent they must suffer even as I;* Which suffering caused myself, even God, the greatest of all, to tremble because of pain, and to bleed at every pore, and to suffer both body and spirit—and would that I might not drink the bitter cup, and shrink—Nevertheless, glory be to the Father, and I partook and finished my preparations unto the children of men."[17]

INFINITE SUFFERING IN ATONEMENT. This is what he did: He carried, in some way that I cannot understand and you cannot understand, the burden of the combined weight of the sins of the world. It is hard enough for me to carry my own transgressions, and it is hard enough for you to carry yours. None of us is perfect. We all have done things we should not, and when we do things we should not do, we do not feel very good; we are troubled. I have seen men in the gall of bitterness, in the torments and the anguish of their souls, because of

---
[16]*Gen. & Hist. Mag.,* vol. 17, pp. 146-148; John 5:21-24; 10:10-18. [17]*D. & C.* 19:16-19.

their sins. I have seen them cry out in anguish because of their transgressions—just one individual's sins. Can you comprehend the suffering of Jesus Christ when he carried, not merely by physical manifestation but in some spiritual and mental condition or manner, the combined weight of sin?

GREATEST SUFFERING WAS IN GETHSEMANE. We speak of the passion of Jesus Christ. A great many people have an idea that when he was on the cross, and nails were driven into his hands and feet, that was his great suffering. His great suffering was before he ever was placed upon the cross. It was in the Garden of Gethsemane that the blood oozed from the pores of his body: "Which suffering caused myself, even God, the greatest of all, to tremble because of pain, and to bleed at every pore, and to suffer both body and spirit—and would that I might not drink the bitter cup, and shrink."

That was not when he was on the cross; that was in the garden. That is where he bled from every pore in his body.[18]

Now I cannot comprehend that pain. I have suffered pain, you have suffered pain, and sometimes it has been quite severe; but I cannot comprehend pain, which is *mental anguish more than physical,* that would cause the blood, like sweat, to come out upon the body. It was something terrible, something terrific; so we can understand why he would cry unto his Father:

"If it be possible, let this cup pass from me: nevertheless not as I will, but as thou wilt."[19]

RIGHTEOUS ESCAPE SUFFERING THROUGH ATONEMENT. A mortal man could not have stood it—that is, a man such as we are. I do not care what his fortitude, what his power, there was *no man ever born into this world that could have stood under the weight of the load that was upon the Son of God, when he was carrying my*

---

[18]Matt. 26:36-46; Mark 14:32-42; Luke 22:39-44; Mosiah 3:7. [19]Matt. 26:39.

sins and yours and making it possible that we might escape from our sins. He carried that load for us if we will only accept him as our Redeemer and keep his commandments. Some of us find it so hard, so terribly hard, to do the little things that are asked of us, and yet he was willing to carry all that tremendous load and weight of sin—not his own, for he had no sin. He did it that we might escape. He paid the price, the penalty of our sinning.

So I say there never was a sin committed that was not atoned for. Christ paid the debt of my sins on one condition, and that is that I will believe in him and keep his commandments. He did that for you and for every other person in the world; but he never paid any debt on the cross, or before he went on the cross, for the sins of any of us, if we will be rebellious. *If we are rebellious, we will have to pay the price ourselves.*[20]

ATONEMENT AND OUR LACK OF GRATITUDE

CHRIST PAID AN INFINITE PRICE FOR US. It is impossible for weak mortals, and we are all weak, fully to comprehend the extent of the suffering of the Son of God. We cannot realize the price he had to pay. . . . It is, however, within our grasp to know and realize that this excruciating agony of his sacrifice has brought to us the greatest blessing that could possibly be given. Moreover, we are able to realize that this extreme suffering —which was beyond the power of mortal man either to accomplish or endure—was undertaken because of the great love which the Father and the Son had for mankind.

INGRATITUDE OF DISOBEDIENCE. We are extremely ungrateful to our Father and to his Beloved Son when in all humility with "broken hearts and contrite spirits" we are unwilling to keep the commandments. The violation of any divine commandment is a most ungrateful

---
[20]*Church News,* Apr. 22, 1939, pp. 5, 7.

act, considering all that has been accomplished for us through the atonement of our Savior.[21]

We will never be able to pay the debt. The gratitude of our hearts should be filled to overflowing in love and obedience for his great and tender mercy. For what he has done, we should never fail him. He bought us with a price, the price of his great suffering and the spilling of his blood in sacrifice on the cross.[22]

Now, he has asked us to keep his commandments. He says they are not grievous, and there are so many of us who are not willing to do it. I am speaking now generally of the people of the earth. We are not willing to do it. That certainly is ingratitude. We are ungrateful.

Every member of this Church who violates the Sabbath day, who is not honest in the paying of his tithing, who will not keep the Word of Wisdom, who wilfully violates any of the other commandments the Lord has given us, is ungrateful to the Son of God, and when ungrateful to the Son of God is ungrateful to the Father who sent him.

INGRATITUDE TO CHRIST. If our Savior would do so much for us, how in the world is it that we are not willing to abide by his commandments, which are not grievous, which do not cause us any suffering if we will only keep them? And yet, people break the Word of Wisdom; they refuse to attend to their duties as officers and members in the Church; many of them stay away from meetings the Lord has called upon them to support. They follow their own desires if they are in conflict with the commandments of the Lord.

If we understood our position, and if we loved the Lord our God with all our heart, with all our soul, and with all our mind, . . . then we would keep his commandments. When we will not do this, I tell you, my brethren and sisters, we show ingratitude to Jesus Christ.[23]

The crime of ingratitude is one of the most preva-

---
[21]*Rel. Soc. Mag.*, vol. 30, pp. 591-592.
[22]*Church News*, June 12, 1949, p. 21.
[23]Conf. Rep., Oct. 5, 1947, pp. 147-149.

THE ATONEMENT OF CHRIST

lent and I might say at the same time one of the greatest with which mankind is afflicted. The more the Lord blesses us the less we love him. That is the way men show their gratitude unto the Lord for his mercies and his blessings towards them![24]

THE DOCTRINE OF BLOOD ATONEMENT[25]

CLEANSING POWER OF BLOOD OF CHRIST. The Latter-day Saints believe in the efficacy of the blood of Christ. They believe that through obedience to the laws and ordinances of the gospel they obtain a remission of sins; but this could not be if Christ had not died for *them*.[26] If you did believe in blood atonement, I might ask you *why* the blood of Christ was shed, and *in whose stead was it shed?* I might ask you to explain the words of Paul, "Without shedding of blood is no remission."[27]

Are you aware that *there are certain sins that man may commit for which the atoning blood of Christ does not avail?* Do you not know, too, that this doctrine is taught in the *Book of Mormon?* And is not this further reason why you should discard the book as well as the name? Is it not safe for us to rely upon the scriptures for the solution of problems of this kind?[28]

TRUE DOCTRINE OF BLOOD ATONEMENT. Just a word or two now, on the subject of blood atonement. *What is that doctrine?* Unadulterated, if you please, laying aside the pernicious insinuations and lying charges that have so often been made, it is simply this: Through the atonement of Christ all mankind *may* be saved, by

---

[24]*Millennial Star*, vol. 94, p. 385; D. & C. 59:5-6; Matt. 22:36-40.
[25]This material on "Blood Atonement" was first published some 50 years ago to refute the evil, false, and slanderous charges of the so-called elders of the "Reorganized" church, including one R. C. Evans, second counselor in the presidency of that sect. Similar false charges are made, even to this day, by some who choose to walk in darkness and fight the truth with lies. B. R. M.
[26]1 Ne. 12:10; 2 Ne. 9:7; Mosiah 3:11, 15; Alma 21:9; Mark 14:22-25; D. & C. 29:1, 17; 45:4; 74:7; 76:39-41.
[27]Heb. 9:22.
[28]2 Ne. 9:35; Alma 1:13-14; 42:19; *Inspired Version*, Gen. 9:12-13; Luke 11:50; Heb. 9:22; 10:26-29; 1 John 3:15; 5:16; D. & C. 42:18-19, 79; 87:7; 101:80.

obedience to the laws and ordinances of the gospel. Salvation is twofold: *General*—that which comes to all men irrespective of a belief (in this life) in Christ—and, *Individual*—that which man merits through his own acts through life and by obedience to the laws and ordinances of the gospel.

But man may commit certain grievous sins—according to his light and knowledge—that will place him beyond the reach of the atoning blood of Christ. If then he would be saved he must make sacrifice of his own life to atone—so far as in his power lies—for that sin, for the blood of Christ alone under certain circumstances will not avail.

MURDERERS AND THE ATONEMENT. Do you believe this doctrine? If not, then I do say you do not believe in the *true doctrine of the atonement of Christ!* This is the doctrine you are pleased to call the "blood atonement of Brighamism." This is the doctrine of Christ our Redeemer, who died for us. This is the doctrine of Joseph Smith, and I accept it.

In whose stead did Christ die? I wish your church members could be fair enough to discuss this subject on *its merits.*

I again recommend you to a careful reading of the quotations in my open letter. You will find them as follows: *Book of Mormon*—2 Nephi 9:35; Alma 1:13-14 and 42:19. *Bible—Inspired Version,* Genesis 9:12-13; Luke 11:50; Hebrews 9:22 and 10:26-29; 1 John 3:15 and 5:16. *Doctrine and Covenants* 42:18-19, 79; 87:7; 101:80.

To these I will add: "Whoso killeth any person, *the murderer shall be put to death* by the mouth of witnesses; but one witness shall not testify against any person to cause him to die. Moreover ye shall take no satisfaction for the life of a murderer, which is guilty of death; but *he shall be surely put to death.* . . . So ye shall not *pollute* the land wherein ye are; for blood it defileth the land; and *the land cannot be cleansed of the blood that is shed therein, but by the blood of him that shed it.*"²⁹

ANCIENT MEN SLAIN TO ATONE FOR SINS. Do you want a few references of where *men were righteously slain to atone for their sins?* What about the death of Nehor?³⁰ Of Zemnarihah and his followers?³¹ What about Er and Onan, whom the Lord slew?³² Of Nadab and Abihu?³³ And the death of Achan?³⁴

Were not these righteously slain to atone for their sins? And it was of this class of cases that President Young referred in his discourse you *misquote.* He tells us so, in the same discourse in the portion which you *did not quote.* It is:

"Now take the wicked, and I can refer you to where the Lord had to slay every soul of the Israelites that went out of Egypt except Caleb and Joshua. He slew them by the hand of their enemies, by the plague and by the sword. Why? Because he loved them and promised Abraham he would save them."³⁵

ATONEMENT AND SINS UNTO DEATH. *Joseph Smith taught that there were certain sins so grievous that man may commit, that they will place the transgressors beyond the power of the atonement of Christ. If these offenses are committed, then the blood of Christ will not cleanse them from their sins even though they repent. Therefore their only hope is to have their own blood shed to atone, as far as possible, in their behalf.* This is scriptural doctrine, and is taught in all the standard works of the Church. The doctrine was established in the beginning, that "Whoso sheddeth man's blood, *by man shall his blood be shed;* for man shall not shed the blood of man. For a commandment I give, that every man's brother

---

²⁹*Inspired Version,* Nu. 35:30-31, 33.
³⁰Alma 1:15.
³¹3 Ne. 4:27-28.
³²Gen. 38:7, 10.
³³Lev. 10:2.
³⁴Joshua 7:24-25.
³⁵*Blood Atonement and the Origin of Plural Marriage,* pp. 14, 47-48; *Journal of Discourses,* vol. 4, p. 220.

shall preserve the life of man, for in mine own image have I made man."[36]

This was the law among the Nephites: "Wo unto the murderer who deliberately killeth, for *he shall die.*"[37]

John says: "If any man see his brother sin a sin which is not unto death, he shall ask, and he shall give him life for them that sin not unto death. *There is a sin unto death*: I do not say that ye shall pray for it."[38]

UNIVERSAL PRACTICE OF BLOOD ATONEMENT. *Every nation* since the world began has practiced blood atonement, at least in part, as that doctrine is based upon the scriptures. And men for certain crimes have had to *atone* as far as they could for their sins wherein they have placed themselves beyond the redeeming power of the blood of Christ.

But that the Church practices "Blood Atonement" on apostates or any others, which is preached by ministers of the "Reorganization" is a damnable falsehood for which the accusers must answer.[39]

LAW OF CAPITAL PUNISHMENT. In pursuance of, and in harmony with this scriptural doctrine, which has been the righteous law from the days of Adam to the present time, the founders of Utah incorporated in the laws of the Territory provisions for the capital punishment of those who wilfully shed the blood of their fellow men. This law, which is now the law of the State, granted unto the condemned murderer the privilege of choosing for himself whether he die by hanging, or whether he be shot, and thus have his blood shed in harmony with the law of God; and thus atone, so far as it is in his power to atone, for the death of his victim. Almost without exception the condemned party chooses the latter death.

This is by the authority of the law of the land, not that of the Church. This law was placed on the statutes

---

[36]*Inspired Version*, Gen. 9:12-13.
[37]2 Ne. 9:35.
[38]1 John 5:16.
[39]*Origin of the "Reorganized" Church*, pp. 95-96.

THE ATONEMENT OF CHRIST   137

through the efforts of the Mormon legislators, and grants to the accused the right of jury trial. It is from this that the vile charge, which you are pleased to repeat, has been maliciously misconstrued by the enemies of the Church, who prefer to believe a lie. When men accuse the Church of practicing "Blood Atonement" on those who deny the faith, or, for that matter, on any living creature, they know that they bear false witness, and they shall stand condemned before the judgment seat of God.[40]

CHURCH NEVER PRACTICED BLOOD ATONEMENT. Your report says: "This doctrine was introduced by Brigham Young" and that it meant "death to anyone who left the Church . . . that the apostate whose throat was cut from ear to ear . . . saved his soul." Why you made this statement you best know; but were you not aware that it was but the repetition of the *ravings of enemies of the Church, without one grain of truth?*

Did you not know that *not a single individual was ever "blood atoned,"* as you are pleased to call it, *for apostasy or any other cause?* Were you not aware, in repeating this *false charge, that it was made by the most bitter enemies of the Church before the death of the Prophet Joseph Smith?* Do you know of anyone whose blood was ever shed by the command of the Church, or members thereof, to "save his soul?" Did you not know that you were embittering the people against the Mormon elders, and that just such malicious charges and false insinuations have made martyrs for the Church, whose blood does not "cease to come up into the ears of the Lord of Sabaoth?"[41]

Never in the history of this people can the time be pointed to when the Church ever attempted to pass judgment on, or execute an apostate as per your statement. There are men living in Utah today who left the Church in the earliest history of our State who feel as secure, and are just as secure and free from molestation from

---
[40]*Blood Atonement and the Origin of Plural Marriage*, pp. 15-16. [41]D. & C. 87:7.

their former associates as you or any other man could be.[42]

INFINITE SCOPE OF ATONEMENT

NATURE OF THE ATONEMENT. In the *Compendium*, which was first published in a very early day, this is found: "*The word atonement signifies deliverance through the offering of a ransom, for the penalty of a broken law.* The sense is expressed in Job 33:24: 'Deliver him from going down to the pit: I have found a ransom.' *As effected by Jesus Christ, it signifies the deliverance, through his death, and resurrection, of the earth and everything pertaining to it, from the power which death has obtained over them through the transgression of Adam.*"

On the following page, this: "These passages evidence that *redemption from death, through the suffering of Christ, is for all men, both the righteous and the wicked; for this earth, and all things created upon it.*"[43]

ATONEMENT FOR EARTH AND ALL LIFE. I believe in Jesus Christ as the Son of God and the Only Begotten Son of the Father in the flesh: that he came into the world as the Redeemer, as the Savior; and through his death, through his ministry, the shedding of his blood, he has brought to pass redemption from death to *all men*, to *all creatures*—not alone to man, but to *every living thing*, and *even to this earth itself*, upon which we stand, for we are informed through the revelations that it too shall receive the resurrection and come forth to be crowned as a celestial body, and to be the abode of celestial beings eternally.[44]

---

[42]*Op. cit.*, pp. 13-14.
[43]Pers. Corresp.; *Compendium*, pp. 8-9.
[44]Conf. Rep., Oct. 6, 1934, pp. 64-65; D. & C. 29:23-25; 88:25-26.

Chapter 9

EVOLUTION

ORIGIN OF LIFE[1]

THEORY OF SPONTANEOUS GENERATION. The theory which prevails today regarding the origin of man is that all life has developed from some common origin, spontaneously; that man, fish, fowl, and beast, and even the vegetation upon the earth, all have sprung from the same original germ, which formed itself out of the sea, millions of years ago, in the vague and distant past. . . .

This theory *assumes* as a fact that life, millions of years ago, originated itself spontaneously. This is the foundation of the theory of evolution. The question naturally arises, if spontaneous generation could be possible then, is it possible now? If not, why not?

LIFE TRANSPLANTED FROM OTHER EARTHS. I tell you, *life did not commence upon this earth spontaneously. Its origin was not here. Life existed long before our solar system was called into being.* The fact is, *there never was a time when man—made in the image of God, male and female—did not exist.* The Lord revealed to Joseph Smith the truth that man was also in the beginning with God.[2] . . .

The Lord has given us the information regarding his creations, and how he has made many earths, for there never was a beginning, never was a time when man did not exist somewhere in the universe, and *when the time came for this earth to be peopled, the Lord, our God, transplanted upon it from some other earth, the*

---

[1]President Joseph Fielding Smith has written a scholarly work of 563 pages entitled, *Man: His Origin and Destiny,* to which reference may be made for both a scientific and religious analysis of the doctrine of organic evolution.
[2]D. & C. 93:21-26.

life which is found here. Man he created in his own image. If it were our privilege to go out and visit some of the other creations, other worlds in space, we should discover that they are peopled with beings who *look like us,* for they, too, are the offspring of God, and of the *same race* from whence we came. Perhaps they would be more exalted, but, nevertheless, they would be in the image of God, and so are we. *Adam was not a "cave man," but perhaps the most nearly perfect man in form and feature to our Father and Creator.*[3]

EVOLUTIONARY THEORY FALSE. This idea that everything commenced from a small beginning, from the scum upon the surface of the sea, and has gradually developed until all forms of life, the beasts of the field, the fowls of the air, the fishes of the sea, and the plants upon the face of the earth, have all sprung from that one source, is a falsehood absolutely. *There is no truth in it,* for God has given us his word by which we may know, and all who are led by the Spirit of God can understand through that Holy Spirit, the truth of these things.[4] . . .

How foolish, how narrow, how contemptible it is for men professing to be men of intelligence and possessing scientific knowledge and wisdom, to declare that all life upon this earth is spontaneous, and to confess that they know *nothing* of any life upon any other world, and, moreover, to declare that the life here has all developed from the same single, simple source.

GOD SOLE SOURCE OF LIFE. It is true that all life does come from the same source, but that is not the scum of the sea, a jellyfish or a pollywog. *God, our Father, is the creator of life, and he placed life on this earth in varied forms, and also on other worlds.* He will continue his work on this earth and upon other planets, or worlds, which will take the place of this earth when it has been exalted and gone on to its celestial glory. He will con-

---
[3]*Era,* vol. 23, pp. 378-379, 391-393; [4]1 Cor. 2:11-16. Moses 1:27-40.

tinue to bring to pass his purposes by peopling worlds and bringing to pass the immortality and eternal life of his children.

Now I think this is a noble thought. I think it is something that will enlighten the minds of men and buoy them up. It will strengthen our faith and give us encouragement to continue on in well doing, because it gives us hope of better things, even immortality and eternal life as the sons and daughters of God. But this false theory, which prevails in the world so extensively, is one that is debasing and not ennobling nor uplifting.[5]

EVOLUTION AND RELIGION CANNOT BE HARMONIZED

ADAM DID NOT EVOLVE FROM LOWER FORM OF LIFE. *Do you think that Adam, this great and important prince, the archangel before the presence of God, was a half-breed monkey?* In other words, that he had just developed gradually from the animal kingdom, from some animal form, so that the Lord could put a spirit in him and call him a man? Do you think that? There are people who do believe that. That is why I ask you that question.

Of course, I think those people who hold to the view that man has come up through all these ages from the scum of the sea through billions of years do not believe in Adam. Honestly I do not know how they can, and I am going to show you that they do not. There are some who attempt to do it but they are inconsistent—absolutely inconsistent, because *that doctrine is so incompatible, so utterly out of harmony, with the revelations of the Lord that a man just cannot believe in both.*[6]

CANNOT BELIEVE BOTH GOSPEL AND EVOLUTION. I say most emphatically, *you cannot believe in this theory of the origin of man, and at the same time accept the plan of salvation as set forth by the Lord our God. You must choose the one and reject the other, for they*

---
[5]Conf. Rep., Oct. 1917, pp. 69-71.   [6]*Church News*, Apr. 15, 1939, p. 6.

are in direct conflict and there is a gulf separating them which is so great that it cannot be bridged, no matter how much one may try to do so.

If you believe in the doctrine of the evolutionist, then you must accept the view that man has evolved through countless ages from the very lowest forms of life up through various stages of animal life, finally into the human form. The first man, according to this hypothesis known as the "cave man," was a creature absolutely ignorant and devoid of any marked intelligence over the beasts of the field.

THEORY OF EVOLUTION DENIES CHRIST. Then Adam, and by that I mean the first man, was not capable of sin. He could not transgress, and by doing so bring death into the world; for, *according to this theory, death had always been in the world. If, therefore, there was no fall, there was no need of an atonement, hence the coming into the world of the Son of God as the Savior of the world is a contradiction, a thing impossible.* Are you prepared to believe such a thing as that? Do you believe that the first man was a savage? That he lacked in the power of intelligence? That he has been on the constant road of progression? These are the teachings of such theorists. . . .

ALL MAY KNOW ORIGIN OF LIFE ON EARTH. From whence came man? What is his destiny? It is to me exceedingly strange that men will travel so far, following a will-o-the-wisp until they are overcome in the quagmire, and reject the truth at their door. For an answer to these questions, why not accept the statement of the One who knows? This knowledge is within the reach of all. The story is a simple one, but its grandeur is as far above the doctrine of the evolutionist as the heavens are above the depths of hell.

DILEMMA OF THE THEISTIC EVOLUTIONISTS. It is true that the school of evolutionists is divided into the two great classes, the Theistic and the Atheistic branches.

But the *Theistic evolutionist is a weak-kneed and unbelieving religionist, who is constantly apologizing for the miracles of the scriptures, and who does not believe in the divine mission of Jesus Christ.*

Again I repeat, *no man can consistently accept the doctrine of the evolutionist and also believe in the divine mission of our Redeemer.* The two thoughts are in absolute conflict. You cannot harmonize them and serve both masters.

IF EVOLUTION IS TRUE, THE CHURCH IS FALSE. If life began on the earth, as advocated by Darwin, Huxley, Haeckel (who has been caught openhanded perpetrating a fraud), and others of this school, *whether by chance or by some designing hand, then the doctrines of the Church are false.* Then there was no Garden of Eden, no Adam and Eve, and no fall. *If there was no fall; if death did not come into the world as the scriptures declared that it did*—and to be consistent, if you are an evolutionist, this view you must assume—*then there was no need for a redemption, and Jesus Christ is not the Son of God, and he did not die for the transgression of Adam, nor for the sins of the world. Then there has been no resurrection from the dead!* Consistently, logically, there is no other view, no alternative that can be taken. Now, my brethren and sisters, are you prepared to take this view?[7]

EVOLUTIONISTS REJECT FATHERHOOD OF GOD. The modern world is fulfilling the scriptures which say that in the last days men would be "ever learning, and never able to come to the knowledge of the truth."[8] Today the world has discarded the great truth concerning the Fatherhood of God and has *turned to fables.* It has adopted and is promulgating in textbooks and schools the *debasing doctrine* that man is not the offspring of God, but a natural development through countless ages from the lowest forms of physical life to his present form and intelligence.

---
[7]*Era,* vol. 23, pp. 386-387, 389, 390.   [8]2 Tim. 3:7.

Such a doctrine is an *insult* to our Father in whose image we were created, and yet in this teaching vast multitudes seem to glory. Paul saw our day and by prophetic vision declared that such conditions would prevail in this dispensation and the Lord should "send them strong delusion, that they should believe a lie: That they all might be damned who believe not the truth, but had pleasure in unrighteousness."[9]

LIFE: ITS CREATION AND FALL. All life upon this earth has come from antecedent life. Man has never been able to create life, notwithstanding the many attempts so to do.

All life, having been created by our Eternal Father, must be eternal, as he is eternal.

If all life is eternal, then it must have been subject to a fall.

If all life fell because of Adam's fall, then all life is entitled to a resurrection, through the atonement of Jesus Christ.

If life was produced, or can be produced, spontaneously without the power of God, but in a natural state, then such life would not be entitled to a redemption, or restoration, since it never had anything to which it could be restored.[10]

INTELLIGENCE OF THE ANCIENTS

MEN IN FORMER AGES INTELLIGENT. It is quite generally believed that the people living now are more intelligent than were those who lived in former ages. I cannot accept this view because, with the understanding I have of the restoration of the gospel and of the dealings of our Eternal Father with his children from the very beginning, I know that he would *not* choose and send into this world in the beginning *inferior intelligences* to stand at the *head* of his work.

---
[9]*Church News,* June 12, 1949, p. 21; 2 Thess. 2:11-12.   [10]Pers. Corresp.

INTELLIGENCE DEVELOPED IN PRE-EXISTENCE. We are informed that in the councils that were held in the heavens, when tests were made, the spirits of the men, then living in the pre-mortal state in the presence of the Father and the Son, were chosen to stand upon the earth in the various ages of the world's history to hold particular positions of responsibility because of *superior intelligence* manifested in the spirit world. I am satisfied with the thought that among these spirits there was *none greater, except the Savior of the world himself, than the one who was called to stand at the head of the human family.*[11]

CERTAIN KNOWLEDGE RESERVED FOR FINAL DISPENSATION. So it is not because of greater intelligence, but because, no doubt, of the greater accumulation of knowledge, together with the inspiration that comes from the Lord as he grants it unto men, that we receive the benefit of these latter-day blessings. The time has come for the Father to gather together in one all things in Christ, both which are in heaven, and which are on earth, that the fulness of his work may be consummated. For *this reason* we are seeing and enjoying the great advantages of our time. The prophets anciently, I am sure, spoke of these marvelous events that should come to pass in the dispensation of the fulness of times.[12]

MODERN INVENTIONS RESERVED FOR LAST DAYS. Abraham, as he sat in his tent, could not receive the news of the world published in the daily press and have it delivered to him at his door; he could not push a button and turn on the electric light, but is that saying that Abraham was less intelligent than men are who dwell on the earth today?

The truth of the matter is that these things were *not intended for Abraham's day,* and they would not be

---
[11]Abra. 3:21-26; 5:7; Moses 3:5; 6:51; Ether 3:6-16; 1 Ne. 11:18, 29; 14:27; 2 Ne. 3:6-11, 14-18; Jer. 1:5; Rev. 12:7-9.   [12]Conf. Rep., Oct., 1926, p. 118; Eph. 1:9-10.

known and utilized today if the Lord had not revealed them to men, and had not inspired men to make the discoveries which have been made, by which we are able to receive the news as it is gathered from the telegraph and from wireless telegraphy and have it printed by machinery which is run by electricity.

We can sit in our comfortable homes and turn on the light by pressing a button; we can read the public press, and we will know what is going on today in all the world; but does that prove that we today are more intelligent, or that we have greater understanding than Abraham, than Moses, than Elijah, or any of the prophets of those early times, pertaining to those things which are *most* essential to the salvation of mankind? Not by any means!

ANCIENT PROPHETS SAW OUR CIVILIZATION. I read in the scriptures, if I understand them correctly, that many of the prophets of old had opened to their vision scenes pertaining to the history of the children of men down to the end of time, and the Lord revealed unto them the conditions that would prevail in the earth in this generation.

They saw, if I understand the matter correctly, our automobiles, our railroad trains; they saw, very probably, the communication that was taking place upon the face of the earth so wonderfully by wireless communication, or by means of wires by which news is conveyed. They saw, I believe, the airplanes flying in the midst of the heavens, because we can read in the prophecies of these ancient scriptures many things that indicate that these things were revealed unto those ancient prophets.[13]

INVENTIONS WITHHELD FROM MEN ANCIENTLY. But these wonderful discoveries and conveniences were not intended for their day. They could not sit in an automobile and travel from city to city, or in a railroad

---
[13]Isa. 5:26-30; Nahum 2:2-5; Rev. 9:6-10.

EVOLUTION

train, and ride comfortably, nor could they ride in a modern carriage drawn by horses, but upon the back of an ass would they journey from place to place, or walking by the side of their beast of burden they would travel a few miles each day and call it a day's journey.

And yet the prophets saw the time in the latter days when an ensign should be lifted up that those gathering to Zion should come with speed swiftly; they should not be weary, neither should they be under the necessity of slumber, nor the loosing of their girdle or the shoes from off their feet.

INVENTORS INSPIRED OF GOD. But these advantages were not for their times, and the customs and conditions which prevail now, were held in reserve, not because we are any better or more worthy than the saints of former time, nor because we have greater intelligence, but because we are living in the dispensation of the fulness of times, when the Lord is gathering all things in one and preparing the earth for the great millennial reign; and, it is necessary now that all these discoveries, these wonderful inventions and conveniences should be made known to the children of men.

Those who make these discoveries are inspired of God or they would never make them. The Lord gave inspiration to Edison, to Franklin, to Morse, to Whitney and to all of the inventors and discoverers, and through their inspiration they obtained the necessary knowledge and were able to manufacture and invent as they have done for the benefit of the world. Without the help of the Lord they would have been just as helpless as the people were in other ages.

ABRAHAM: GREATEST ASTRONOMER OF ALL AGES. Abraham knew far more in his day regarding the planets and the great fixed stars out in space than the greatest astronomer knows today. How did he get his knowledge? Not through the telescope; not through the spectroscope; but through the opening of his vision by the Spirit of God. *He was taught by the Lord himself* who revealed unto him all these things and explained the great heavenly bodies and their workings, also the earth, in a manner that never has been approached and cannot be approached by the scientific man with all his instruments to aid him and inspired by worldly learning, and don't you forget it![14]

These ancient seers and saints were just as intelligent as we are. They were just as full of inspiration. They had the Spirit of the Lord to guide them and were directed by it. They hearkened unto those things which God taught and they understood the truth and knew far more of that which is essential, in a minute, than some of these so-called scientists, who declare that life is spontaneous and commenced upon this earth, know in a year.[15]

THE DEVOLUTION NOT EVOLUTION OF CIVILIZATION

TRUE DOCTRINE OF EVOLUTION. It was not until man forsook the divine guidance which the Lord was always willing to extend to him, that *retrogression set in. The "cave-man" and the savage are products of transgression and sin;* for, *in the beginning man was intelligent,* and directed by light and truth, even by the Savior, Jesus Christ, who is the Mediator between man and God. The destiny of man is to become, through stages of progression, like unto his Father; and after the resurrection from the dead, he shall be added upon, as the scriptures say, until he shall receive all things "which the father hath," and shall be counted as a son and joint-heir with Jesus Christ, the first-fruits of the resurrection and the Savior of the world.[16]

EVOLUTION A DOCTRINE OF THE DEVIL. This, then, is true evolution, which all Latter-day Saints believe. There is something inspiring, ennobling and grand in this view of things, but the other view—which is the

---
[14]Abra. 1:31; 3:1-28; Book of Abraham, explanation of figure 2, p. 35.
[15]Conf. Rep., Oct., 1917, pp. 71-73.
[16]D. & C. 76:54-60; 84:33-41; 93:20-22.

doctrine of the devil, who desires all men to be miserable like unto himself, for he was denied a body and the privilege of progression upon this earth—is debasing, and contains not one uplifting or ennobling thought.[17]

MEN BECAME SAVAGES THROUGH RETROGRESSION. It was not until *after* man rebelled and rejected the word of God that he fell into *mental degeneracy,* and *lost* the power to converse in written language. Man was intelligent in the beginning, and understood many fundamental truths, but when he refused to receive divine guidance, the Spirit of the Lord withdrew, and then he was left alone and *became a savage, for the light in him was turned to darkness.*

Tubal-Cain was "an instructor of every artificer in brass and iron," long before the flood.[18] Yet, as late as the middle of the 19th century, when Speke, Grant, Livingstone, and others explored the wilds of Africa they found the descendants of Cain living in savagery in the depths of the "stone age." Columbus, in 1492, found the "stone age" flourishing in all its glory here in America. Likewise our Utah pioneers, in 1847, discovered similar conditions in the valleys of these mountains.

STONE AGE MAY FOLLOW HIGH CIVILIZATION. Shall we argue from this that the poor, benighted savage of Africa, and the equally uncultured Indian of America, were slower in their development than the people in Europe and Asia? If we do, our conclusion will be hastily reached, without an investigation of all the facts to be considered. *The "stone age," the "copper age," the "age of iron," and the age of culture and refinement, run in parallel directions at one and the same time, but the age of knowledge and inspiration preceded all.* . . .

The fact that there has been a "stone age," a "copper age," or any other age or degree of development in the civilization of the world, does not prove that there has been a constant and steady advancement in knowledge

---

[17]*Era,* vol. 23, p. 393.   [18]Moses 5:46; Gen. 4:22.

and skill from the beginning, whenever that may have been. The evidence in history is abundant to show sufficient proof that even where enlightenment has prevailed and men have refused to continue in the light, degenerating influences have set in, and the ages of brass, copper, or stone, are just as likely to follow the age of progress and development as to precede it.[19]

RISE AND FALL OF CIVILIZATIONS Nations have risen to great power and dominion, only to fall into decay and be superseded by other nations. So it has been from the beginning. Egypt, Assyria, Babylonia, Persia, Greece and Rome, all had their day of greatness, culture and might, but their glory has departed forever. In some respects, also, much of their culture and knowledge of the arts and sciences perished with them, and cannot be duplicated in this great age of wonderful advancement. All this reminds us of the words of Byron, so aptly expressed:

There is the Moral of all human tales;
  'Tis but the same rehearsal of the past.
First Freedom, and then Glory—when that fails,
  Wealth, vice, corruption—barbarism at last.
And History, with all her volumes vast,
  Hath but one page.

DECAY OF JAREDITE CIVILIZATION. Here in America, thousands of years ago, there flourished a civilization equal, if not superior, to that which could be found in Egypt or Asia at that time. These ancient people developed the arts and were especially skilled in agriculture to a marked degree. . . .

Nevertheless this people forsook the Lord. They turned from the covenants they had made with him. Contentions arose, bloody conflicts followed, until they were entirely destroyed. There are in parts of the United States and in other places on this continent some mute

---
[19]*Era*, vol. 22, p. 468, 473.

EVOLUTION 151

evidences of their former glory. In Michigan the ruins of ancient copper mines have been found.

Likewise in other localities there are indications that ore has been extracted from the earth, great heaps have been thrown up that still remain. Was it not done by these ancient people?[20]

DECAY OF NEPHITE CIVILIZATION. Six hundred years before the birth of Christ another civilization supplanted that previously mentioned which was destroyed about that time. This second civilization flourished about 1,000 years. The people multiplied and spread over the face of the entire continent. They were highly cultured, and when they hearkened to the voice of their prophets and kept the commandments of the Lord, they prospered, and, like the nation which preceded them, they became skilled in the weaving of all manner of fine linen and other cloth. They tilled the soil and delved into the earth, having also among them many "curious workmen, who did work all kinds of ore and did refine it; and thus they did become rich."[21]

But, like their predecessors, they forgot the Lord; his Spirit was withdrawn, and the greater part of the people was destroyed. *Their civilization perished.* Those who remained *became* ferocious and bloodthirsty. In their decadence they *lost* their knowledge of agriculture, and the working of the metals, and became more or less nomadic tribes. Their descendants, the American Indians, were wandering in all their wild savagery when the Pilgrim Fathers made permanent settlement in this land.[22]

---

[20]Ether 1:41-43; 10:20-28; 15:1-34.   [22]*Era,* vol. 22, p. 468, 470-472.
[21]Hela. 6:9-13.

CHAPTER 10

EVERLASTING COVENANTS

NATURE OF GOSPEL COVENANTS

GOD OFFERS COVENANT OF SALVATION. *The gospel covenant is the promise of God to grant to man, through man's obedience and acceptance of the ordinances and principles of the gospel, the glory and exaltation of eternal life. It is the Father in Heaven who stipulates the terms of the covenant. Man has no say in the matter or right to alter or annul any provision of the covenant.* His duty is to *accept* on the terms which are presented to him from the Almighty, in full faith and obedience, without complaint or desire because of personal weakness to alter or annul, what the Father offers for man's salvation.[1]

BAPTISM AN EVERLASTING COVENANT. *Each ordinance and requirement given to man for the purpose of bringing to pass his salvation and exaltation is a covenant.* Baptism for the remission of sins is a covenant. When this ordinance was revealed in this dispensation, the Lord called it "a new and an everlasting covenant, even that which was from the beginning."[2]

This covenant was given in the beginning and was lost to men through apostasy, therefore, when it was revealed again, it became to man a *new covenant*, although it was from the beginning, and it is everlasting since its *effects* upon the individual endure forever. Then again, whenever there is need for repentance, baptism is the method, or law, given of the Lord by which the remission of sins shall come, and so *this law is everlasting.*

EXAMPLES OF MANY EVERLASTING COVENANTS. Keeping the Sabbath day holy is a covenant between man

[1]*Church News*, May 6, 1939, p. 3.   [2]*D. & C.* 22:1-4.

EVERLASTING COVENANTS 153

and the Lord for he said: "Ye shall keep the Sabbath therefore; for it is holy unto you: everyone that defileth it shall surely be put to death: for whosoever doeth any work therein, that soul shall be cut off from among his people."[3] All of the Ten Commandments are everlasting covenants.[4] The law of tithing is a form of an everlasting covenant, the covenant of revenue for the Church, although some day we shall be given a higher form of this law known as consecration.[5]

Marriage is an everlasting covenant, but *not* as some believe, *the* new and everlasting covenant.[6] The law of marriage to the Church, like the covenant of baptism, is new because it is not the marriage of the world, but for time and for all eternity. Yet this everlasting law of marriage is that which was in the beginning.

PROPHETS FORETELL LATTER-DAY COVENANTS. There are many covenants which the Lord promised Israel he would establish with them in the latter days. These have been spoken of by Isaiah, Jeremiah, Ezekiel and other prophets. Isaiah said: "And many people shall go and say, Come ye, and let us go up to the mountain of the Lord, to the house of the God of Jacob; and he will teach us of his ways, and we will walk in his paths: for out of Zion shall go forth the law, and the word of the Lord from Jerusalem."[7]

Jeremiah, speaking of the covenants which had been given to Israel and which were yet to be given, said: "Behold, the days come, saith the Lord, that *I will make a new covenant* with the house of Israel, and with the house of Judah: Not according to the covenant that I made with their fathers in the day that I took them by the hand to bring them out of the land of Egypt; which my covenant they brake, although I was an husband unto them, saith the Lord: But *this* shall be the covenant that I will make with the house of Israel; After those days,

[3]Ex. 31:13-17.
[4]Ex. 20:1-17; D. & C. 42:18-28.
[5]D. & C. 119; Mal. 3:8-12.
[6]D. & C. 132:4.
[7]Isa. 2:2-3.

saith the Lord, *I will put my law in their inward parts, and write it in their hearts; and will be their God, and they shall be my people.*[8]

And this from Ezekiel: "Moreover I will make a *covenant of peace* with them; it shall be *an everlasting covenant* with them: and I will place them, and multiply them, and will set *my sanctuary* in the midst of them for evermore."[9] These predictions have been partly fulfilled in our day.

LORD STIPULATES TERMS OF HIS COVENANTS. When a covenant is made between two men or parties, it is usual for each man or party to have a voice in the contract and its various stipulations. This is *not* the case with a covenant coming to man from the Lord. It is the duty of man to accept all the provisions of such a sacred covenant established for his eternal benefit.

Man does not have the right to change in any sense whatever, or reject in the slightest degree any part of a covenant which the Lord presents for his benefit and salvation. For a man to presume to change any ordinance offered by the Lord is absurd and should be considered a sad reflection on man's intelligence. Yet such a thing has been done in many instances, and there are those who presume to say that the Lord permits man to change and even mar the Almighty's laws to suit the convenience and the frailties of mankind.

THE LAWS OF GOD ARE UNALTERABLE. They are as fixed and immutable as any of the laws of nature, in fact the laws of nature are the laws of God, and the laws governing in the celestial kingdom are similar in their duration and unchangeableness to the natural laws of the universe.

COVENANTS WITHDRAWN BECAUSE OF UNWORTHINESS. It has become necessary, at times however, for the Lord to withdraw from mankind some of his covenants,

[8]Jer. 31:31-34. [9]Ezek. 37:26.

and give in the stead thereof a lesser law. This was the case in the days of Moses, when the Lord withdrew the higher ordinances and the Melchizedek Priesthood, because of the rebellion or failure of the Israelites to heed the laws of the Lord. In the place of these laws he gave to them the carnal law to be to them as a schoolmaster to bring them unto Christ.[10]

Moreover, there have been times when it has been necessary for covenants to be withdrawn, and man has been left to grope in spiritual darkness without the guidance of the Holy Spirit, and without the saving grace of the ordinances and covenants of the gospel. Such was the case in Israel preceding the coming of John the Baptist and Jesus Christ. The long dark day of apostasy, preceding the middle ages and continuing until the restoration of the gospel through Joseph Smith, was another benighted period of this kind.[11]

No UNNECESSARY COVENANTS OR COMMANDMENTS. We should fully and sincerely comprehend the fact that *no requirement, request, or commandment made of man by the Father or the Son is given except for the purpose of advancing man on the path of eternal perfection.* Never at any time has the Lord given to man a commandment which was not intended to exalt him and bring him nearer to eternal companionship with the Father and the Son. Too many of us receive the commandments of the Lord in the spirit of indifference or with the attitude of mind toward them that they have been given for the sole purpose of depriving us of some comfort or pleasure without any real profit to be derived in the observance of them.

Every covenant, contract, bond, obligation, and commandment we have received by revelation and coming from the Almighty has the one purpose in view, the exaltation and perfection of the individual who will in full faith and obedience accept it. He that "receiveth a com-

---

[10]D. & C. 84:25-28; Gal. 3:7-8, 16-19, 24. [11]*Church News*, Feb. 4, 1933, p. 2.

mandment with doubtful heart, and keepeth it with slothfulness, the same is damned," the Lord has said.[12] Unfortunately there are a great many who receive covenants in that way.[13]

THE NEW AND EVERLASTING COVENANT

GOSPEL IS THE EVERLASTING COVENANT. What is the new and everlasting covenant? I regret to say that there are some members of the Church who are misled and misinformed in regard to what the new and everlasting covenant really is. *The new and everlasting covenant is the sum total of all gospel covenants and obligations,* and I want to prove it. In the 66th section of the *Doctrine and Covenants,* verse 2, I read:

"Verily I say unto you, blessed are you for receiving *mine everlasting covenant, even the fulness of my gospel,* sent forth unto the children of men, that they might have life and be made partakers of the glories which are to be revealed in the last days, as it was written by the prophets and apostles in days of old."[14]

More definitely stated is the definition of the new and everlasting covenant given to us in section 132 of the *Doctrine and Covenants.* Now I am going to say before I read this that marriage is *not* the new and everlasting covenant. If there are any here that have that idea I want to say that right to them. Baptism is not the new and everlasting covenant. Ordination to the priesthood is not the new and everlasting covenant. In section 22 of the *Doctrine and Covenants* the Lord says that baptism is "a new and an everlasting covenant, even that which was from the beginning." Marriage in the temple of the Lord for time and for eternity is "a" new and everlasting covenant.

MEN DAMNED BY REJECTING COVENANTS. But when we get to thinking that one of the covenants belonging to the gospel of Jesus Christ is "the" new and

---
[12]*D. & C.* 58:29.
[13]*Church News,* May 6, 1939, p. 3.
[14]*D. & C.* 1:22; 39:11; 45:9; 49:9; 76:101; 88:131, 133; 98:14; 101:39.

everlasting covenant, that is where we make a mistake, and I am going to point it out to you now. See how clearly and definitely the Lord speaks. I begin by reading verses 4 and 5, section 132:

"For behold, I reveal unto you *a new and an everlasting covenant; and if ye abide not that covenant, then are ye damned;* for no one can reject this covenant and be permitted to enter into my glory.

"For all who will have a blessing at my hands shall abide the law which was appointed for that blessing, and the conditions thereof, as were instituted from before the foundations of the world."

That applies to any covenant. It is not merely this one that the Lord is speaking of here that is going to bring upon us a condemnation if we violate it or refuse to receive it. That is true of every covenant that belongs to the gospel. Take for instance the covenant of baptism. If you will not have that covenant, you will be damned. If you will not have the covenant of repentance, you will be damned. If you will not take upon you the covenant of faith, you will be damned. And so it is with any covenant of the gospel.

The Lord says in section 84 of the *Doctrine and Covenants* that we "shall live by every word that proceedeth forth from the mouth of God"—not by this word and that word and reject these others.[15] *We have got to accept every covenant that he gives us if we want exaltation.* So the Lord is speaking here of introducing what he calls "a new and an everlasting covenant." Now mark what he says in verse 6:

"And as pertaining to *the new and everlasting covenant,* it was instituted for the fulness of my glory; and he that receiveth a fulness thereof must and shall abide the law, or he shall be damned, saith the Lord God."

PROVISIONS OF THE EVERLASTING COVENANT. The Lord is very definite here. In these first verses he uses the

---
[15]*D. & C.* 84:44.

article "*a*" and in verse 6 it is "*the.*" "*A*" covenant means one of many, does it not? But *the* covenant singles out one particular covenant, and that is what the Lord has done right here in this revelation. After calling attention to *the* new and everlasting covenant he gives the definition, and I am going to read it to you (verse 7):

"And verily I say unto you, that the *conditions of this law [i.e. the new and everlasting covenant]* are these: All covenants, contracts, bonds, obligations, oaths, vows, performances, connections, associations, or expectations, that are not made and entered into and sealed by the Holy Spirit of promise, of him who is anointed, both as well for time and for all eternity, and that too most holy, by revelation and commandment through the medium of mine anointed, whom I have appointed on the earth to hold this power (and I have appointed unto my servant Joseph to hold this power in the last days, and there is never but one on the earth at a time on whom this power and the keys of this priesthood are conferred), are of no efficacy, virtue, or force in and after the resurrection from the dead; for all contracts that are not made unto this end have an end when men are dead."

GOSPEL COVENANT EMBRACES ALL COVENANTS. Now there is a clear-cut definition in detail of the new and everlasting covenant. *It is everything—the fulness of the gospel.* So marriage properly performed, baptism, ordination to the priesthood, everything else—*every contract, every obligation, every performance that pertains to the gospel of Jesus Christ, which is sealed by the Holy Spirit of promise* according to his law here given, *is a part of the new and everlasting covenant.*[16]

Man-made covenants, contracts, obligations, vows, associations or expectations, must come to *an end,* for *they are not everlasting.* In the end all things that are not of God shall pass away, and only that which he has established and decreed shall stand. Therefore, all who

---
[16]*Church News,* May 6, 1939, p. 5.

seek a place in the kingdom of God are under the obligation and commandment to abide in the new and everlasting covenant, which is the fulness of the gospel with *all* its rites, covenants, gifts, and obligations, or they "shall be damned, saith the Lord."[17]

THE GOSPEL COVENANT

THE GOSPEL NEVER CHANGES. *This work is based upon fundamental principles that do not change.* They must not, they cannot change, because *they are eternal.* I believe in progression; we all believe in progression; and the Lord has not curtailed us in any respect, but *we cannot substitute the ideas of men for that which the Lord has given,* or the plan which he has adopted and revealed to us, by which we may be saved.

For instance, there is no name other than that of Jesus Christ by which men shall be saved. Men may formulate plans and adopt theories and introduce strange works and gather and teach many peculiar doctrines, but this teaching is fundamental and from it we cannot depart, that all things are concentrated in and around the Lord Jesus Christ, who is the Redeemer of the world.

DOCTRINES OF CHRIST ALWAYS THE SAME. So we accept him as the Only Begotten of the Father in the flesh, the only one who has dwelt in the flesh who had a Father who was immortal. We must accept, and do accept the great truth that because of his birthright, and of the conditions surrounding his coming into the earth, he became the Redeemer of men, and that through the shedding of his blood we are privileged again to return into the presence of our Father, on conditions of our repentance and acceptance of the great plan of redemption.

We must believe in the resurrection of the dead, absolutely so, that every soul born upon the face of this earth shall come forth in the resurrection, either of the

---

[17]*Church News,* Feb. 4, 1933, p. 2; D. & C. 132:8-14.

just or of the unjust, for the resurrection shall be universal, and that, too, through the great atonement which was made by the Savior of the world.[18]

GOSPEL TAUGHT FROM BEGINNING. These principles were taught to Adam after he was driven from the Garden of Eden, who repented and was baptized in water for the remission of his sins, and received the Holy Ghost.[19] . . .

The principles of the gospel were taught from the beginning among the children of Adam. Some believed and accepted them; many others rejected them, bringing down upon their heads the wrath of God, for his anger was kindled against them because of their rebellion. In course of time, when the inhabitants of the earth were sufficiently corrupt, he caused the floods to come upon them, sweeping them off the earth. Noah, who was a preacher of righteousness, continued to preach these saving principles. The gospel was also taught to Abraham, and has always been among men when they were prepared to receive it.[20]

FULNESS OF THE GOSPEL. *By fulness of the gospel is meant all the ordinances and principles that pertain to the exaltation in the celestial kingdom.* . . .

While the saints in former dispensations were granted every privilege and power by which they, through their faithfulness, could obtain exaltation even to the fulness, the fact remains that the Lord has reserved many privileges, authorities, powers, and much knowledge for the dispensation of the fulness of times, into which all things are to be eventually gathered and made perfect in the consummation of the purposes of the Lord towards the earth and its inhabitants.[21]

GOSPEL DISPENSATIONS

NATURE OF A DISPENSATION. *A dispensation of the*

---

[18]Conf. Rep., Apr., 1921, pp. 39-40.
[19]Moses 6:51-68.
[20]*Salvation Universal*, pp. 6-7; Moses 5:10-59; D. & C. 20:21-28.
[21]*Era*, vol. 30, pp. 736-738; Acts 1:6; Eph. 1:9-10; Rom. 11:25-27; D. & C. 124:41; 128:18.

EVERLASTING COVENANTS 161

gospel is defined as the granting to divinely chosen officers, by a commission from God, of power and authority to dispense the word of God, and to administer in all the ordinances thereof. However, a dispensation has frequently embraced additional power and included a special commission or warning to the people, the making of a special and definite covenant with man, and the conferring of special powers upon chosen prophets beyond what other prophets may have received.

PARTIAL LIST OF DISPENSATIONS. The first dispensation of the gospel was given to *Adam,* and he was promised that he and his posterity should be redeemed from death through the atonement of the Messiah[22]. *Enoch* had a dispensation granted to him, and through his faithfulness he and his people were translated.[23] *Noah* received a dispensation of warning when the whole world had fallen into apostasy, and he was commanded to build the ark in which he and his family were saved from the flood, while all the rest of the world perished.[24] To *Abraham* was given a dispensation, and with him the Lord made a special covenant that through him and his posterity all nations of the earth should be blessed. Moreover, he was promised that all who received the gospel should be numbered among his posterity.[25] *Moses* was given a dispensation of gathering and led Israel from Egypt to their promised land.[26] *John the Baptist* was given the dispensation of preparation before the coming of our Redeemer,[27] and Jesus Christ granted a dispensation of the gospel to his *disciples* in the restoration of its fulness and the commission that they should go into all the world and preach the gospel.[28]

---

[22] Moses 5:10-15, 56-59; 6:51-68.
[23] Moses 6:26-68; 7:1-69.
[24] Moses 8:13, 16-20, 23-27.
[25] Abra. 2:6-11; Gal. 3:7-8, 16-19, 23-29.
[26] Moses 1:1-41; D. & C. 84:19-25; Heb. 4:2; 11-24-26; 1 Cor. 10:1-4.
[27] John 1:19-37; Luke 7:24-30; D. & C. 84:26-28.
[28] John 15:16; Matt. 16:18-19; 17:1-5; 18:18; Mark 16:14-17; D. & C. 27:12-13; 128:20.

GOSPEL LOST BY APOSTASY. There have been times when the gospel has been taken from men because of their transgression. Such was the case in the days of Noah. Israel turned from the Lord and was left in darkness for many generations preceding the advent of Jesus Christ, and when he came among men, he *restored* the fulness of the gospel. He sent his disciples to proclaim his message in all the world, but not many centuries had passed before the people had again fallen into error and lost the authority to act in the name of the Lord. This made it necessary for the opening of the heavens, and for the introduction of a new dispensation, to make ready for the second coming of our Lord in the clouds of heaven to reign upon the earth in glory for a thousand years. This event is near, even at our doors."[29]

NUMBER OF DISPENSATIONS. I do not know how many dispensations there have been. Some brethren, basing the statement upon an article by Elder David W. Patten in the early days of the Church, have declared that there are seven; but this does not include the *Jaredites,* the *Nephite nation,* nor the *Lost Tribes of Israel,* whom the Lord visited in the meridian of time following his appearance to the Nephites, and surely, also, the Lord gave dispensations to *Lehi and Nephi* who lived at the time of the coming of the Savior.[30]

CHRIST RESTORED GOSPEL IN HIS DAY. When Christ came, he found Israel—the remnant that remained of Judah—in apostasy and wickedness. Scarcely was there a man remaining who had faith and comprehension enough to worship the true and living God. Our Lord endeavored to bring the wicked nation of Jews to repentance. He offered them the fulness of his gospel— that same gospel which had been declared to Adam, to

---

[29]*Church News,* Dec. 5, 1931, p. 6.

[30]Pers. Corresp.; Ether 1:41-43; 3:6-16; 1 Ne. 2:2-4; Hela. 10:3-17; 11: 19-23; 3 Ne. 7:15-19; 9:15-22; 11:7-40; 16:1-4.

EVERLASTING COVENANTS 163

Enoch, to Noah and to Abraham—the higher principles of which had been taken away with Moses, who left with Israel *the law* instead as *a schoolmaster to bring them unto Christ.*

There were few among the Jews who would hear the Savior when he came. His mighty works, his spoken words given in authority, his miracles, all that he did, fell on eyes that were blind, ears that were deaf, and hearts without understanding. The Lord *again* established his Church, and the gospel was declared to the contrite, the oppressed and the poor. He gave his authority to the humble fishermen of Galilee, and after his resurrection, sent them into all the world with the message of salvation to every creature.[31]

GOSPEL IN MERIDIAN OF TIME. The dispensation of the meridian of time is the name given to the dispensation of the ministry of Christ and his apostles. It is so called because *our Lord came into the world in the meridian of its mortal history.* By revelation we know that it was about 4,000 years from the time of the fall of Adam to the birth of Christ and that it will be about 3,000 years, plus "a little season" from his birth until the end of the mortal earth. We are now living near the close of the sixth thousandth year, or the period known as the "last days," or the time immediately preceding the second advent of Jesus Christ.[32]

When the gospel was restored by our Lord in the day of his ministry, it was his will, of course, that it should remain among men as a means of eternal salvation. However, Jesus knew that this would not be the case, and that the time would come when darkness would take the place of gospel light and the priesthood would be withdrawn from men and the Church driven into the wilderness.[33] However, the disciples were sent into all the world to proclaim the plan of salvation, and to give to

---

[31]*Millennial Star*, vol. 90, p. 307; Mark 16:14-15.
[32]*D. & C.* 77:12-13; 88:108-116.
[33]Rev. 12:1-6.

mankind the privilege of worshiping God in spirit and in truth, if they were willing to receive the truth.

A DISPENSATION RESERVED FOR LAST DAYS. The Lord indicated to the apostles, before his ascension, that *the restoration of all things was not for their day or time,* and that it was not for them "to know the times or the seasons, which the Father hath put in his own power." Peter and Paul made it very clear in their teachings that *there should come another dispensation of the gospel* to succeed that in which they lived, and *this final dispensation should be given shortly before the second coming of the Son of God, to prepare mankind and the earth for the restoration of all things spoken of by all the holy prophets.*[34]

THE ABRAHAMIC COVENANT

CHILDREN OF THE COVENANT. Because of Abraham's faithfulness, the Lord promised to make of him—through his posterity—a great nation and a blessing to all nations to the end of time. Said the Lord: "And I will bless them through thy name; for as many as receive this Gospel shall be called after thy name, and shall be accounted thy seed, and shall rise up and bless thee, as their father."[35]

The descendants of Abraham, the tribes of Israel, became the chosen people of the Lord according to the promise. The Lord honored them, nourished them, watched over them with a jealous care, until they became a great nation in the land the Lord had given to their fathers. Notwithstanding this tender care and the instructions and warnings this people received from time to time through their prophets, they failed to comprehend the goodness of the Lord and departed from him. Because of their rebellion they were driven out of their land and eventually were scattered among the nations. Their

---
[34]*Church News,* Dec. 12, 1931, p. 7; Acts 1:6-7; 3:19-21; Eph. 1:9-10; Rev. 14:6-7.
[35]Abra. 2:6-11; Gen. 17:1-14; 22:15-18; Acts 3:25; 7:1-8; 3 Ne. 20:25-28.

priesthood was lost and they were left in spiritual darkness.[36]

ABRAHAMIC COVENANT CONTINUED TO ISRAEL. These covenants that were made with Abraham continued down and were *amplified—not changed—*as time progressed, and *in the days of Moses the Lord gave many commandments based upon these original covenants with the house of Israel.* If you will read the 26th chapter of Leviticus and the 28th chapter of Deuteronomy—there are many other chapters also in the *Bible* but these two especially—you will find recorded many things by way of covenant and promise and admonition that the Lord gave to Israel. He told them what would happen if they kept his commandments. He told them the consequences of breaking his commandments. All that was clearly set forth in these scriptures before the Israelites entered the promised land.

ISRAEL SCATTERED FOR REJECTING COVENANTS. As time went on they violated these covenants. They turned away from the admonitions, the commandments, the instructions that the Lord gave them through the Prophet Moses, and eventually, *because of that rebellion, the curses came upon them* and they were scattered among the nations of the earth. The 10 tribes were led off captive and later went into the north, and where they are no man knows; but among the children of Israel many were scattered among the nations.

Israel, you know, was divided into two nations before that scattering was completed, the nation of Israel being composed of 10 tribes and the nation of Judah of two tribes, after the days of Solomon, under Rehoboam, Solomon's son. Eventually, I say, the 10 tribes, because of their rebellion and their extreme wickedness, were carried off captive.

ANCIENT COVENANTS RENEWED. The Jews continued, possessing the land of Palestine until after the

---
[36]*Millennial Star,* vol. 90, pp. 306-307.

days of Christ. Then, because of their wickedness and the fact that they had risen up against the Son of God, they too were scattered among the nations of the earth and became a hiss and a byword, and were so to remain until, the Lord says, the times of the gentiles shall be fulfilled. Now the Jews are being gathered again, because the times of the gentiles are coming to their close.

The Lord, through his prophets before Israel was completely scattered, spoke of our day. He spoke of the covenants and how in these latter times he would renew these covenants upon Israel, after Israel had been gathered.[37]

---
[37]*Church News*, May 6, 1939, p. 3; Jer. 31:31-34; 32:36-42; Ezek. 37:24-28; Deut. 4:29-31.

Chapter 11

THE RESTORATION OF ALL THINGS[1]

A MARVELOUS WORK AND A WONDER

WHY THE RESTORATION. The everlasting covenant had been broken; the correct understanding of gospel principles had disappeared through apostasy; the right to officiate in the ordinances of the gospel had ceased among men. It became necessary that all this might be restored, and that faith might increase among the people through an opening of the heavens and a restoration of the gospel.[2]

HOW RESTORATION COMES ABOUT. To bring to pass this restoration, there must come an opening of the heavens. Messengers from the presence of God, of necessity, must come to earth. How else could things in heaven be revealed? Men on earth must be chosen and endowed with priesthood to conduct the labor of the Lord on the earth. This is, in the economy of the Almighty, *always* the plan.

Witnesses must be sent as in former dispensations, clothed with divine authority, to warn the people and preach the gospel of repentance, that men may come into harmony with the revealed word of God. It was for this reason that the Lord declared, "This gospel of the kingdom shall be preached in all the world for a witness unto all nations," before the end of unrighteousness shall come.[3]

WHAT IS TO BE RESTORED. In this restoration it is necessary that the Church of Jesus Christ in its simplicity

---

[1] For a more extensive treatment of this subject see *The Restoration of All Things*, a 320 page work by President Joseph Fielding Smith.
[2] Conf. Rep., Oct., 1944, p. 141.
[3] Matt. 24:14.

and truth be restored. All the keys and powers of priesthood held by the prophets of former dispensations must be conferred upon God's chosen representatives on the earth. In this manner all the authority and keys of priesthood of the past are to flow into the most glorious and greatest of dispensations, like clear streams flowing into a mighty river. The everlasting covenant once given to the ancients, and which Isaiah says was broken, must be restored.[4]

Covenants which the Lord promised Israel—and which the gentiles may share through faith and repentance—are to be conferred. "And they shall teach no more every man his neighbour, and every man his brother, saying, Know the Lord: for they shall all know me, from the least of them unto the greatest of them, saith the Lord: for I will forgive their iniquity, and I will remember their sin no more."[5]

MILLENNIUM AND THE RESTORATION. When that time shall come, the "earth shall be full of the knowledge of the Lord, as the waters cover the sea." Wickedness shall be destroyed, for with righteousness shall Jehovah "judge the poor, and reprove with equity for the meek of the earth: and he shall smite the earth with the rod of his mouth, and with the breath of his lips shall he slay the wicked."[6]

In that day there shall be no *"divided Christianity." All who will not repent and receive the gospel shall soon be removed, and they who shall remain shall learn to worship the true and living God in spirit and in truth. The Church of Jesus Christ shall have sway over all the earth, for Christ shall be the King and Deliverer.* Peace shall prevail both among men and among beasts. Satan shall be bound and his dominion, which he has held by usurpation and fraud since the beginning of the earth's temporal existence, shall come to an end. The rightful King shall

---

[4]Isa. 24:5; *D. & C.* 1:15-16. [6]Isa. 11:4, 9.
[5]Jer. 31:34.

reign and his saints shall possess the kingdom according to the vision of Daniel.[7]

Jerusalem shall become a righteous city when Israel is gathered and redeemed. Zion also shall be cleansed of all iniquity, and in that day, when Christ shall rule, the word of the Lord to Isaiah shall be fulfilled, "for out of Zion shall go forth the law, and the word of the Lord from Jerusalem."[8]

RESTORATION OF THE EARTH. Isaiah has predicted as a part of this great restoration the coming of "new heavens, and a new earth: and the former shall not be remembered, nor come into mind."[9] These new heavens and earth are but *part* of the great restoration as proclaimed in the tenth article of our faith:

"We believe in the literal gathering of Israel and in the restoration of the Ten Tribes; that Zion will be built upon this [the American] continent; that Christ will reign personally upon the earth; and, that *the earth will be renewed and receive its paradisiacal glory.*"

The land surface of the earth is to be returned to one place as it was before it was divided, and the land of Jerusalem and the land of Zion shall be turned back into their own place, and the earth shall be like it was in its paradisiacal glory. The mountains shall be broken down, and the valleys shall not be found, and the great deep shall be driven back into the north, and the islands shall become one land.[10]

A PROPHET NEEDED FOR RESTORATION. Since the prophets predicted that in the last days the Lord would gather Israel and once more reveal to them his covenants, *reason demands that these covenants and the keys of this restoration must be given to some chosen messenger.* Joseph Smith is that messenger. He was to come in the day when the people drew near to the Lord with their mouths, and with their lips they honored him, but had

---
[7]Isa. 65:17-25; *D. & C.* 101:23-31; Dan. 7:14, 22, 27.
[8]Isa. 2:3.
[9]Isa. 65:17.
[10]*Church News,* Aug. 19, 1933, p. 4; *D. & C.* 133: 22-25.

removed their hearts far from him, and their fear toward him was taught by the precepts of men. It was to be in that day, said the Lord, that "I will proceed to do a marvellous work among this people, even a marvellous work and a wonder: for the wisdom of their wise men shall perish, and the understanding of their prudent men shall be hid."[11]

RESTORATION: LINE UPON LINE. There is a beautiful thread of consistency running through the scheme of gospel restoration. Joseph Smith and Oliver Cowdery could not foresee the end from the beginning, but the Lord was the Architect, and made known to them little by little, as knowledge and organization were needed, until the perfect structure of the Church was restored.

Inspiration is discovered in the fact that each part, as it was revealed, dovetailed perfectly with what had come before. *There was no need for eliminating, changing, or adjusting any part to make it fit; but each new revelation on doctrine and priesthood fitted in its place perfectly to complete the whole structure,* as it had been prepared by the Master Builder. The organization of the Church in all of its parts and functions has been proclaimed, even by enemies of the Church, as being equal in its nearness to perfection to any organization on the earth.[12]

ELIAS, ELIJAH AND THE RESTORATION

ELIJAH: A LINK BETWEEN DISPENSATIONS. It seems to be most fitting that the last of the old prophets should close his predictions with a promise to future generations, and in that promise speak of a time to come when there would be a linking of the dispensations past with those of latter times.

Malachi's prophetic sayings have proved to be an insurmountable mystery to most commentators. Especially is this true of his declaration of the coming of Elijah.

[11]*Era.,* vol. 55, p. 82; Isa. 29:14.   [12]*Church News,* Sept. 9, 1933, p. 4.

THE RESTORATION OF ALL THINGS

The reason for this stumbling is due largely to the failure of *Bible* commentators to comprehend that it is both possible and reasonable for an ancient prophet, who lived nearly 1,000 years before the time of Christ, to be sent in these days with such remarkable power as that described by Malachi and possessed by Elijah.[13]

JOHN THE BAPTIST: AN ELIAS. It has been the popular interpretation to say that this prophecy was fulfilled in the coming of John the Baptist as an Elias, with power to turn the hearts of the fathers to children and children to fathers. One reason for this interpretation is the failure of these scholars to understand the words of the angel to Zacharias, in relation to John, which are as follows:

"And he shall go before him in the spirit and power of Elias, to turn the hearts of the fathers to the children, and the disobedient to the wisdom of the just; to make ready a people prepared for the Lord."[14]

It is true that *John came in the spirit and power of Elias,* but not to fulfill the promise made by Malachi, which is shown in the context to be something designed to take place in the last days and shortly preceding the great and dreadful day of the Lord, when Christ should make his second advent on the earth.

Neither should it appear unreasonable to one who has faith in the scriptures to believe that an ancient prophet could be sent to the earth in latter times. There is a very vivid story by the writers of the gospels of the appearance of Moses and Elias to Peter, James, and John, while they were with Christ on the Mount of Transfiguration.[15] Now if Moses and Elias could appear, hundreds of years after they lived on the earth, to these disciples, is it not just as reasonable to believe that they could be sent again with a message of salvation, and with authority to men on the earth in our own day?

---

[13]Mal. 4:5-6.
[14]Luke 1:17.

[15]Matt. 17:1-8; Mark 9:2-10; Luke 9:28-36.

ELIAS TO RESTORE ALL THINGS. When the Savior and these disciples came down from the Mount of Transfiguration, the Lord charged them that they were to tell no man of this manifestation until after he should come from the dead. However, they were anxious to know something about the coming of Elias and in answer to their inquiry the Lord said to them: *"Elias truly shall first come, and restore all things.* But I say unto you, That Elias is come already, and they knew him not, but have done unto him whatsoever they listed."[16] Then the disciples knew that the Master spoke of John.

The Savior made it very clear that *John the Baptist came as an Elias,* or to prepare the way before him, but he also made it clear that *there was yet to come at some future time another Elias with the power to restore all things. John did not restore all things during his brief ministry,* important though it was. His work was that of preparation for the ministry of Jesus Christ, and in this respect he was an Elias.

The name *Elias* is more than a proper name; it is also a title. *An Elias is one who goes before one greater than himself to prepare the way for the greater who is to follow.* In this calling John served, but *not as the restorer of all things.* It is apparent that the restoration of all things was not the purpose to be accomplished during the meridian of time, when Christ was in his ministry. This great work was reserved for the last days. Let us consider this point for a moment.

RESTORATION TO COME AFTER NEW TESTAMENT TIMES. Just before the ascension of our Lord, the disciples put to him this question: *"Lord, wilt thou at this time restore again the kingdom to Israel?"* He answered them: "It is not for you to know the times or the seasons, which the Father hath put in his own power."[17]

This answer has but one meaning, which is, that *the restoration was not for their day.* Later this truth

---

[16]Matt. 17:11-12.   [17]Acts 1:6-7.

THE RESTORATION OF ALL THINGS 173

became very clear to these disciples. It was shortly after this occurrence when Peter admonished some of the Jews who were instrumental in the death of the Lord. He told them they should repent and be converted, that their sins might be blotted out, *"when the times of refreshing shall come from the presence of the Lord; And he shall send Jesus Christ, which before was preached unto you: Whom the heaven must receive until the times of restitution of all things, which God hath spoken by the mouth of all his holy prophets since the world began."*[18]

Paul, also, when writing to the Ephesian Saints, said that in the dispensation of the fulness of times, the Father was to gather together in one all things in Christ, "both which are in heaven, and which are on earth."[19]

RESTORATION TO PRECEDE SECOND COMING. The disciples knew that the restitution was not to come until the approach of the second coming of Jesus Christ, and it was to be in that day that Elijah was to bring back to the earth his priesthood and restore to men the power to seal on earth and in heaven, so that mankind might have means of escape from the destruction which awaited the wicked in that great and dreadful day of the Lord. This great and dreadful day can be no other time than the coming of Jesus Christ to establish his kingdom in power on the earth, and to cleanse it from all iniquity. It will not be a day of dread and fear to the righteous, but it will be a day of fear and terror to the ungodly. This we have learned from the words of our Savior himself.[20]

KEYS OF ALL DISPENSATIONS RESTORED. In the restoration of authority it was necessary that John the Baptist—the messenger who was formerly sent to prepare the way—should first come.[21] Then Peter, James and John, who held the keys of the greater priesthood had to come and give their power that the Church could be organized in the earth. Peter, James and John, the

---
[18] Acts 3:19-21.
[19] Eph. 1:9-10.
[20] *Church News,* Apr. 29, 1933, p. 4, D. & C. 2:1-3; 133:50-53.
[21] D. & C. 13.

three chief apostles, *who constituted the Presidency of the Church in that day*, were the logical personages to come with this authority.[22]

But others had to come. After the coming of the apostles we do not know just what order was observed. It is natural for us to conclude that the authorities revealed and restored would begin with Adam, "who was the first man."[23] Then would come Enoch, Noah, and so on down the line of authority to the dispensation of the meridian of time.[24]

ELIAS OF ABRAHAM'S DAY. We have not been informed as to the identity of the man Elias who lived in the days of Abraham. Some think him to be Melchizedek. But we do know that this man Elias held the keys of the dispensation in which Abraham lived. *He, too, came and restored his authority, which is the restoration of the gospel with all its covenants as given in the days of Abraham.*[25]

ELIAS OF THE RESTORATION. *The Elias who was to restore all things is a composite Elias. In other words, the restoration was not made by one personage, but many,* and in speaking of Elias coming to restore all things, *the Lord was using that title in a plural meaning, having in mind all the prophets who came to restore the fulness of the gospel.* This would include John the Baptist, Peter, James and John, and every ancient prophet who restored keys from the days of Adam down.[26]

WORLD-WIDE SCOPE OF THE RESTORATION

REFORMERS PREPARED WAY FOR RESTORATION. In preparation for this restoration the Lord raised up noble men, such as Luther, Calvin, Knox and others whom we call reformers, and gave them power to break the shackles which bound the people and denied them the sacred right to worship God according to the dictates

---

[22]*D. & C.* 27:12-13; 81:1-2.
[23]*D. & C.* 84:16.
[24]*D. & C.* 128:20-21.

[25]*Church News*, Sept. 16, 1933, p. 4.
[26]Pers. Corresp.; *D. & C.* 27:6-7; 77:9, 14; 110:11-16.

THE RESTORATION OF ALL THINGS 175

of conscience. The Almighty gave men their agency, or the power to act for themselves in choosing good or evil, before the foundation of the earth was laid; but the dragon, from the beginning when he was cast out of heaven, has endeavored to deprive men of this great gift of God.

In the days of greatest spiritual darkness, when evil raged, the Lord raised up honorable men, who rebelled against the tyranny of the dragon and his emissaries who held dominion on the earth, and had subdued in abject slavery the consciences of men.[27]

Latter-day Saints pay all honor to these great and fearless reformers, who shattered the fetters which bound the religious world. The Lord was their Protector in this mission, which was fraught with many perils. In that day, however, the time had not come for the restoration of the fulness of the gospel. The work of the reformers was of great importance, but *it was a preparatory work,* and they shall in no wise lose their well earned reward.

It was not until the close of the first quarter of the nineteenth century that the time fully came for the restoration of light and truth in its primitive fulness. At that time the world had been *prepared* sufficiently, both by the establishment of political and religious liberty, for the Church of Jesus Christ and the holy priesthood to be again returned safely to the earth.[28]

JOEL'S PROPHECY OF LAST DAYS. The second chapter of Joel, beginning with the 27th verse, is as follows:

"And ye shall know that I am in the midst of Israel, and that I am the Lord your God, and none else: and my people shall never be ashamed. And it shall come to pass *afterward,* that *I will pour out my spirit upon all flesh;* and your sons and your daughters shall prophesy, your old men shall dream dreams, your young men shall

---
[27]Rev. 12:1-17; 1 Ne. 13:1-34; 14:1-26.   [28]*Church News,* Sept. 2, 1933, p. 4; 3 Ne. 21:4.

see visions: And also upon the servants and upon the handmaids in those days will I pour out my spirit. And I will shew wonders in the heavens and in the earth, blood, and fire, and pillars of smoke. The sun shall be turned into darkness, and the moon into blood, before the great and terrible day of the Lord come. And it shall come to pass, that whosoever shall call on the name of the Lord shall be delivered: for in mount Zion and in Jerusalem shall be deliverance, as the Lord hath said, and in the remnant whom the Lord shall call."[29]

Of course we understand that there shall be two headquarters: Zion and Jerusalem, and out of these cities shall go forth the word of the Lord, and his commandments, not only to those who are members of the Church, but unto the nations of the earth, when his kingdom is fully established.[30]

LORD TO POUR OUT SPIRIT UPON ALL FLESH. The time for the darkening of the sun and the turning of the moon as blood has not yet arrived; but *the Lord has already commenced to pour out his Spirit upon all flesh,* and we do find even now that the sons and daughters prophesy; the old men dream dreams, and the young men see visions.

Now, my brethren and sisters, *I am not going to confine this prophecy to the members of the Church.* The Lord said he would pour out his Spirit upon *all* flesh. *That does not mean that upon all flesh the Holy Ghost should be sent,* and that they should be participants in the blessings which those are privileged to receive who have been baptized and endowed and become members of the Church;[31] but *the Lord would pour out his blessings and his Spirit upon all people and use them to accomplish his purposes.*[32]

RENAISSANCE PREPARED WAY FOR RESTORATION. I think, properly, we could go back into the days of the

[29]Joel 2:27-32.
[30]Isa. 2:3
[31]John 14:17.
[32]D. & C. 88:6-13.

THE RESTORATION OF ALL THINGS

revival of learning—the renaissance, as it is called—and the reformation in the fifteenth and sixteenth centuries, to find *the beginning of the fulfilment of this promise. The Lord had to begin in those days to prepare the way for the ushering in of the dispensation of the fulness of times, because in the fourteenth and fifteenth centuries, the Christian world was in absolute darkness; a pall of darkness hung over the earth, such as I suppose it had never seen before, and the corruption of the so-called Christian Church was almost beyond belief.*

But during the fifteenth and sixteenth centuries, the revival of learning broke through this darkness and paved the way for the reformation which in the sixteenth century gained a foothold. This was really the dawn of our present day. The yoke of that great power, which kept the nations bound, not merely physically but spiritually, was broken; and rays of light commenced to find their way through so that freedom of religious belief and liberty were established.

INVENTIONS PREPARED WAY FOR RESTORATION. If you will take time to reflect, you will find that in the matter of discovery and invention things have come about in a logical way, step by step, as the people were prepared to receive them, and each step has been in the direction of establishing the truth of the everlasting gospel upon the earth. Thus, when people began to study and to learn, as they did in those days, and learning began to spread, the printing press came along and made it easy to publish books and other matters and to distribute them amongst the people, so that the entire people could learn to read and write.

Before that time a man who could read and who had education was of the privileged class, usually of the clergy; and if a man were accused of an offense, if he could read and write and show that he had some education, he could demand a trial before the ecclesiastical court, rather than before the civil court, and that was greatly to his advantage, because it took more witnesses to prove a case against men before the ecclesiastical court than it did before the civil courts.

IGNORANCE PREVAILED IN DARK AGES. A man with learning could enter the ministry, and the common people were kept in darkness, more particularly concerning the scriptures, and the idea prevailed that the scriptures were not to be had by the common people. One of the great leaders of religious thought at that time said that he regretted the fact of printing, because through its means the scriptures, the jewel of the Church, he said, were becoming common to the laity; and he deplored it because it was a desecration of sacred things; and that was the spirit of the times.

And so, we can follow these things down step by step: and we see that the *discoveries and inventions came logically when most needed.* Before the days of Columbus the people thought that beyond the borders of the Atlantic ocean was a sea of darkness, upon the other side of which were dragons, and if anyone should sail out into the deep, they would become a prey to those terrible monsters.

INVENTIONS COME BY SPIRIT OF LORD. *There has never been a step taken from that day to this, in discovery or invention, where the Spirit of the Lord (that is, the spirit of which Joel spoke, the Light of Christ, not the Holy Ghost!) was not the prevailing force, resting upon the individual, which caused him to make the discovery or the invention.* The world does not understand that, but it is perfectly clear to me; *nor did the Lord always use those who have faith, nor does he always do so today. He uses such minds as are pliable and can be turned in certain directions to accomplish his work, whether they believe in him or not.*

America had to be discovered, because it was upon this land that the gospel was to be restored. There had to be a breaking down of despotic power; feudalism had to come to an end; men had to be freed. If was necessary that parliaments be organized, that the magna charta be given to the people, and that they have a voice in what should and what should not be, in regard to government.

THE CONSTITUTION AND THE RESTORATION. All of this had to be *before* the establishment of the Church of Jesus Christ of Latter-day Saints upon the earth. These things took place in Europe before the discovery of America. After America was discovered liberty upon this land received an impetus which the old world could not give to it; and through the shedding of blood, the land was redeemed (the Lord has said it) and freedom proclaimed in the constitution of the country, so that all peoples of the earth could find a place of refuge in America, the Land of Promise.[33] When that was accomplished, the time had come for the bringing forth and establishing of the gospel of Jesus Christ upon the earth.

INVENTIONS RESERVED FOR ERA OF RESTORATION. Since that time, there have been a great many discoveries. In fact, since the establishment of the gospel, these discoveries and inventions have been increasing more rapidly and we have seen more, perhaps, let me say in the last quarter of a century, than was seen during all the years from the days of the revival of learning and the reformation down to the visitation of Moroni to the Prophet Joseph Smith.

Among other things that have been discovered and invented—and I am not confining myself now to this side of the restoration of the gospel, but things which led up to it—we find: labor saving machinery, weaving, knitting, sewing, farm machinery, and machinery for all kinds of employment. Some of them, of course, came before the establishment of the gospel. The discovery of steam power was before that time, but since that time, see how it has developed; see how all of these things have developed. Everyone of these discoveries, which were made known before the coming of Moroni, or let us say,

---
[33]*D. & C.* 98:4-9; 101:76-80; 109:54.

before the establishment of the Church in 1830, have since been developed and perfected in thousands of ways, most marvelously.

INVENTIONS HELP FULFIL PROPHECY OF JOEL. Now, I have referred to these things as being the *fulfilment* of this prediction made by the Prophet Joel, and which Moroni said to the Prophet Joseph Smith was to be fulfilled in this dispensation of the fulness of times.[34] I have only touched it here and there, for time will not permit greater detail. Look at these electric lights here. We are able to sit in this room and see each other, and I am able to read to you by the aid of these lights, which come from electricity. We have known of that for a long time, but it has not been such a long time that we have been using an electric globe, and see how they have been perfected.

Then, too, as already stated, electricity is used as a propelling force, to drive machinery, to drive our cars through the streets and from town to town! It is used for the raising of great weights; great magnets are made through the power of electricity, by which great loads of metal can be raised in the air, and moved from place to place; and in various ways man has learned to use the great force of which they know so little.

INVENTORS USED BY THE LORD. Now, do you think that these discoveries and inventions by Marconi, by Edison, by Bell, by Stephenson and by the other inventors and discoverers without naming them, have come just because these men have been sitting down and concentrating their minds upon these matters and have discovered them through their thought or accidentally? Not in the least, but *the Spirit of the Lord, the Light of Christ, has been back of it, and has been impelling them to do these very things; and why? Because the time is here; it is ripe. We are ready for these discoveries, these inventions, and they all have a bearing upon the restoration*

---
[34]Joseph Smith 2:41.

THE RESTORATION OF ALL THINGS 181

of the gospel and preparation for the time which is yet future, but which is shortly to come, when Christ shall reign on the earth, and for a thousand years peace shall be established. That is what it is all for.

Now, a man like Edison may say, "I do not believe in a supreme being." I do not know whether he does or not; some of these men do not. However, the Lord, in his great mercy, overlooks that and uses the man because he is adapted to a certain work, and he, through his Spirit, can inspire this man to do this great work, and so he goes ahead and does it, all for the establishment of the kingdom of God.

SAINTS HAVE MESSAGE OF SALVATION. Sometimes we, in our narrow way of looking at things, think that because we are the Lord's people, he is using us and us only. Because it is our purpose to go forth and preach the gospel, and lead the honest to Zion with songs of everlasting joy, we may have an idea that "we are the people," as Job would say, "and wisdom shall die with us."[35] But the Lord is using other forces, other peoples, other powers as well.

We have the great work to perform of salvation for the living and the dead, and those other people are preparing the way in other directions, which we cannot be called upon to do, because our time is to be given to something else.

LORD USES PEOPLE OF WORLD FOR HIS PURPOSES. I am not looking for these great discoveries to come particularly from among the Latter-day Saints, because the Lord has given unto us another work to do, and therefore he is using these people who have the time and who are on the outside to make great scientific discoveries. Not altogether is he using them. He may be using some of us, too, for that matter, but he is doing that, and it looks to me very reasonable that he would pour out his Spirit upon these people abroad.

---
[35] Job 12:2.

You know Peter had an idea that the gospel was only for the Jews. The Lord had a hard time convincing him that Cornelius was worthy of baptism and salvation.[36] *Do not let us get so narrow as to think that because we have the gospel and salvation is with us, that the Lord is confining the fulfilment of these scriptures to the Latter-day Saints alone and that in the pouring out of his Spirit, it is only upon our sons and our daughters, and upon our handmaids and our servants, and upon our old men and upon our young men.* We must not think that the Lord uses only those of his Church and kingdom. He is using all that he sees fit to use, even those who revile him, to bring to pass his purposes. These men may say, "I do not believe," and "I have accomplished this," and they may take the honor to themselves, but *the honor belongs to God.*[37]

INVENTIONS BY THOSE OUT OF CHURCH. The voice is heard and recognized, perhaps a thousand miles away, and the words leave their impression on the mind of those who are listening almost the same as if they were sitting in the presence of the speaker, as you are doing. I think this is very wonderful; and yet, this great discovery did not come through revelation to a member of the Church; it was not sent through one who holds the priesthood, but it came through one not of the Church, but who was inspired of the Lord to give this great blessing to the world. So with many other things: the automobile and the airplane as means of transportation; the talking machine, and all of these great discoveries that have come through scientific research; they have come, most of them, from outside of the Church.

MODERN INVENTIONS PART OF FULNESS OF TIMES. Yet I maintain that had there been no restoration of the gospel, and no organization of the Church of Jesus Christ of Latter-day Saints, there would have been no radio; there would have been no airplane, and there would not

---
[36]Acts 10:1-48. [37]*Gen. & Hist. Mag.,* vol. 14, pp. 5-14.

have been the wonderful discoveries in medicine, chemistry, electricity, and the many other things wherein the world has been benefited by such discoveries.

Under such conditions these blessings would have been withheld, for *they belong to the dispensation of the fulness of times of which the restoration of the gospel and the organization of the Church constitute the central point,* from which radiates the Spirit of the Lord throughout the world. The inspiration of the Lord has gone out and taken hold of the minds of men, though they know it not, and they are directed by the Lord. In this manner he brings them into his service that his purposes and his righteousness, in due time, may be supreme on the earth.

Now let me say briefly that I do not believe for one moment that these discoveries have come by chance, or that they have come because of superior intelligence possessed by men today over those who lived in ages that are past. *They have come and are coming because the time is ripe, because the Lord has willed it, and because he has poured out his Spirit on all flesh."*[38]

---
[38]Conf. Rep., Oct., 1926, p. 117.

Chapter 12

JOSEPH SMITH: PROPHET OF THE RESTORATION

NATURE OF THE PROPHETIC CALLING

PROPHETS CHOSEN IN PRE-EXISTENCE. In the far distant past before the foundations of this earth were laid, a grand council was held in heaven. At that council plans were perfected and an organization formed for the government of this earth during its mortal probation. Our Eternal Father, knowing the end from the beginning, chose from among the spirits those to be his rulers and prophets to assist in carrying through his eternal purposes on this earth in relation to the final destiny of men.[1] . . .

JOSEPH SMITH FOREORDAINED. In this grand council, Michael was chosen to come as the progenitor of the human family and to bring mortality into the world. Jesus Christ was chosen to come in the meridian of time to redeem man from the mortal state, and, on condition of repentance and faithfulness to the eternal plan, to extend redemption from individual sin. Abraham was appointed to become the "father of the faithful," and the founder of the house of Israel. Moses was chosen to lead Israel from Egyptian bondage, and Joseph Smith to stand at the head of the greatest of all dispensations, that of the fulness of times.[2] . . .

Joseph Smith was chosen to stand at the head of the work of the Lord in the last days, and his work was assigned to him through the fore-knowledge of our Eternal Father in the eternities before he was born. He came in the spirit of Elias to prepare the way for the coming of our Lord. No prophet since the days of Adam,

---
[1]Abra. 3:22-28; Jer. 1:5; Titus 1:1-2. [2]*Inspired Version,* Gen. 50:26-37.

save, of course, our Redeemer, has been given a greater mission.[3]

WHAT IS A PROPHET? *A prophet is one who teaches by the voice of inspiration the words of eternal life, and who officiates in the saving ordinances of the gospel.* Predicting is only one qualification of a prophet.

When John was on the Isle of Patmos, a messenger came to him, and John fell to his knees and was about to worship him. But this messenger said unto him, "See thou do it not: I am thy fellowservant, and of thy brethren that have the testimony of Jesus: worship God: for *the testimony of Jesus is the spirit of prophecy."*[4]

In other words, every person who is baptized and confirmed should have the spirit of inspiration, and should know that Jesus Christ is the Son of God. Every person should live in harmony with the revealed truth; and in doing that, and receiving the testimony through the Holy Spirit that Jesus lives and is the Son of God, he or she becomes a prophet or prophetess, and is entitled to the guidance of and inspiration from the Holy Ghost, which is the spirit of prophecy.[5]

ALL SAINTS SHOULD BE PROPHETS. *Every man who can say knowingly that the Lord Jesus Christ is the Redeemer of the world and the Only Begotten Son of God, is a prophet.* Every man that holds the priesthood, and magnifies his calling, is a prophet; and he has a right to the inspiration of the Holy Spirit, so far as he is concerned —but not to receive revelation for the Church. There is only one who is appointed to that office.[6]

A president of a stake has a right to revelation in his stake, and for the guidance of it; a bishop, in his ward; and likewise a missionary in his mission field. Every other member of the Church who is called to an office has the right to the inspiration and the guidance of the

---
[3]*Era*, vol. 44, pp. 716-717.
[4]Rev. 19:10.
[5]*Rel. Soc. Mag.*, vol. 28, pp. 3-4; 1 Cor. 12:28; 14:1-6, 24, 31-39.
[6]D. & C. 43:3-6.

Spirit of the Lord in that which is given him to do. *If he is so inspired, he is a prophet.*[7]

Not only Joseph Smith was to be a prophet, not only his counselors and the Council of the Twelve were to be prophets, but *every* person who would be willing to accept the truth, who would humble himself, and come into the Church, might speak in the name of God, the Lord, even the Savior of the world.[8] . . .

WHAT IS SCRIPTURE? *When one of the brethren stands before a congregation of the people today, and the inspiration of the Lord is upon him, he speaks that which the Lord would have him speak. It is just as much scripture as anything you will find written in any of these records,* and yet we call these the standard works of the Church. We depend, of course, upon the guidance of the brethren who are entitled to inspiration.

There is only one man in the Church at a time who has the right to give revelation for the Church, and that is the President of the Church. But that does not bar any other member in this Church from speaking the word of the Lord, as indicated here in this revelation, section 68, but a revelation that is to be given as these revelations are given in this book, to the Church, will come through the presiding officer of the Church; yet, the word of the Lord, as spoken by other servants at the general conferences and stake conferences, or wherever they may be when they speak that which the Lord has put into their mouths, is *just as much the word of the Lord as the writings and the words of other prophets in other dispensations.*[9]

Now the reason for prophets in this day is that we might be guided in all truth, that we might draw near unto God, that we might know his ways and walk in his paths in righteousness.[10]

---

[7]*Elijah the Prophet and His Mission,* pp. 3-5.
[8]*D. & C.* 1:20.
[9]*D. & C.* 11:25; 50:23-27; 68:2-6; Prov. 29:18; Amos 3:7.
[10]*Rel. Soc. Mag.,* vol. 28, pp. 6-7.

JOSEPH SMITH: PROPHET OF THE RESTORATION 187

PROPHETIC UTTERANCES CONFORM TO REVELATIONS. *When is a prophet a prophet? Whenever he speaks under the inspiration and influence of the Holy Ghost.* Men frequently speak and express their own opinions. The Lord has not deprived men of individual opinions. Good men, men of faith, have divergent views on many things. There is no particular harm in this if these views are not in relation to the fundamentals. Some men are Democrats, some Republicans. Some believe in a particular political philosophy and some are bitterly opposed to it, and yet they are faithful men with a testimony of the gospel.

When prophets write and speak on the principles of the gospel, they should have the guidance of the Spirit. If they do, then all that they say will be in harmony with the revealed word. If they are in harmony then we know that they have not spoken presumptuously.[11] *Should a man speak or write, and what he says is in conflict with the standards which are accepted, with the revelations the Lord has given, then we may reject what he has said, no matter who he is.* Paul declared that he, at times, gave his own opinion in his writing.[12]

PROPHETS FALSELY LABELLED AS MAJOR AND MINOR. This division, generally classing Isaiah, Jeremiah, Ezekiel, and Daniel as *major* prophets and the others whose records have come down to us as *minor* prophets, is without any basis in fact. It is nothing but a man-made segregation and *has no inspiration in it* or approval in any way by revelation or coming from the Lord.

Truthfully, man has no authority to class certain prophets as great and others as inferior, for no uninspired man has been given any authority or commandment to make such a classification. According to the thoughts back of this division, John the Baptist would be only a very minor prophet. We have little of a prophetic nature

---

[11]Deut. 18:22.   [12]D. & C. 1:38; 74:5; 1 Cor. 7:14.

coming from him, and it was the nature of the prophetic utterances which determined this division. Yet we have the word of the Lord definitely declaring to us that there was no greater prophet than John.[13]

By the same token Elijah would be classed as a very minor prophet, because we do not have any but local predictions coming from him, yet he was one of the greatest among the prophets because of his authority, and because of that authority he was sent in this dispensation to restore the fulness of authority—the keys of the sealing power.

It would be very foolish for a man to say that President Heber J. Grant, for instance, was a minor prophet, for he holds the keys and the powers and stands at the head, with all the authority that has been revealed and bestowed on man on the earth. Such a conclusion would certainly come out of a narrow construction and misunderstanding of the nature of the prophetic calling.[14]

THE DIVINE MISSION OF JOSEPH SMITH

CHURCH STANDS OR FALLS WITH JOSEPH SMITH. Mormonism, as it is called, must *stand or fall on the story of Joseph Smith*. He was either a prophet of God, divinely called, properly appointed and commissioned, or he was one of the biggest frauds this world has ever seen. *There is no middle ground.*[15]

If Joseph Smith was a deceiver, who wilfully attempted to mislead the people, then he should be exposed; his claims should be refuted, and his doctrines shown to be false, for the doctrines of an impostor cannot be made to harmonize in all particulars with divine truth. If his claims and declarations were built upon fraud and deceit, there would appear many errors and contradictions, which would be easy to detect. *The doctrines of false teachers will not stand the test when tried by the accepted standards of measurement, the scriptures.*[16]

---

[13]Luke 7:28; Matt. 3:2, 10-12.
[14]Pers. Corresp.
[15]*Church News*, Apr. 1, 1939, p. 1.
[16]*Millennial Star*, vol. 96, pp. 33-34.

ALL ATTACKS ON WORK OF JOSEPH SMITH FAIL. There is no possibility of his being deceived, and on this issue we are ready to make our stand. I maintain that Joseph Smith was all that he claimed to be. His statements are too positive and his claims too great to admit of deception on his part. No impostor could have accomplished so great and wonderful a work. Had he been such, he would have been detected and exposed, and the plan would have failed and come to naught.

In the plan of salvation, as it was made known through Joseph Smith to the world, there are no flaws. Each part fits perfectly and makes the whole complete. Attacks have been made from the beginning to the present, and yet every one has failed. The world has been unable to place a finger upon anything that is inconsistent, or out of harmony in the revelations to Joseph Smith, with that which has been revealed before, or predicted by the prophets and the Lord himself.[17]

MAN CANNOT CREATE A PERFECT RELIGION. No man, in and of himself, without the aid of the Spirit of God and the direction of revelation, can found a religion, or promulgate a body of doctrine, in all particulars in harmony with revealed truth. If he has not the inspiration of the Lord and the direction of messengers from his presence, he will not comprehend the truth, and therefore such truth as he teaches will be hopelessly mixed with error. This is proved to be the case with many professed founders of religious creeds. Their teachings cannot be made to square themselves with the revelations of Jesus Christ and his prophets.

NO SALVATION WITHOUT ACCEPTING JOSEPH SMITH. If Joseph Smith was verily a prophet, and if he told the truth when he said that he stood in the presence of angels sent from the Lord, and obtained keys of authority, and the commandment to organize the Church of Jesus Christ once again on the earth, then this knowl-

---
[17]Conf. Rep., Apr., 1920, p. 106.

edge is of the most vital importance to the entire world. *No man can reject that testimony without incurring the most dreadful consequences, for he cannot enter the kingdom of God.* It is, therefore, *the duty of every man to investigate* that he may weigh this matter carefully and know the truth.

Had Joseph Smith been a fraud, the work he established would have been destroyed many years ago. The fact is, it would not have survived him. At his death, if it had been possible for him to hold his followers until that time, they would have fallen away, the fraud would have been exposed to the face of the whole world, bringing about its destruction.

Some one might say, "If what you say is true, would it not also be true of any other religious sect founded in error?" In time, yes. All man-made creeds and doctrines shall perish when the fulness of truth is come, when Christ reigns in power upon the earth, and when those who abide the day of his coming have all been converted to the one true Church.

NO FRAUD FOUND IN JOSEPH SMITH'S WORK. Had the work been based on fraud, it would have been exposed many years ago in some of the many publications and attacks made against it.

For upwards of 100 years the revealed gospel has stood the test of criticism, attack, and bitter opposition. I think we can say that *never before in recorded history do we have an account of truth passing through such a crucible and being put to such a test as has the truth known in the world as Mormonism.*

Every attack has failed, whether that attack has been waged against Joseph Smith in person or against the *Book of Mormon,* which by the power of God he translated from ancient records, or against the revelations received by him personally from the Lord. *No error in his doctrine has been shown.* The organization effected by him through the blessing and guidance of the Lord harmonizes with the Church of Jesus Christ in former days.

Through him the predictions of ancient prophets have been fulfilled, and now are being fulfilled. He sealed his testimony with his blood, knowing he was going to his death for proclaiming the eternal truths of heaven. His testimony is now binding on the world. It cannot be ignored in safety. Obedience to it has brought joy to thousands, and will yet prove to be a help in the salvation of other thousands who receive it with all their heart.[18]

THE MESSENGER OF THE RESTORATION

WORK OF JOSEPH SMITH COMPARED TO REFORMERS. The fact, so conclusively proved, that there has been an apostasy, shows the necessity of a restoration of the gospel. It is a remarkable fact that Martin Luther, John Knox, John Calvin, the Wesleys, and the other reformers who attempted to correct the evils of the Catholic church, did not think of this great truth. It was left for Joseph Smith to make the wonderful discovery.

It is also strange that the reformers did not discover the necessity for the restoration of the Church as in primitive days with its divine authority, but *assumed* to take the authority upon themselves to organize churches and societies of their own. It was reserved for Joseph Smith to teach the world the necessity for these things.[19]

RESTORATION BY ANGELIC MINISTRATION. The gospel was to be restored as it was in primitive times, before the coming of the Lord. All will admit, whether they believe in the mission of Joseph Smith or not, that at least there has been a departure from the teachings and the organization which existed in the days of the Savior's ministry and the ministry of the apostles. That must be, and is, conceded. You cannot find that organ-

---
[18]*Millennial Star*, vol. 96, pp. 34-35.   [19]*Era*, vol. 23, p. 499.

ization anywhere in the world, and you cannot find those doctrines anywhere except as they have been given through the agency of Joseph Smith.

This ancient gospel was to be declared, so John the Revelator has written in the fourteenth chapter and sixth verse of Revelation, by an angel, who was to fly through the midst of heaven having the everlasting gospel to preach unto them that dwell on the earth, and to every nation, and kindred, and tongue, and people, calling on them to repent for the hour of judgment is come. *Nobody else, except Joseph Smith, ever claimed that an angel did fly and did appear to him with this message, and that he was commissioned to send it forth to all the world.*

ONLY JOSEPH SMITH FULFILS ANCIENT PROMISES. Joseph Smith declared that he, with Oliver Cowdery, his companion, received the keys of the gathering of Israel. *No one else ever claimed to have had them revealed to him.* If Joseph Smith did not receive them, then someone must be empowered with this authority before the coming of the Lord: for Israel is to be gathered, and it must be by authority given to someone. *Israel is being gathered, which indicates that Joseph Smith must have held those keys.*

Malachi has said that the Lord would send Elijah before the coming of the great and dreadful day of the Lord. The Prophet Joseph Smith said he (Elijah) came to him and Oliver Cowdery with the keys of that power. If he did not, and they have told a falsehood, then Elijah must come before the great day of the Lord, or the earth will be smitten with a curse. But Elijah did come, and the earth will be spared that curse.

No one, save Joseph Smith, has claimed that these keys have been revealed. No one else even knew what was meant by this passage of scripture. The hearts of the children are turned to their fathers, as Malachi predicted would be the case, after the coming of Elijah.

*This indicates that Elijah has come, and it must have been to Joseph Smith.*²⁰

LORD TO SEND A MESSENGER BEFORE HIM. Malachi speaks of the Lord sending his messenger to prepare the way before him, and while that does have reference to the coming of John the Baptist, it is one of those prophecies in the scriptures that has a *double fulfilment. It has reference also to the coming of the Prophet Joseph Smith, because that messenger which was to come and prepare the way before him, was to come in this day.* I am going to take just a moment for that because it is important, and I will show you when this messenger was to deliver his message.

"Behold, I will send my messenger, and he shall prepare the way before me: and the Lord, whom ye seek, shall suddenly come to his temple, even the messenger of the covenant, whom ye delight in: behold, he shall come, saith the Lord of hosts."

I went to a service of the Baptist Church and the preacher took that for his text, and told how this was fulfilled in the coming of John. He did come as a messenger. He did come to prepare the way of the Lord, but there are some things written here that *cannot apply to Christ's first ministry on the earth.*

THE MESSENGER TO PRECEDE SECOND COMING. "But who may abide the day of his coming? and who shall stand when he appeareth? for he is like a refiner's fire, and like fullers' soap: And he shall sit as a refiner and purifier of silver: and he shall purify the sons of Levi, and purge them as gold and silver, that they may offer unto the Lord an offering in righteousness. Then shall the offering of Judah and Jerusalem be pleasant unto the Lord, as in the days of old, and as in former years."²¹

Was that fulfilled in John and in the days of Christ's ministry on the earth? Was the sacrifice of Levi pleasant

---

²⁰Conf. Rep., Apr., 1920, pp. 105-108.   ²¹Mal. 3:1-4.

before the Lord? Was the offering of Judah pleasant before the Lord? Levi and Judah rose up in rebellion against Christ and cried out against him: "His blood be on us, and on our children."[22] And they put him to death. He did not sit then as a refiner and purifier, in the sense in which this is meant. He did not purge Levi and Judah and make things pleasant as in former years, as stated here.

That indicates that this had reference, and does have reference, to the dispensation of the fulness of times, when Christ comes again—and I think *he has already come and fulfilled that,* at least very largely, for Christ did, if you please, "suddenly come to his temple" on the 3rd day of April, 1836, and minister to Joseph Smith and Oliver Cowdery, and then send other messengers to confer upon them keys of priesthood of the various dispensations. As to the offering of Judah and the offering of Levi, that is yet to be fulfilled, for these are yet to become "pleasant unto the Lord." That is a revelation that is yet to come.[23]

JOHN AND JOSEPH SMITH BOTH MESSENGERS. The Lord, in the former dispensation, sent a messenger to prepare the way before him, and in this dispensation it was just as necessary that a messenger be sent to prepare the way for the coming of the Lord and the establishment of the reign of peace. If Joseph Smith was not that man, then we must look for another. . . .

The Lord declared, through one of his prophets, that before his second coming a messenger should be sent to prepare the way and make it straight. You may apply this to John if you will, and it is true. John, the messenger who came to prepare the way before the Lord in the former dispensation, also came in this dispensation as a messenger to Joseph Smith; so it applies, if you wish to apply it so, to John who came as a messenger to prepare the way before the Lord.

[22]Matt. 27:25.   [23]D. & C. 110:1-16.

JOSEPH SMITH: PROPHET OF THE RESTORATION 195

But I go farther and maintain that *Joseph Smith was the messenger whom the Lord sent to prepare the way before him.* He came, and under direction of holy messengers laid the foundation for the kingdom of God and of this marvelous work and a wonder that the world might be prepared for the coming of the Lord.[24]

DETAILS PROVING TRUTH OF PROPHET'S MISSION

RESTORATION OF AARONIC PRIESTHOOD. I have answered the question as to why the Father introduced the Son, and why it was the Son who spoke to Joseph Smith, because all revelations since the day of Adam's casting out of the Garden of Eden have come through Jesus Christ.[25]

Why did John confer the priesthood upon Joseph Smith and Oliver Cowdery on the bank of the Susquehanna River? Because there was no authority upon the earth authorized to give it. That is why.

Now suppose Joseph Smith had found another man, Oliver Cowdery, who was willing to enter into collusion to deceive, and they had thought—without any inspiration—that it would be a wonderful thing to say, that a man could not act in the name of God without authority from God, so they would come before the world claiming a restoration of priesthood.

Would they say, if they were deceivers, "We went out into the woods; we prayed, and John the Baptist came and laid his hands upon our heads and then commanded us to baptize each other?" Would they have said that if they had been deceivers? I cannot for the life of me believe they would.[26]

WHAT ANGELS WILL DO FOR US. I'll tell you what would have happened, had they discovered in some way, *which no other religious teacher in all the ages had ever thought of,* that they had to have authority from the heavens—when others just assumed authority. They

---
[24]Conf. Rep., Apr., 1920, pp. 105-108.   [26]*D. & C.* 13; Joseph Smith 2:68-72.
[25]Sub. topic, "First Vision and Revelation," chapter 2.

would have come back and said: "We went out to pray and a messenger came"—they might have called him John or they might have called him someone else—"He laid his hands on our heads and gave us authority and baptized us." They would likely have come back and said: "An angel came and said he was John the Baptist, and then he baptized us."

We would know now, if such had been the case, that Joseph Smith was a fraud, because John would not baptize them. Why? Because it would be contrary to the order of heaven. *It is contrary to the law of God for the heavens to be opened and messengers to come to do anything for man that man can do for himself.*

The only reason that Jesus Christ became the Redeemer of the world, and came here to atone for the transgressions of man, was that we could not redeem ourselves. It required an infinite atonement, as the *Book of Mormon* says.[27] He came to do what no one else could do.

You cannot point to anywhere in the scriptures where a messenger has come from the heavens and bestowed upon man something man could do for himself, but angels have come and told men what to do and sent men to do it. So if they had come back and said John baptized them, it would have been fatal to their story.

JOHN THE BAPTIST'S DIRECTIONS TO JOSEPH AND OLIVER. They came back and said: "After we baptized each other the angel said, 'Joseph, you lay your hands upon Oliver and *reconfirm* the ordination that I have given you, and Oliver, put your hands upon the head of Joseph Smith and reconfirm the ordination that I have given you' "—or the restoration of the priesthood, which is a better term. And they did that. Why? Because of this very thing I am telling you.

It was out of order to ordain men and then baptize them. We never think today of doing that. We do not

---
[27] 2 Ne. 9:7.

take a man and confer upon him the Aaronic Priesthood and then baptize him, or send him to be baptized. Why? Because we have a Church organization. So the angel did what was essential—the only thing that was, as far as he was then concerned—and then he commanded them to baptize each other, and then had them lay hands on each other and *reseal* those blessings in the proper order. That is a little detail, but suppose Joseph Smith had not thought of it. It would have been fatal—fatal to his mission.

JOSEPH SMITH REQUIRED TO TRANSLATE BOOK OF MORMON. Then when Moroni came to Joseph Smith, he told him that in the hill Cumorah there were certain records of the ancient people of this land, and that he was going to turn them over to him. He had Joseph Smith call on him four times, at a certain time in September each year for four years, and there instructed him. That was a school for Joseph Smith. Then he turned the record over to Joseph Smith together with the Urim and Thummim, and told him to translate it.

Why didn't he translate it himself? Moroni could read those writings. He wrote some of them. He was familiar with the language. How easy it would have been for him to say to Joseph Smith, "Here is the record. I sealed it up. I did the writing of two of these books. My father did the writing of others. I understand the language perfectly, and I am going to write this in your language and give it to you."

It seems to me that is what a fraud would have said. If Joseph Smith had been an impostor he would have said: "The angel revealed this record to me, but I couldn't read it so the angel, who understood the language, interpreted it and I wrote it at his dictation."

But if he had said that it would have been fatal. Instead of doing that he said, "The angel placed in my hands the Urim and Thummim and said: 'These interpreters will enable you to translate this record. Now you go and do it.'" That, in substance, is what he said.

He has been ridiculed for it, and the great people of the earth, the scientists, say it is an impossibility, but that is the consistent thing.

JOSEPH SMITH FOLLOWED SCRIPTURAL PATTERN. Now I am going to call your attention to some of the examples we have in the scriptures, for instance, the case of Peter and Cornelius. Cornelius was a devout man. He sought the Lord and an angel appeared, but he did not say, "Cornelius, the gospel has been restored, and since you are a devout man and you believe, I will take you and baptize you." He did not say that, but he told Cornelius where to go.

Then a messenger appeared to Peter and taught him and directed him, so that when Cornelius came he would know what he was coming for, and Peter would not refuse to attend to the ordinances. *The angel did only that which was essential—that is all.*[28]

When the Savior appeared to Paul and stopped him in his mad course in the persecution of the saints, what did he do? He sent him into the city, there to find one named Ananias, who would tell him what to do. Then he sent word to Ananias where Paul, who had been persecuting the saints, was. The Savior said he had a mission for Paul, and told Ananias to go and find him at such and such a place, and lay his hands on him.

That is the way the Lord works. *Joseph Smith was in perfect harmony all through his mission. It never fails —every little detail works harmoniously, perfectly, with the plan the Lord has instituted, and never in one case has it failed.*[29]

DETAILS OF MORONI'S VISIT PROVE JOSEPH A PROPHET. On the night of September 21, 1823, when Moroni appeared to Joseph Smith, he said that the time was at hand for the fulfilment of many of the prophecies relating to the last times. This angel quoted to the young

[28]Acts 10:1-48.   [29]*Church News*, Apr. 1, 1939, pp. 7-8; Acts 9:1-18; 22:6-16.

man, Joseph Smith, part of the third and all of the fourth chapters of Malachi, with some variations from the reading as we find it in the King James translation of the *Bible.*

He also quoted the 11th chapter of Isaiah, saying that it was about to be fulfilled; also the 22nd and 23rd verses of the third chapter of Acts, and the second chapter of Joel, verses 28 to the end, which he said were shortly to be fulfilled. He also said that the time for the fulness of the gentiles would soon come in, and many other scriptures were quoted which pertain to the dispensation of the fulness of times.[30]

The significant thing about this statement coming from Joseph Smith is the *frankness* with which he has given it to the world, presenting chapters and verses in definite order, with the declaration that the time is at hand for their fulfilment.

How would he dare to make such a statement, if the presentation of it was only an act of imagination, or a falsehood presented to deceive? He would know that if this information was not given by the angel it surely would be proved untrue, for the promised fulfilment of the predictions would not come to pass.

Joseph Smith, then but a boy, did not have the knowledge of the times by which he could of himself make such predictions. In fact, the learned men of the world could not make such predictions in that day, for they also were without the power of discernment and could not read the signs of the times. The fact that some of the words of Moroni to Joseph Smith have been fulfilled, and that others are now being fulfilled, lends credence to the fact that this young man spoke the truth, as he received it from a messenger sent from the presence of the Lord.[31]

PERSONAL SENTIMENTS ABOUT JOSEPH SMITH

PRAYER FOR CHILDREN OF THE PROPHET. *All my life I have prayed and hoped that the Lord would touch*

---
[30]Joseph Smith 2:36-41.   [31]*Church News,* Sept. 5, 1931, p. 2.

the hearts of the children of the Prophet Joseph Smith and bring them to repentance. I still pray that he may do so. No man would hold out the hand of fellowship more quickly than I would to welcome them into the fold of truth. But I cannot countenance their actions in opposition to this great work which the Lord established through the Prophet Joseph Smith.

While I regret the fact that they stand aloof and in opposition to the fulness of the gospel which that Prophet restored, yet I pray and hope that the time will speedily come when some of them, at least, will see the error of their ways, and come humbly seeking the favor of God, and membership in the Church. They who will not repent, but who persist in the opposition to the truth, may they be confounded; may that which they propose come to nought; may all their works fail and may they stand exposed in the full error of their ways before the world.

May the Lord bless the family of the Prophet Joseph Smith and bring them to repentance. May he bless the descendants of Hyrum Smith that they also may walk in the light of the everlasting gospel. May they never falter nor turn from the path in which their father walked, and may they honor and uphold his good name. And so I pray for all who receive the gospel, for we are all brothers and sisters. May the Lord guide and bless all who love the truth.[32]

ON REMOVING BONES OF JOSEPH AND HYRUM. *Those sacred remains should not have been disturbed. Such a despicable act could only be performed by those who are lacking in all the finer feelings and in whom the spirit of reverence for things held sacred and holy by all faithful Latter-day Saints, does not exist. Frederick M. Smith has debased himself in the sight of all honorable men, as well as in the sight of God, in this unholy and sacrilegious act. It is almost beyond belief that even he*

---
[32]Conf. Rep., Apr., 1930, p. 94.

could stoop so low as to photograph the remaining bones of God's prophets, and show them on screens to a morbid following. The Lord will reward Frederick M. Smith according to his works.[33]

TESTIMONY CONCERNING JOSEPH SMITH. *Joseph Smith, the humble farmer boy, was trained and instructed as, perhaps, no other prophet was ever taught and trained, by divine instructors sent from the throne and presence of our Eternal Father.*[34]

I have a *perfect knowledge* of the divine mission of the Prophet Joseph Smith. There is no doubt in my mind that the Lord raised him up and gave him revelation, commandment, opened the heavens to him, and called upon him to stand at the head of this glorious dispensation. I am perfectly satisfied in my mind that in his youth, when he went out to pray, he beheld the actual presence, stood in the actual presence of God the Father and his Son, Jesus Christ; in my mind there is no doubt; I know this to be true. I know that he received later the visitations from Moroni, the Aaronic Priesthood under the hands of John the Baptist, the Melchizedek Priesthood under the hands of Peter, James, and John, and that the Church of Jesus Christ of Latter-day Saints was organized on the sixth day of April, 1830, by divine command.

ALL MAY GAIN TESTIMONY CONCERNING JOSEPH SMITH. These things I know. The Lord has revealed them to me, and this knowledge I have had since the day I was baptized. I know that the power of the Almighty is guiding this people, that we are under covenant to keep his commandments, to walk in light and truth. It is my firm conviction that every member of this Church should be able to bear witness and declare by words of soberness that these things are true, that the *Book of Mormon* is true, that the destiny of this latter-day work

---

[33] *Millennial Star*, vol. 90, p. 158. [34] *Era*, vol. 44, p. 763.

is true, and, according to the revelations, must and will be fulfilled.[35]

And every soul upon the face of the earth who has a desire to know it, has the privilege of knowing for himself, for every soul that will humble himself, and in the depths of humility and faith, with a contrite spirit, go before the Lord, will receive that knowledge just as surely as he lives.[36]

---
[35]Conf. Rep., Apr., 1951, p. 58.   [36]Conf. Rep., Oct., 1949, p. 89.

Chapter 13

THE DIVINE LAW OF WITNESSES

NATURE AND HISTORY OF LAW OF WITNESSES

WITNESSES SENT IN ALL DISPENSATIONS. There is a law definitely stated in the scriptures governing testimony and the appointment of witnesses. This law the Lord has *always* followed in granting new revelation to the people.[1]

All down through the ages this law has been a fixed and definite one. If we had perfect records of all ages, we would find that *whenever the Lord has established a dispensation, there has been more than one witness to testify for him.* Paul in writing to the Corinthians said: "In the mouth of two or three witnesses shall every word be established."[2]

If you will look in your *Bible*, you will find that the Lord gave the law to Israel and it is recorded in Deuteronomy: "At the mouth of two witnesses, or three witnesses, shall he that is worthy of death be put to death; but at the mouth of one witness he shall not be put to death."[3]

Of course, that reference to the trial of an individual is based upon the general law, which was to be applied not merely in trial where life was at stake, but in every important undertaking. In one of the discourses of our Lord, he said: "Moreover if thy brother shall trespass against thee, go and tell him his fault between thee and him alone: if he shall hear thee, thou hast gained thy brother. But if he will not hear thee, then take with thee one or two more, that in the mouth of two or three witnesses every word may be established."[4]

---
[1] *Era*, vol. 30, p. 950.
[2] 2 Cor. 13:1.
[3] Deut. 17:6; 19:15.
[4] Matt. 18:15-16.

OTHER WITNESSES AIDED NOAH. It is generally thought that the Lord called Noah, when he had determined to cleanse the earth with the flood, and sent him out alone to preach to the wicked inhabitants. It is sometimes said, *without basis in fact,* that Noah preached 120 years; and nothing is said of the preaching of other witnesses.

Let me call your attention to the fact that *Noah was not alone in bearing witness.* It is recorded in the *Pearl of Great Price* that: "It came to pass that Methuselah, the son of Enoch, was not taken, that the covenants of the Lord might be fulfilled, which he made to Enoch; for he truly covenanted with Enoch that Noah should be of the fruit of his loins. And it came to pass that *Methuselah prophesied* that from his loins should spring all the kingdoms of the earth (through Noah), and he took glory unto himself."[5]

Now Methuselah, grandfather of Noah, was a righteous man and a prophet. He knew by the spirit of revelation that the flood would come in the days of Noah. Moreover, he lived until the year of the flood when he died. *Do you not think that this righteous man was also declaring repentance to the perverse world, and warning them of the flood which was to come?* Again, *Lamech,* father of Noah, was also a righteous man and he lived until five years before the flood. It is reasonable to suppose that *he, too, was preaching* to the people, as well as his father and his son.

OTHER WITNESSES IN DAYS OF ABRAHAM AND OF MOSES. We do not know much about the dispensation of Abraham. We speak of it as the dispensation of Abraham, but *what about Elias who held the keys of that dispensation? Melchizedek was living in the days of Abraham,* was the one who blessed him, and without question understood the covenant the Lord had made with Abraham.[6] . . .

---

[5]Moses 8:2-3.   [6]*D. & C.* 84:14; 110:12; *Inspired Version,* Gen. 14:37.

THE DIVINE LAW OF WITNESSES

When Moses was called to lead Israel, that was another great and important event. Moses had to flee from the courts of Egypt. He went out among the Midianites and became a herdsman, tending the flocks of Jethro, sometimes spoken of in the scriptures as Reuel. The Lord appeared to Moses in the burning bush as he was thus employed and called him to a mission. But the Lord did not leave him alone to testify to the Pharaoh of Egypt. What did he do? He sent *Aaron the brother of Moses to assist him.*

Moses said to the Lord, "I am not eloquent, neither heretofore, nor since thou has spoken unto thy servant: but I am slow of speech, and of a slow tongue."[7] So *the Lord appointed Aaron to be a spokesman for him.* Why did Aaron wait 40 years before he came to Moses and then appear just at the right time? Because the Lord sent him, not only to be spokesman, but *to bear witness with Moses that the Lord had spoken.*[8]

The Savior took *Peter, James, and John* with him on the mount at the time of the transfiguration.[9] Why did he not take Peter alone? Because he wanted more than one witness. And we would find, I am confident, if we had the perfect record, *all down the ages, whenever the Lord introduced a dispensation, he did not leave one man to testify alone.*

JOSEPH SMITH OBEYS LAW OF WITNESSES. Joseph Smith was alone when he went into the grove to pray and beheld the Father and the Son. He was alone when Moroni appeared to him in his father's home, and he was alone in meeting the angel at the Hill Cumorah each year for four years. This was true because it was not necessary on these occasions for another witness to be present, anymore than for two witnesses to witness the power of the Lord in the burning bush.

But suppose that this had continued on through the entire mission of Joseph Smith and he had declared to

---
[7]Ex. 4:10. [9]Matt. 17:1-13.
[8]Ex. 3 and 4.

the world: "I received the plates of the *Book of Mormon* and translated them by the gift and power of God, but I was alone. I wrote the translation when I was alone. John the Baptist came to me and gave me the Aaronic Priesthood, but I was alone; there was no other witness. Also Peter, James, and John came to me and conferred upon me the Melchizedek Priesthood, but I was alone."

Suppose that in each instance when keys of authority were bestowed he had declared that it was a personal visitation to himself, and that it was the will of the Lord that he be alone? Then we could with perfect propriety reject the testimony of Joseph Smith, for it would not be true.

CHRIST OBEYS LAW OF WITNESSES. Now let me refer you again to the scriptures: "I can of mine own self do nothing: as I hear, I judge: and my judgment is just; because I seek not mine own will, but the will of the Father which hath sent me. If I bear witness of myself, my witness is not true. There is another that beareth witness of me; and I know that the witness which he witnesseth of me is true. Ye sent unto John, and he bear witness unto the truth."[10]

Let us not misunderstand. When Christ said, "There is another that beareth witness of me," he was not speaking primarily of John, although John did bear such a witness. He was speaking of Another Witness, and what he says is true: "If I stand alone and no one testifies for me, then you can reject my testimony because the witness would not be true." It was his Father he had in mind when he said there was Another Witness.

CHRIST ACCUSED OF BREAKING LAW OF WITNESSES. We turn now to the 8th chapter of John, where we have a statement from our Lord as he was under fire by those wicked Pharisees. I can imagine the Savior surrounded by this group of evil men, trying to teach them the truth and bring them to repentance, and they stood there rid-

---
[10]John 5:30-33.

THE DIVINE LAW OF WITNESSES

iculing him and casting aspersions upon him. This is the conversation as we have it given by John:

"Then spake Jesus again unto them, saying, I am the light of the world: he that followeth me shall not walk in darkness, but shall have the light of life. The Pharisees therefore said unto him, Thou bearest record of thyself; thy record is not true."

It is very evident that they understood the law, and it is as if they had said: "You are alone; nobody testifies for you. You say you are the light of the world, but *the law demands that there shall be another witness if what you say is true.*" That this was in their minds is evident from what follows:

"Jesus answered and said unto them, Though I bear record of myself, yet my record is true: for I know whence I came, and whither I go; but ye cannot tell whence I come, and whither I go. Ye judge after the flesh; I judge no man. And yet if I judge, my judgment is true: for I am not alone, but I and the Father that sent me. It is also written in your law, that the testimony of two men is true."

THE FATHER BEARS WITNESS OF CHRIST. "*I am one that bear witness of myself, and the Father that sent me beareth witness of me.* Then said they unto him, Where is thy Father? Jesus answered, Ye neither know me, nor my Father: if ye had known me, ye should have known my Father also."[11]

Let me ask this question: Jesus Christ being the Only Begotten Son of the Father, and having been sent into this world to perform the greatest mission that was ever performed—he being the Son of God—*who could be a witness for him, logically, except his Father?*

Did not Jesus fill the requirements of this divine law? He acknowledged the law, and said, "It is also written in your law, that the testimony of two men is true." Then he declared that he was one *Man* bearing witness in

---
[11]John 8:12-19.

fulfilment of that law, and his Father was the other what? —*Man,* who bore witness to that fulfilment.

How Christ Testified of Himself. Now let us examine the evidence for a moment. How did Christ become a witness for himself? *By word of mouth;*[12] in the preaching of the gospel, because he taught as one having authority and not as the scribes; *in the great work that he performed:* restoring sight to the blind, healing withered hands, raising the dead, and in many other ways blessing and administering to the people. In this way *his words and his work spoke for him.*

Voice of Father Testifies of Son. Who, I say, could testify for him, other than his Father? Do we find any references in the scriptures where the Father testified for him? Take the baptism of Jesus, for instance, where the Holy Ghost descended and the Father spoke from the heavens.[13] Was not that a witness?

On another occasion, when Jesus was praying to his Father before a group of people, the Father spoke to him from the heavens answering his prayer, saying, "I have both glorified it [the name of Jesus], and will glorify it again."[14] Some who were present said it thundered, some said an angel spoke to him, but it was his Father.

At the transfiguration on the mount, the Savior stood with Peter, James and John, also Moses and Elias, and again the voice of the Father spoke, saying, "This is my beloved Son, in whom I am well pleased; hear ye him."[15]

Lord's System to Use Witnesses. There are other references in the scriptures, but these will suffice.[16] Naturally *the Father was not testifying to all the Jews.* That is not the way he does. You know, if the Lord wished he could preach this gospel to the world by declaring it from the heavens. He could have his angels blow their trumpets and declare the message of salvation

---
[12]John 10:7-36.
[13]Matt. 3:13-17; Mark 1:9-11; Luke 3:21-22.
[14]John 12:28.
[15]Matt. 17:5.
[16]3 Ne. 11:7; Joseph Smith 2:17.

in the ears of all the world. Would not that be a much easier way to get the message of truth before the world than the expensive way of sending messengers clothed with authority at great expense and toil to try to teach the world?

But the ways of the Lord are not man's ways. *He works through his witnesses, and in establishing his work in every age, he uses the few, not the many. Never since the beginning has the Lord declared himself to the unbelieving world, but he has sent out his messengers to preach the gospel to the world.*

How easy it would have been for him to have sent an angel to Nineveh to cry repentance, rather than to ask Jonah who was unwilling to take that message. And what a time Jonah had! It was a great burden to him, and he hesitated, but finally went with his message. Could not the Lord have done it in a much easier way?

We read of the coming forth of the *Book of Mormon* in these last days. The Lord said to us, through Nephi, something of his plans as follows: "And there is none other which shall view it [that is, the Nephite record], save it be *a few* according to the will of God, *to bear testimony* of his word unto the children of men; for the Lord God hath said that *the words of the faithful should speak as it were from the dead.* Wherefore, the Lord God will proceed to bring forth the words of the book; *and in the mouth of as many witnesses as seemeth him good, will he establish his word; and wo be unto him that rejecteth the word of God!*"[17]

No Personal Ministration of Christ to Unbelieving. This is the way the Lord has always worked. When the Savior rose from the dead, how easy it would have been for him to have gone to Pilate and said: "Here I am. You condemned me to death. I said I would rise on the third day. Here I am." But Pilate did not see him after his resurrection.

---
[17] 2 Ne. 27:13-14.

How easy it would have been for him to have gone to the members of the Sanhedrin, before those leaders of the Jews who cried out against him and who were responsible for his death, and said: "Here I am. You had the tomb sealed, but I told you I would rise on the third day; now will you believe." But he did not appear to one of them.

He appeared to Peter, and to the apostles, to Mary at the tomb, and to many others, but never to those who had persecuted him and put him to death. *The Romans did not see him; the unbelieving Jews did not see him; and he sent his chosen witnesses out into all the world to declare the message of his risen glory.* It is true he appeared to Paul, an exception, but the reason for this is made apparent in the scriptures.

After the healing of the lame man through the power of God, by Peter and John, these two apostles were summoned before the leaders of the Jews and commanded to cease preaching about Jesus as the Son of God, but this Peter said they could not and would not do, for they were his witnesses. "Whether it be right in the sight of God to hearken unto you more than unto God," said Peter, "judge ye. For we cannot but speak the things which we have seen and heard."[18]

So we see this is the way the Lord works, through his chosen witnesses.

JOSEPH SMITH AND THE LAW OF WITNESSES

KEYS AND PRIESTHOOD ALWAYS GIVEN TO TWO WITNESSES. Every time that the heavens were opened and keys had to be restored what happened? We have two witnesses. Joseph Smith was not alone. He was alone in the first vision, alone when Moroni brought the message to him, alone when he received the plates; but after that he was not alone. The Lord called other witnesses. Grandmother Smith in her history says that the Prophet came home weeping for joy after the wit-

---
[18] Acts 4:19-20.

THE DIVINE LAW OF WITNESSES

nesses had beheld the plates under the direction of an angel of God, because, he said, "The load has been lifted and I am no longer alone."

Every time keys were restored, two men received them. Why? Because it was necessary according to the divine law of witnesses for Joseph Smith to have a companion holding those keys; otherwise it would not have happened. So, as Oliver Cowdery states, when John the Baptist came, he and Joseph Smith received the Aaronic Priesthood under his hands; and when Peter, James, and John came, he was with Joseph Smith.

It was Oliver Cowdery and Joseph Smith who received the keys in the Kirtland Temple on the 3rd of April, 1836, when Christ appeared, when Moses appeared, when Elias appeared, when Elijah appeared. And every time when the keys of a dispensation were bestowed it was to Joseph Smith and Oliver Cowdery— not Joseph Smith alone. Why? Just because of what the Savior said: "If I bear witness of myself, my witness is not true."[19]

If Joseph Smith had said, "I testify, and I testify alone," his testimony would not be true. There had to be two, that the testimony might be valid.

OLIVER COWDERY STOOD AS ASSISTANT PRESIDENT OF CHURCH. Now let me call your attention to this. In the Kirtland Temple in 1836, when Joseph Smith and Oliver Cowdery were behind the pulpit and received keys from heavenly messengers there was a First Presidency of the Church and the Prophet had counselors, Sidney Rigdon and Frederick G. Williams. But Sidney Rigdon and Frederick Williams did not go behind the veil, or the curtain, when it was drawn; they were not asked to kneel there behind the pulpit. It was Joseph Smith and Oliver Cowdery. Why? Because that was Oliver Cowdery's place.

Now I am going to call your attention to something

---
[19]John 5:31.

that is not, I regret to say, generally known. Oliver Cowdery was called to be what? The "Second Elder" of the Church, the "Second President" of the Church. We leave him out in our list of Presidents of the Church, we do not include Oliver Cowdery; but *he was an Assistant President. Oliver Cowdery's standing in the beginning was as the "Second Elder" of the Church, holding the keys jointly with the Prophet Joseph Smith.* He preceded the counselors in the First Presidency in authority, standing next to the Prophet Joseph Smith. December 5, 1834, Oliver Cowdery was ordained by Joseph Smith, by the command of the Lord, an Assistant President of the High Priesthood, to hold the keys of Presidency jointly with the Prophet in the ministry. I am going to read that record to you.

NATURE OF OFFICE OF ASSISTANT PRESIDENT OF CHURCH. *"The office of Assistant President is to assist in presiding over the whole Church, and to officiate in the absence of the President,* according to his rank and appointment, viz.; President Cowdery, first; President Rigdon, second; and President Williams, third, as they were severally called. *The office of this priesthood is also to act as spokesman, taking Aaron for an example. The virtue of the above priesthood is to hold the keys of the kingdom of heaven or of the Church militant."* That is copied from the history of the Church.

So Oliver Cowdery, through that place as the "Second President," preceded the counselors in the Presidency—naturally so. Why shouldn't he? *He had the same authority, had received the same keys with the Prophet Joseph Smith every time the heavens were opened, and he was an Assistant President of the Church and the second witness of the dispensation of the fulness of times,* which is the greatest of all dispensations, for it was necessary that there be *two Presidents, two witnesses standing at the head of this dispensation.*[20]

---
[20]*Church News*, Apr. 8., 1939, pp. 1-4, 6, 8.

PROPHET ORDAINS OLIVER COWDERY AS ASSISTANT PRESIDENT. In harmony with this law the Lord called Oliver Cowdery as the second witness to stand at the head of this dispensation assisting the Prophet in holding the keys. The records inform us that every time the Prophet received authority and the keys of the priesthood from the heavens, Oliver Cowdery shared in the conferring of those powers with the Prophet. *Had Oliver Cowdery remained faithful and had he survived the Prophet under those conditions, he would have succeeded as President of the Church by virtue of this divine calling.*

This blessing was also confirmed upon the head of Oliver Cowdery by the Prophet, December 5, 1834, in the following words: "I laid my hands upon Brother Oliver Cowdery, and ordained him an Assistant President, saying these words: 'In the name of Jesus Christ, who was crucified for the sins of the world, I lay my hands upon thee and ordain thee an Assistant President of the high and holy priesthood, in the Church of the Latter-day Saints.' "[21]

OTHER WITNESSES SHARED BURDEN WITH PROPHET. In the case of Joseph Smith, his claims are greater than the claims of other religious teachers of the present time. He declared that he stood in the presence of Jesus Christ and the holy angels who instructed him and gave him authority to organize the Church. Not only was such authority given to him, but also to others. In addition to Joseph Smith, Oliver Cowdery, David Whitmer, Martin Harris, Sidney Rigdon, and others have testified that they beheld the presence of angels and were instructed by them.

By heavenly messengers they were taught the doctrines of the restoration. In these things *Joseph Smith did not stand alone.*

COLLUSION AMONG MANY WITNESSES IMPOSSIBLE.

---
[21]*Era,* vol. 45, p. 737; *D.H.C.,* vol. 2, p. 176.

Had there been collusion between these men to practice deceit and organize a church based in fraud, then these men never would have held together, and one or more of them would have exposed the others and revealed the secret of collusion. This certainly would have proved the case for Oliver Cowdery, Martin Harris, and David Whitmer all deserted Joseph Smith while he was living.

For a time they manifested a spirit of opposition, if not of bitterness, towards him. Yet all three of these men remained true to their testimony to the day of death. David Whitmer never returned to the Church, but was always true to his testimony that he stood in the presence of an angel. Oliver Cowdery and Martin Harris, after the death of Joseph Smith, both returned to the Church in its darkest hour, and died in the faith. All of this is evidence that there was no fraud and that these men had from the beginning spoken the truth.[22]

SIGN SEEKERS OF EVERY AGE REJECT LORD'S WITNESSES. We see then, that the methods adopted by Joseph Smith—and that by revelation—in bringing forth the *Book of Mormon* and in organizing the Church, are in perfect harmony with the work of the Lord in all other generations.

We can easily imagine some prominent scribe, lawyer, or Pharisee, saying to Peter and the apostles when they declared that they were witnesses of the resurrection of Jesus Christ: "If what you say is true, why did not Jesus show himself to us and to the world? What a wonderful thing it would be in convincing people of your story if you could only show him to the people that they might know that he is risen from the dead!"

In fact, the contemptuous cry of the chief priests and scribes to the Savior when he was on the cross was: "He saved others; himself he cannot save. If he be the King of Israel, let him now come down from the cross, and we will believe him. He trusted in God; let him

---
[22]*Millennial Star*, vol. 96, pp. 34-35.

THE DIVINE LAW OF WITNESSES

deliver him now, if he will have him: for he said, I am the Son of God."[23]

They knew he saved others. They had been witnesses that he raised the dead, healed the sick and was a benefactor to the afflicted, but they sought a great sign, and how true are the words of the Lord: "An evil and adulterous generation seeketh after a sign."[24]

MEN CONDEMNED FOR REJECTING LORD'S WITNESSES. Our Savior after his resurrection, did not appear to the non-believing Jews, to Herod, or Pilate; he did not go before the Sanhedrin in triumph to convince them that he had risen. It was only to his disciples to whom he appeared, and then he sent them into all the world as witnesses declaring to every nation that he was in very deed the Resurrection and the Life.

Said he to the apostles: "But ye shall receive power, after that the Holy Ghost is come upon you: and *ye shall be witnesses unto me* both in Jerusalem and in all Judea, and in Samaria, and unto the uttermost part of the earth."[25] Again he said as he appeared to them in his glorified body: "Thus it is written, and thus it behoved Christ to suffer, and to rise from the dead the third day: . . . *And ye are witnesses of these things.*"[26]

Does it not appear that when Peter and the other disciples went forth, as they had been commanded, as witnesses having the perfect knowledge that Jesus Christ was risen from the dead and is verily the Son of God, that the people who heard their testimony and rejected it were under condemnation? Moreover, was it not sufficient for these disciples to testify to the world of this truth, to leave men without excuse who would not believe, without the Lord giving a direct manifestation, or making a personal appearance to each individual upon the face of the earth?

OUR RESPONSIBILITY TO ACCEPT LATTER-DAY WIT-

---

[23]Matt. 27:42-43.
[24]Matt. 12:39.
[25]Acts 1:8.
[26]Luke 24:46, 48.

NESSES. The course taken by Joseph Smith is in perfect harmony with this course adopted by our Savior. In truth it is the only consistent course that could be taken. In this life we are expected to walk by faith and not by sight, and yet *the Lord sends among us witnesses who have seen and heard and who can speak with direct knowledge to encourage us to seek and find the truth,* as Paul says: "That they should seek the Lord, if haply they might feel after him, and find him, though he be not far from every one of us."[27]

It is the duty of all men to heed the message of the divinely appointed witnesses of the Lord and to prove their words by obeying the will of God which will be the means, through the guidance of the Spirit of the Lord, in convincing us of the truth.

Yet, how many accepted the story told by Peter, James, and John, while they lived and testified? How many have accepted the testimony of Joseph Smith, Oliver Cowdery, David Whitmer, Martin Harris and other witnesses who have testified in this generation?

The world today, like the world in the day of our Lord's ministry, have before them Moses and the prophets whom, if they will not hear, "neither will they be persuaded, though one rose from the dead."[28]

JOSEPH AND HYRUM: JOINT WITNESSES

JOSEPH AND HYRUM HOLD KEYS OF DISPENSATION. *My grandfather, the Patriarch Hyrum Smith, was called to hold the keys of this dispensation jointly with the Prophet Joseph, his younger brother.* The Lord has said that in the mouths of two witnesses shall all things be established.... Joseph Smith could not have stood alone, else his work would have failed, just as the work of the Savior required the confirmation of another witness, and who could testify for Christ other than his Father? And so the Lord called another man to stand with Joseph

---

[27]Acts 17:27.   [28]*Era,* vol. 30, pp. 953-954; Luke 16:31; D. & C. 5:5-10.

THE DIVINE LAW OF WITNESSES

Smith and to hold the keys of salvation in this dispensation as a witness with him.

The Prophet Joseph was alone in his first vision. He was alone when the Angel Moroni first came to him and revealed the *Book of Mormon,* but *whenever keys were to be bestowed, when the Lord had light and information to reveal in which the power of priesthood was to play a part, Joseph Smith and one other witness received the blessings.*

KEYS FIRST GIVEN TO JOSEPH AND OLIVER. It was Oliver Cowdery who was appointed to stand with Joseph Smith to hold the keys of this dispensation. It was Oliver Cowdery who, with Joseph Smith, received the Priesthood of Aaron under the hands of John the Baptist. It was Oliver Cowdery who received the authority of the Melchizedek Priesthood with Joseph Smith from Peter, James, and John. It was Oliver Cowdery who knelt with the Prophet Joseph in the Kirtland Temple in 1836, when Moses and Elias and Elijah came with the keys of their dispensations.

I am convinced that if we had the full record, we would discover that Oliver Cowdery was associated with Joseph Smith the Prophet when the keys of all the other dispensations were revealed and restored in this dispensation. In this manner *Oliver Cowdery was appointed and ordained to stand with the Prophet Joseph Smith as an associate and witness, holding all the authority and keys of this most glorious of all dispensations*—the dispensation of the fulness of times.

OLIVER COWDERY FELL FROM HIS HIGH STATUS. Unfortunately—at least unfortunately for Oliver Cowdery, who was called to this wonderful and responsible position, jointly associated with Joseph Smith holding all the authority and presidency in this dispensation— Oliver, in a spirit of rebellion and darkness, turned away. He lost his fellowship in the Church, the power of the priesthood was taken from him, and for a season he stood excommunicated from the Church. Fortunately he eventually overcame this spirit of darkness, but never again was he privileged to receive the keys of power and authority which once were placed upon him.

HYRUM SMITH RECEIVES BLESSINGS OF OLIVER COWDERY. That this testimony of witnesses might be continued and made complete, the Lord chose another to take the place of Oliver Cowdery, and that other witness was the Patriarch Hyrum Smith. By revelation through Joseph Smith, Hyrum was called and ordained to the priesthood and standing once held by Oliver Cowdery. *Hyrum Smith received a double portion*, not only was he called to become the Patriarch of the Church, which was his birthright, but at the same time the Lord said to him:

"And from this time forth I appoint unto him that he may be a prophet, and a seer, and a revelator unto my church, as well as my servant Joseph: That he may act in concert also with my servant Joseph; and that he shall receive counsel from my servant Joseph, who shall show unto him the keys whereby he may ask and receive, and be crowned with the same blessing, and glory, and honor, and priesthood, and gifts of the priesthood, that once were put upon him that was my servant Oliver Cowdery; *That my servant Hyrum may bear record of the things which I shall show unto him*, that his name may be had in honorable remembrance from generation to generation, forever and ever."[29]

JOSEPH AND HYRUM JOINT PRESIDENTS OF CHURCH. In accord with this calling and commandment, the Prophet Joseph Smith conferred upon Hyrum Smith all the keys, authority and gifts of the priesthood which he, the Prophet, held, and which were formerly held by Oliver Cowdery. *The Lord also revealed to Hyrum Smith all that was necessary to make him completely and to the full degree, a witness with his brother Joseph,*

---
[29]*D. & C.* 124: 94-96.

THE DIVINE LAW OF WITNESSES

as a prophet, seer, revelator and president of the Church, and to stand through all time and all eternity at the head of this dispensation with his brother Joseph, a witness for Jesus Christ.

Thus, we see, Hyrum Smith became a president of the Church with Joseph Smith, which place Oliver Cowdery might have held had he not wavered and fallen from his exalted station. *I am firmly of the opinion that had Oliver Cowdery remained true to his covenants and obligations as a witness with Joseph Smith, and retained his authority and place, he, and not Hyrum Smith, would have gone with Joseph Smith as a prisoner and to martyrdom at Carthage.*

The sealing of the testimony through the shedding of blood would not have been complete in the death of the Prophet Joseph Smith alone; it required the death of Hyrum Smith who jointly held the keys of this dispensation. It was needful that these martyrs seal their testimony with their blood, that they "might be honored and the wicked might be condemned."[30]

PROPHET'S TRIBUTE TO HIS BROTHER HYRUM. Now if I may take just a moment or two longer—there are many things I would like to say, but time forbids—I would like to read to you the opinion of the Prophet expressed of his brother Hyrum, who was almost six years older. This is what the Prophet says:

"Brother Hyrum, what a faithful heart you have got! Oh may the Eternal Jehovah crown eternal blessings upon your head, as a reward for the care you have had for my soul! O how many are the sorrows we have shared together; and again we find ourselves shackled with the unrelenting hand of oppression. Hyrum, thy name shall be written in the book of the Law of the Lord, for those who come after thee to look upon, that they may pattern after thy works."

On another occasion the Prophet said: "I could

---
[30]*D. & C.* 136:39.

pray in my heart that all my brethren were like unto my beloved brother *Hyrum, who possesses the mildness of a lamb, and the integrity of a Job, and in short, the meekness and humility of Christ;* and I love him with that love that is stronger than death, for I never had occasion to rebuke him, nor he me, which he declared when he left me today.[31]

ORDER OF SUCCESSION IN PRESIDENCY. Oliver Cowdery turned away and lost his place, and he ceased to be the second President, although he could always bear witness and did. He ceased, as far as the priesthood was concerned, to be the "Second Elder," the "Second President," in the Church. So time went on. Frederick G. Williams turned away and Hyrum Smith was called to take the place of Second Counselor.

It went on in that way—Joseph Smith, President, Sidney Rigdon and Hyrum Smith counselors—until the 19th day of January, 1841. On that day the Lord commanded Joseph Smith to ordain Hyrum Smith and confer upon him all the keys, authority, and privileges placed upon the head of Oliver Cowdery, and make him the "Second President" of the Church. Hyrum Smith, like Oliver Cowdery, has not received his place properly in the minds of many as the "Second President" of the Church—but that was his place.

President Brigham Young, after the death of Joseph Smith, when they were discussing the matter of succession, said: "Did Joseph Smith ordain a successor? Who was it? Hyrum Smith. But Hyrum Smith fell martyr before the Prophet did." Well, he did not ordain him as his successor, exactly, but if Hyrum Smith had hearkened to the Prophet and taken his family to Cincinnati, there would have been a President of the Church and it would not have been Brigham Young. Brigham Young was President of the Council of the Twelve, and Hyrum Smith would have been President of the Church by virtue

---
[31]Conf. Rep., Apr., 1930, pp. 91-94.

THE DIVINE LAW OF WITNESSES 221

of his ordination, holding the place held by Oliver Cowdery.

That is as plain and simple as it can be, as it is stated in our scriptures and in the history of the Church. Joseph Smith and Hyrum Smith, after 1841, signed documents as Presidents of the Church. With many members of the Church Hyrum Smith was just the Patriarch. Hyrum Smith received a double portion. He received the office of Patriarch which belonged to his father and came to him by right, and also received the keys to be "Second President" and precede the counselors as Oliver Cowdery had done. So he would have remained as President of the Church had he not died a martyr.

DEATH OF TWO TESTATORS REQUIRED. But here is another point. He had to die. Why? Because we read in the scriptures that the testimony is not of force without the death of the testator—that is, in his particular case, and in the case of Christ.[32] *It was just as necessary that Hyrum Smith lay down his life a martyr for this cause as a witness for God as it was for Joseph Smith, so the Lord permitted them both to be taken in that way and both sealed their testimony with their blood.* Both of them held the keys of the dispensation of the fulness of times jointly, and they will through all the ages of eternity. Then naturally the Council of the Twelve came into its place, and *by right* Brigham Young became President of the Church.

Had Oliver Cowdery remained true, had he been faithful to his testimony and his calling as the "Second Elder" and Assistant President of the Church, I am just as satisfied as I am that I am here that Oliver Cowdery would have gone to Carthage with the Prophet Joseph Smith and laid down his life instead of Hyrum Smith. That would have been his right. Maybe it sounds a little strange to speak of martyrdom as being a right, but it was a right. Oliver Cowdery lost it and Hyrum Smith

---
[32]Heb. 9:15-17; D. & C. 135:5.

received it. According to the law of witnesses—and this is a divine law—it had to be.[33]

NO ASSISTANT PRESIDENT NEEDED TODAY. The question is sometimes asked: If Oliver Cowdery was ordained to hold the keys jointly with the Prophet, and after his loss by transgression, this authority was conferred on Hyrum Smith, then why do we not have today in the Church the same order of things, and an Assistant President as well as two counselors in the First Presidency?

The answer to this is a simple one. It is because the peculiar condition requiring two witnesses to establish the work, is not required after the work is established. Joseph and Hyrum Smith stand at the head of this dispensation, jointly holding the keys, as the two necessary witnesses fulfilling the law as it is set down by our Lord in his answer to the Jews. Since the gospel will never again be restored there will be no occasion for this condition to arise again. We all look back to the two special witnesses, called to bear witness in full accord with the divine law.[34]

WITNESSES OF THE BOOK OF MORMON

THREE WITNESSES ADHERE TO TESTIMONY. What the three witnesses saw was in the presence of the angel; and they heard the voice of God speaking to them. All three witnesses became disaffected for varying reasons and left the Church. If you will read the history of the Church, you will find that charges were brought against each of these three men, and that they were brought before the Prophet and the councils of the Church and were excommunicated.

Do you think for one moment if Joseph Smith and these witnesses had entered into collusion to defraud and deceive, that no matter what the cause Joseph Smith could under any circumstances have permitted a falling

---
[33]*Church News*, Apr. 8, 1939, p. 8. [34]Pers. Corresp.

THE DIVINE LAW OF WITNESSES

out with these witnesses? Do you think he would have dared to permit a high council of this Church to excommunicate these men and cast them out, if the testimony were not true?

It is absolutely out of the question, because under those conditions immediately Oliver Cowdery, David Whitmer, and Martin Harris would have come out and said: "We just entered into a fraud to deceive. It is not true. We did not see an angel. What Joseph Smith is saying is not true." But they never said it. All the days of their lives they were true to their testimony, though they became bitter toward the Prophet Joseph Smith personally. All three got over that bitterness before they died, but there was a time when they were very, very bitter in their feelings toward him.

TESTIMONY OF DAVID WHITMER. I have here the testimony given by David Whitmer. I copied this from the original in his handwriting, signed by his own name, as we have it in the Historian's Office. We got it not so very long ago, obtained it by purchase from the grandson of David Whitmer. He said he thought we ought to have it here.

It is filed in the archives of the Church, and with the signatures of the men I am going to name attached to it—non-members of the Church, none believing in the mission of Joseph Smith. This testimony was given in 1881, because a certain individual had said that David Whitmer had declared to him that his testimony was not true. David Whitmer calls attention to the fact that this man lied.

"Unto all nations, kindred, tongues and people unto whom these presents shall come—

"It having been represented by one John Murphy of Polo (Caldwell County) Missouri that I had in a conversation with him last summer, denied my testimony as one of the three witnesses to the *Book of Mormon*—

"To the end therefore, that he may understand me now, if he did not then, and that the world may know the truth, I wish now, standing as it were, in the very sunset of life, and in the fear of God, once for all to make this public statement:

"That *I have never at any time, denied that testimony or any part thereof,* which has so long since been published with that book, as one of the three witnesses.

"Those who know me best, will know that I have always adhered to that testimony."

ENDORSEMENT OF DAVID WHITMER'S STANDING AS A CITIZEN. I cannot take time to read it all. I copied it so I could say I copied it from the original document in the handwriting of David Whitmer, with his own signature and with these names attached to it:

A. W. Doniphan, (Alexander W. Doniphan—who was an old man too. He was the attorney for the Prophet at one time.)

George W. Dunn, Judge of the Fifth Judicial Circuit.

T. D. Woodson, President, Ray County Savings Bank.

Jacob O. Child, Editor of *Conservator,* (In which this was also published.)

H. C. Garner, Cashier, Ray County Savings Bank.

W. A. Holman, County Treasurer.

J. S. Hughes, Banker, Richmond, Mo.

James Hughes, Banker, Richmond, Mo.

D. P. Whitmer, Attorney at Law, (He was a grandson of David Whitmer.)

James W. Black, Attorney at Law.

L. C. Cantwell, Postmaster, Richmond, Mo.

Geo. I. Wassen, Mayor.

Jas. A. Davis, Revenue Collector.

C. J. Hughes, Probate Judge and P. J. Ray County Court.

Geo. W. Trigg, County Clerk.

W. W. Mosby, M.D.

Thos. McGinnis, Late Sheriff, Ray Co.

W. R. Holman, Furniture Merchant.
J. P. Queensbury, Merchant.
Lewis Slaughter, Recorder of Deeds.
George W. Buchanan, M.C.
A. K. Reyburn.

Thus some of the leading citizens of the town of Richmond, in Ray County, Missouri, put their names to that document, and it was published in the local newspaper in 1881.

Now David Whitmer was a sober man, in his right mind when he wrote that. He lived for a number of years after that, and *that is his testimony when he was out of the Church. What are you going to do with it?*

EDITOR APPROVES DAVID WHITMER'S TESTIMONY. And these men testify as to his integrity. I will read what the editor said: "Elsewhere we publish a letter from David Whitmer, Sen., an old and well known citizen of Ray, as well as an endorsement of his standing as a man, signed by a number of the leading citizens of this community, in reply to some unwarranted aspersions made upon him.

"There is no doubt that Mr. Whitmer, who was one of the Three Witnesses of the authenticity of the gold plates, from which he asserts that Joe Smith translated the *Book of Mormon* (a facsimile of the same he now has in his possession with the original records)—is firmly convinced of its divine origin, and while he makes no effort to obtrude his views or belief, he simply wants the world to know that so far as he is concerned there is no 'variableness or shadow of turning.' Having resided here for a half of a century, it is with no little pride that he points to his past record, with the consciousness that he has done nothing derogatory to his character as a citizen and a believer in the Son of Mary to warrant such an attack on him, come from what source it may, and now, with the lilies of seventy-five winters crowning him like an aureole, and his pilgrimage on earth well nigh ended, he reiterates his former statement and will leave futurity to solve the problem that he was but a passing witness of its fulfilment."

That is what they said of David Whitmer, and I ask you, What you are going to do with it? Do you not think it should have some weight?

TESTIMONY OF MARTIN HARRIS. Now let me say something about Martin Harris. The High Council in Kirtland excommunicated him as a dissenter in December, 1837. While continuing true to his testimony of the Book of Mormon he was for many years disgruntled with the Church. But some time after the saints came to Utah some of our good brethren went after him, found him and warmed him up, and brought him back. He came out here, was re-baptized, and lived here for a number of years, bearing witness of his testimony among the settlements. He died here and was buried up in Cache Valley.

TESTIMONY OF OLIVER COWDERY. Now we come to Oliver Cowdery. What about Oliver Cowdery, the most important of the three, who was with Joseph Smith so many times at the appearing of angels and the restoration of keys? What about him? He left the Church and became extremely bitter, but never denied the testimony. Some people have said he did, but he did not. Always he was true to that testimony. I have his testimony in his own handwriting, and I have copied it from his own handwriting so I could say I did. It is taken from a letter from Oliver Cowdery written to his brother-in-law, and I am going to read to you what he says. He was out of the Church when he wrote it.

"I have cherished a hope, and that one of my fondest, that I might leave such a character as those who might believe in my testimony, after I should be called hence, might do so, not only for the sake of the truth, but might not blush for the private character of the man who bore that testimony. I have been sensitive on this subject, I admit, but I ought to be so; you would be, under the circumstances, had you stood in the presence of John with our departed brother Joseph, to receive the lesser priesthood, and in the presence of Peter, to receive the greater and looked down through time, and witnessed the effects these two must produce—you would feel, what you have never felt, were wicked men conspiring to lessen the effects of your testimony to man, after you have gone to your long sought rest."

OLIVER COWDERY'S RETURN TO THE CHURCH. We have other testimonies of Oliver Cowdery. We have the testimony of Oliver Cowdery when he returned to the Church at Kanesville. Oliver Cowdery came back to the Church, and I want to call your attention to the conditions and circumstances under which he came.

When the Prophet Joseph Smith was in Nauvoo and very shortly before the martyrdom, he said to his clerk, "I wish you would write to Oliver Cowdery and ask him if he hasn't eaten husks long enough." Evidently the letter was written, because the very day of the martyrdom a letter was received from Oliver Cowdery. The contents of that letter I have always regretted I did not know; in the perilous times it was lost and no record was made of it. But I believe it was Oliver Cowdery's answer to that communcation, and he was feeling his way back to the Church.

Well, after the saints were driven from Nauvoo and were out on the plains and everything looked the darkest (Sidney Rigdon said they had gone to their destruction and there was no hope for them, and the newspapers said they could not survive!), under those conditions, Oliver Cowdery found his way out to Kanesville and asked to come back to the Church. *If he had been a fraud do you think he would have done it?* If you think that, I pity you. He came back and asked humbly for a place in the Church. He was received back, and was preparing to take a mission to Great Britain when he was taken ill and died. He died at the home of David Whitmer, bearing testimony to the truth.

PENALTY FOR REJECTING TESTIMONY OF WITNESSES. *The Lord says: "Wo be unto him that rejecteth the word of God"*[35]—*as it comes to us through two, three, or eight witnesses. And that testimony will stand against the world at the last day, and every man that is living who has heard the testimony of Oliver Cowdery, David Whitmer, Martin Harris, and Joseph Smith and has refused to receive this message will have to give a reason why he rejected it before the judgment seat of God, because that testimony has gone out solemnly and they were God's witnesses to all the world.*[36]

---

[35] 2 Ne. 27:14; D. & C. 84:94. [36] *Church News*, Apr. 8, 1939, pp. 1, 4, 6.

CHAPTER 14

THE CHURCH AND KINGDOM

THE KINGDOM OF GOD ON EARTH

Two Kingdoms: The Ecclesiastical and Political. *The kingdom of God is the Church.*[1]

After Christ comes, all the peoples of the earth will be subject to him, but there will be multitudes of people on the face of the earth who will not be members of the Church; yet all will have to be obedient to the laws of the kingdom of God, for it will have dominion upon the whole face of the earth. These people will be subject to *the political government,* even though they are not members of *the ecclesiastical kingdom which is the Church.*

This government which embraces all the peoples of the earth, both in and out of the Church, is also sometimes spoken of as the kingdom of God, because the people are subject to the kingdom of God which Christ will set up; but they have their agency and thousands will not be members of the Church until they are converted; yet at the same time *they will be subject to the theocratic rule.*

The Kingdom During the Millennium. When our Savior comes to rule in the millennium, all governments will become subject unto his government, and this has been referred to as the kingdom of God, which it is; but this is the *political kingdom* which *will embrace all people whether they are in the Church or not.*[2] Of course, when every kindred, tongue and people become subject to the rule of Jesus Christ such will be in that political

---

[1]*D. & C.* 27:4; 29:5; 35:27; 38:9, 15; 41:6; 50:35; 62:9; 64:4; 65:1-6; 72:1; 81:2; 84:34, 76, 86; 88:70, 74; 90:2-3, 6; 94:3; 136:41; Dan. 2:44; Joseph Fielding Smith, *Teachings of the Prophet Joseph Smith,* pp. 271-275.
[2]*D. & C.* 38:22.

kingdom.³ We must keep these two thoughts in mind. *But the kingdom of God is the Church of Jesus Christ, and it is the kingdom that shall endure forever.* When the Savior prayed, "Thy kingdom come," he had reference to the kingdom in heaven which is to come when the millennial reign starts.⁴

*When Christ comes, the political kingdom will be given to the Church.*⁵ The Lord is going to make an end to all nations; that means this nation as well as any other.⁶ The kingdom of God is the Church, but during the millennium, the multitudes upon the face of the earth who are not in the Church will have to be governed, and many of *their officers,* who will be elected, may not be members of the Church.⁷

THE KINGDOM SET UP ON EARTH

CHURCH ORGANIZED IN THIS DISPENSATION. The Church of Jesus Christ of Latter-day Saints was organized Tuesday, April 6, 1830, at the home of Peter Whitmer, at Fayette, Seneca county, N. Y., with six members.⁸ These six members, who had been baptized previous to the organization of the Church, were all *again baptized* on the day of the organization. They are: Joseph Smith, Jr., Oliver Cowdery, Hyrum Smith, Peter Whitmer, Jr., Samuel H. Smith, and David Whitmer. All of these died in the Church, excepting David Whitmer.

At this time Joseph Smith, Jr., and Oliver Cowdery were sustained as the *first* and *second* elders of the Church. A revelation was given to the Prophet on this day, in which the Church just organized was commanded to keep a record in which Joseph Smith, Jr., was to be called a seer, translator, prophet and apostle of Jesus Christ, and an elder of the Church.⁹

FIRST CONFERENCES OF THE CHURCH. On the 9th

---
³Dan. 7:14.
⁴Matt. 6:10; *D. & C.* 65:5-6.
⁵Dan. 7:27.
⁶*D. & C.* 87:6; Rev. 11:15.
⁷Pers. Corresp.
⁸*D. & C.* 20.
⁹*D. & C.* 21.

day of June, 1830, the first conference of the Church was held at Fayette, N. Y., and the following officers were present:

Joseph Smith, Jr., Oliver Cowdery, David Whitmer, Peter Whitmer and Ziba Peterson, each of whom held the office of elder in the Church. At this conference Samuel H. Smith was ordained an elder; Joseph Smith, senior, and Hyrum Smith were ordained priests. Martin Harris was also ordained a priest, and Hyrum Page and Christian Whitmer, teachers. At the close of this conference there were in the Church *seven* ordained elders —including Joseph Smith and Oliver Cowdery—*three* priests and *two* teachers. The total membership of the Church was 27.

Oliver Cowdery was appointed to keep the Church record and conference minutes until the next conference to be held in September.

The second conference of the Church was held September 26, 1830. On that date the Church had the following officers: *eight* elders (Thomas B. Marsh having been ordained an elder); *four* priests (Newel Knight having been ordained a priest); and *two* teachers: eight holding the Melchizedek Priesthood and six the Aaronic —14 in all, so far as we know, who had been ordained to the priesthood.

David Whitmer was appointed to keep the Church record and conference minutes, until the next conference. The membership at the close of the conference was 62.

The third conference was held at Seneca, January 2, 1831, but no minutes were kept.

FIRST HIGH PRIESTS ORDAINED. At the fourth conference, held in Kirtland, June, 1831, the first high priests in this dispensation were ordained. There were 23 in all, among them being the Prophet Joseph Smith, who was ordained a high priest under the hands of Lyman Wight, he (Lyman Wight) having first been ordained to that office by the Prophet. Owing to his absence, Oliver

Cowdery was not ordained a high priest at this conference, but was ordained by Sidney Rigdon, August 28, following.

At this conference Edward Partridge was also ordained a high priest; he had previously been called to the bishopric, and on this date chose as counselors—or assistants as they were then called—John Corrill and Isaac Morley. This was the *first bishopric* in the Church.

From this time forth the Church grew rapidly in power and strength, notwithstanding the many trials, apostasies and hardships through which it was forced to pass.

FIRST PRESIDENCY ORGANIZED. March 18, 1833, the First Presidency of the Church was organized, with Joseph Smith, president; Sidney Rigdon and Frederick G. Williams, counselors. Prior to this, the Prophet was sustained and ordained president of the high priesthood, at a conference held at Amherst, Ohio, January 25, 1832.

Joseph Smith, Sen., was called and ordained by his son Joseph as presiding patriarch, December 18, 1833. In this ordination he was also called a president of the high priesthood. Oliver Cowdery was also associated with the First Presidency.

The first apostles and seventies in this dispensation were ordained at Kirtland, Ohio, in February, 1835, after the return of Zion's Camp, from the members of that camp. The apostles were by revelation chosen and ordained by the witnesses to the *Book of Mormon,* February 14, 1835, and the first of the seventies were ordained 14 days later. Two quorums of seventies were ordained beginning at this time.

FIRST FOREIGN MISSIONS OPENED. The first foreign mission was the British, which was opened in Lancashire, England, by Elders Heber C. Kimball, Orson Hyde, Willard Richards, Joseph Fielding, John Goodson, Isaac Russel and John Snider, in 1837. From here the work spread to Ireland, Scotland, Wales and the various

THE CHURCH AND KINGDOM

parts of England; also to Australia, South America, and East India.

Joseph Ball was set apart in 1842 to South America. Ten years later, Parley P. Pratt and Rufus Allen visited Chile, but met with little success.

The gospel was taken to Jamaica, in 1842, by Henry Sagers. That same year Orson Hyde went to Jerusalem and dedicated the land of Palestine to the return of the Jews. While on this mission he did some work in Germany.

In 1843, Addison Pratt, Noah Rogers, Benjamin F. Grouard and Knowlton F. Hanks were set apart to visit the Islands of the Pacific. Elder Hanks died November 3, following, and was buried at sea. The others labored in the Society Islands and were quite successful.

Elder William Howell was the first missionary to France. He went from England in 1848, and organized a branch. In 1850 Elder John Taylor and others went to France and labored there.

MISSIONS OPENED IN MANY NATIONS. That same year (1850) Erastus Snow and Peter O. Hansen arrived in Denmark, John E. Forsgren, in Sweden, Lorenzo Snow and Joseph Toronto, in Italy, and later that same year Thomas H. B. Stenhouse opened the door in Switzerland, and Elder George Q. Cannon and others, in the Hawaiian Islands.

Elder Joseph Richards was the first successfully to carry the gospel to India, where he organized a branch, June 22, 1851. William Donaldson, of the British Army, was the first elder to visit that land, but his labors were without apparent success.

In 1852 missionaries were called to India, China, Siam, Cape of Good Hope, (Africa), Prussia, Gibraltar, the West Indies and Norway. Elders went to New Zealand in 1854, and to Mexico in 1877.

Since that time the gospel has been preached in most of Europe, parts of Asia, South America, the Islands of the Sea, where many of the descendants of the Nephite race reside; and in Japan, which land was dedicated by President Heber J. Grant, September 1, 1901.

In 1903, President Francis M. Lyman also dedicated Finland and Russia for the preaching of the gospel and the gathering of the blood of Israel.

From the time when the first company of saints sailed from Liverpool, June 6, 1840, until the close of the year 1908, over 100,000 saints took passage for Zion. Of the *many ships* that carried this mighty host *not one was lost,* and while some of the saints died on the way, and others met with accidents, the result is most marvelous.[10]

THE SAINTS: A PECULIAR PEOPLE

HOW THE SAINTS ARE PECULIAR. *The saints are peculiar. This is true of them both regarding their habits and their religious belief. If they are true to their faith, they cannot help being different from other peoples.* Their religion requires it of them. This same thing could be said of any other people should they endeavor to serve the Lord according to his teachings.

The saints of former days were peculiar. Peter called them peculiar because they were "called out of darkness into his [Christ's] marvellous light." The Latter-day Saints believe that they too, are a "chosen generation, a royal priesthood," and the true successors of the former-day saints. This calling makes them peculiar.[11]

One of the outstanding peculiarities of the Latter-day Saints is the fact that they call themselves *saints.* They have been criticized, and often condemned by well meaning but misinformed people, because they take upon themselves the name of saints. In the eyes of many this

---
[10]*Era,* vol. 12, pp. 554-558; D. & C. 1:2, 4, 11, 34-35; 18:28; 39:15; 42:58; 43:20-28; 68:8; 84:62, 75-76; 90:8-11; 133:7-25, 63-74.
[11]*Church News,* May 2, 1931, p. 2; 1 Pet. 2:9.

indicates a spirit of arrogance, and the assumption of a title which should only be given to those whose benevolence and Christian living have been outstanding, and then given after such individuals have been dead many years. Among many the idea prevails, falsely, that a person worthy of this title should be duly chosen by proper ecclesiastical authority and canonized.

WHY CHURCH MEMBERS ARE CALLED SAINTS. The Latter-day Saints should be all that their name implies. They should live free from sin; their lives should be in strict harmony with the principles of the gospel. They should live "by every word that proceedeth out of the mouth of God."[12] Thus they are commanded.

However, in accepting the title of saints they are not arrogant, pretentious or self-righteous. *They did not choose the name, it was given them by divine commandment.* It is the Lord who said: "For thus shall my church be called in the last days, even The Church of Jesus Christ of Latter-day Saints." That the members might be properly impressed with the significance of this title, there follows this admonition: "Verily I say unto you all: Arise and shine forth, that thy light may be a standard for the nations."[13]

In accepting this title, the Latter-day Saints are only conforming to the custom which prevailed among the people of God in all past ages of the earth. The members of the Church in the days of Peter and Paul were called saints. "And it came to pass, as Peter passed throughout all quarters, he came down also to the saints which dwelt at Lydda."[14] Paul wrote: "To all that be in Rome, beloved of God, called to be saints: Grace to you and peace from God our Father, and the Lord Jesus Christ."[15] It is clear, then, that *the members of the Church today are conforming to the custom of former times,* for they are called in these last days by command-

---

[12]Matt. 4:4; Deut. 8:3.
[13]D. & C. 115:4-5.
[14]Acts 9:32.
[15]Rom. 1:7.

ment, "to be saints," and members of the Church of Jesus Christ.[16]

SAINTS ARE THE BEST PEOPLE. *We are, notwithstanding our weaknesses, the best people in the world.* I do not say that boastingly, for I believe that this truth is evident to all who are willing to observe for themselves. We are morally clean, in every way equal, and in many ways superior to any other people. The reason is that we have received the truth, the gospel of the Lord Jesus Christ. It is not to us a dead letter, something perhaps to be followed on the Sabbath day and forgotten on the six other days of the week, but our religion is an everyday religion. We are expected to live in accordance with the principles of truth every day of our lives, for these principles are just as true in the middle of the week as they are on the Sabbath day.[17]

PRIVILEGES AND DUTIES OF SAINTS

PRIVILEGE OF LIVING WHEN GOSPEL ON EARTH. My desire is to see others share in the light of truth as it has been revealed. *We can all rejoice in the fact that we have been born in this dispensation when the opportunity is given us to know and understand the truth.* I have thanked the Lord many times that I was not sent to the earth during the dark ages or when the gospel was not found among men. If we have nothing else, this great privilege of living now, when the fulness of truth has been revealed, is nearly as wonderful a blessing as we could wish.

One of the strangest things that I know is the fact that people live within the shadows of the gospel but will have none of it. They shut their eyes and refuse to see, their ears and refuse to hear, and even among members of the Church we find many who will not live in the light according to their own convictions.[18]

---

[16]*Church News*, May 9, 1931, p. 2.   [18]Pers. Corresp.
[17]Conf. Rep., Oct., 1913, p. 71.

CONDEMNATION FOR SLOTHFUL SAINTS. *The man who has received the truth and yet will not walk in it deserves the greater condemnation.* A member of this Church who will indulge in the use of tobacco, who will violate the Word of Wisdom, who refuses to pay his tithing, to keep the Sabbath day, or who in any other way will not hearken to the word of the Lord, is not loyal to the Church of Jesus Christ of Latter-day Saints. . . .

Here at home in the stakes of Zion, in the shadows of temples, are to be found those who are numbered with the Church who will not keep the commandments of the Lord. Some of them have made covenant in holy places, and yet they do not value the truth; they do not value the teachings of the servants of the Lord, and they will not walk in the knowledge which they possess, much less by every word that proceeds forth from the mouth of God. *These shall receive the greater condemnation.*[19]

OUR PURPOSE: TO BUILD UP KINGDOM. Every individual radiates some influence. Our influence should be for good, for the building up of the kingdom of God. We should have no other purpose, only to bring to pass this great work and see it established in the earth as the Lord would have it.

In the early days of the Church the brethren came to the Prophet Joseph Smith asking what the Lord would have them do. The answer given to them was "to bring forth and establish the cause of Zion." That is our work, to establish Zion, to build up the kingdom of God, to preach the gospel to every creature in the world, that not one soul may be overlooked where there is the possibility for us to present unto him the truth.[20]

KEEP NAME OF CHURCH ABOVE REPROACH. We must, as a Church and as individuals, keep ourselves clean, our minds pure, our souls clean, uncontaminated by the sins of the world. *It is the duty of each one of us*

---

[19]Conf. Rep., Oct., 1926, pp. 119-120; D. & C. 41:1; 82:2-4. [20]Conf. Rep., Apr., 1951, pp. 152-153; D. & C. 6:6; 11:6; 12:6; 14:6.

individually to keep the good name of this Church unsullied.

Now we have been accused of a great many things. There is not a crime in the category that has not been laid to the charge of the members of the Church. And the Lord said it would be so, that wicked men would speak evil of the truth. We should rejoice when they do that, not in the fact that we are so accused by those who bear false witness, but in the fact that we are innocent from all those things. In that we should rejoice.[21]

But it is our duty as a Church, as communities, to keep the good name of this Church above reproach, and it is the duty of each individual member of this Church to keep himself clean, for each one of us carries with him the good name of the Church. Whenever we do anything that is contrary to righteousness, if we are unclean in our lives, if we do not keep the commandments the Lord has given, the whole Church suffers, not merely the guilty individual who sins; and we ought to think of that. *If one man sins and his sin is published, the world blames the whole Church. They would not do that with any other organization under the sun.*[22]

THE KINGDOM: ITS ORGANIZATION AND GIFTS

CHRIST PERSONALLY ORGANIZED THE CHURCH. *During his mortal ministry Christ himself organized the Church. It is nothing but sectarian stupidity that proclaims that the Savior did not organize the Church. He called attention to the fact that the kingdom of heaven was at hand. He spoke frequently of the kingdom of heaven, and that is the Church.*[23]

Moreover, you will find advice given to a brother who cannot be reconciled with another brother; and *he is to tell it to the Church.*[24] *How could he tell it to the Church if there wasn't a Church?* And Peter declares on the day of Pentecost that *the Lord added to the Church*

---

[21]Matt. 5:10-12; D. & C. 121:11-25.
[22]Conf. Rep., Apr., 1944, pp. 51-52.
[23]Mark 1:15; Matt. 13:47-50.
[24]Matt. 18:17.

daily such as should be saved, so they must have had a Church, and there is no evidence that the apostles organized it. In fact, the apostles were awaiting the endowment that came on the day of Pentecost *before* commencing their ministry.[25]

ORGANIZATION AND GIFTS PART OF TRUE CHURCH. The Church of Jesus Christ, as it was established in the days of the apostles, was governed by apostles, prophets, evangelists, high priests, seventies and other officers, who are not found in the churches of the world today. It is quite generally taught that the apostles and prophets, with the need of revelation and additional scripture, were not needed after the first century; that these officers with revelation from the heavens, were given to the Church for the purpose of establishing it, and then they were taken away and man was left to depend upon the things which had been written.

The apostles, however, taught that the Church as it was established in the first century was to continue with *the same officers indefinitely, or through all time.* Paul informed the Ephesian Saints that the Lord had given to the Church apostles, prophets, evangelists, pastors and teachers, "For the perfecting of the saints, for the work of the ministry, for the edifying of the body of Christ," and that they were to *remain* in the Church, "Till we all come in the unity of the faith, and of the knowledge of the Son of God, unto a perfect man, unto the measure of the stature of the fulness of Christ."[26]

Moreover, he taught the Corinthian Saints that these officers, and the gifts of the gospel, were always needed, and that God had set in the Church, "first apostles, secondarily prophets, thirdly teachers, after that miracles, then gifts of healings, helps, governments, diversities of tongues." He also said that all these officers and gifts were essential to the body of Christ,

---
[25]Pers. Corresp.; Luke 24:49; Acts 2:46-47.   [26]Eph. 4:11-14.

240				DOCTRINES OF SALVATION

and one part could not say to another, "I have no need of you."[27]

CHURCH AND KINGDOM RESTORED. The Lord taught Joseph Smith and his associates that it is due to apostasy that these officers with their authority were taken away; and when the Church of Jesus Christ of Latter-day Saints was restored, it was by divine command that apostles, high priests, seventies and elders, were again ordained and with authority sent forth to proclaim the message of salvation to the nations of the earth.[28]

Where can we go and find the words of eternal life? We cannot turn to the right hand neither to the left, for there spiritual darkness reigns. Right here are to be found the words of eternal life, as they are given by revelation and inspiration to the people of Zion, and we know, as Peter did, that Jesus is the Christ, the Son of the living God. This is our message to the world.[29]

THE KINGDOM TO STAND FOREVER

MAJORITY OF SAINTS TO REMAIN TRUE. *I have that assurance in my heart through the teachings I have received from the Spirit of the Lord, and from the inspiration that has come to me from the revelations of the Lord through his servants, that the majority of this people will always remain true. . . .*

All things that pertain to the salvation of man have been restored in this dispensation preparatory to the coming of Christ and the setting up of his kingdom with absolute authority over all the earth. When that time comes, and Christ reigns, all that now exists contrary to that kingdom and in conflict with it must come to an end.

If people are engaged in works which are not approved of the Lord, the earlier they come to an understanding of the truth and come out of them and learn to serve the Lord, the better it is for them. It is far better

---
[27]1 Cor. 12:21, 28.
[28]*Church News*, Aug. 29, 1931, p. 2.
[29]Conf. Rep., Apr., 1916, p. 70; Matt. 16:13-16.

to know the truth and forsake error than to remain in the systems of the world which are not approved by the Lord and therefore in due time must cease to exist. That day is near at hand, and because of it the Lord has sent forth his servants in the world proclaiming his gospel and crying repentance, that all who will may hear and escape. It is within the reach of all who are willing to forsake error, to know the truth and the established work of the Lord. . . .

CHURCH NEVER TO BE OVERCOME. He has given to us the kingdom. *He has made us the promise that the enemy of the kingdom shall not overcome.*[30] We may have trouble. We have had trouble. We may meet with opposition, but that *opposition shall fail in its endeavor to destroy the work of God.* . . .

The gospel has been restored, and the kingdom given to his saints according to the prophecy of Daniel.[31] *It is not again to be removed, destroyed, or given to other people, and in his own way and time he is going to break down all other systems, that his kingdom may prevail* and that he may come and reign as Lord of lords and King of kings upon the face of the whole earth. . . .

The Lord has called attention to the fact that *he is going to destroy systems and organizations and combinations that are false. And how is he going to do it? By giving their members the truth, if they will receive it;* by giving them the privilege of coming out of those organizations to receive the truth and have every opportunity to come into his kingdom, for his hand is outstretched ready to greet them. *If they will not come; if they will not receive his message;* then, of course, *they must fall with their systems. Truth will prevail; truth will stand when all else is removed, and it is destined to cover the face of the earth.*

ANGELS ARE NOW REAPING THE EARTH. In one of these scriptures the Lord said the angels are waiting

---

[30]D. & C. 38:9, 22.   [31]Dan. 2:44; D. & C. 65:2.

to reap down the earth.[32] I heard President Wilford Woodruff make the statement, in this very spot where I now stand, at a conference of the Church, that these *angels had been sent forth on their mission to reap down the earth, to tie in bundles the tares for the burning and to gather the saints of God.* I heard him make this statement on several occasions. Moreover, he said, from that time forth—and that was about the year 1894—earthquakes, pestilence, war, famine, plague, and other commotions among both men and the elements would *increase* and continue until the coming of Christ.

In the revelation known to us as the "revelation on war," the Lord declared that he had *decreed the overthrow of nations,* "until the consumption decreed hath made a full end of all nations."[33] In that day, when this shall come to pass, *the nation set up by the Lord must reign supreme and all other powers, kingdoms, organizations and societies shall pass away,* for so it is decreed.[34]

SAINTS WILL ALWAYS HAVE A PROPHET TO LEAD THEM. Although the Prophet who stands at the head of the dispensation of the fulness of times, and the Patriarch who stood with him have been taken from us, the *Lord has not left us helpless. There has never been a time since the restoration of the gospel when we have not had a prophet, some one to lead us, to direct us, to teach us the commandments of God that we might walk in the strait and narrow path. We are not without leaders; and the time shall never come when the Lord will not find some one that he can trust, in whom he has confidence, and who will be qualified to stand to represent him among the people.* This is my testimony, and I rejoice in its truth.

I do not feel that because the Prophet was taken and the Patriarch, because President Young was taken, or President Taylor and other leaders were taken, that the time has come when we have not an inspired leader

---

[32]*D. & C.* 1:35; 38:12.   [34]Conf. Rep., Apr., 1927, pp. 108-110.
[33]*D. & C.* 87:6.

THE CHURCH AND KINGDOM 243

to teach us the truth. *The time will never come when we will not be able to put confidence and exercise faith in the teachings and in the instruction of those who lead us.* I am satisfied of this for I know the promises of the Lord are sure. I know that these things are true; the *Lord has not forsaken his people,* and will be with them even to the end. Therefore it behooves us, as Latter-day Saints, to put our trust in the presiding authorities of the Church, in the priesthood of God; and accept of their teachings.

SAINTS SAFE IN FOLLOWING CHURCH AUTHORITIES. No man ever went astray by following the counsel of the authorities of the Church. *No man who ever followed the teachings or took advice or counsel from the one who stands as the representative of the Lord ever went astray;* but men who refused to accept counsel have gone astray and into forbidden paths, and in some instances have even denied the faith. Others who went astray because they failed to understand and to heed the counsels that were given unto them for their eternal good, have humbled themselves and come back to the Church acknowledging their error. . . .

We must put our faith in those whom the Lord hath called, if we want to have a standing before the Lord, and none of us desire, if we have the proper Spirit, to be cut off from among the people. But this punishment will befall those who do not prove faithful and will not pay that heed or give that attention to the counsel of those who are called and appointed and inspired of the Lord to teach and direct us in all things.[35]

YOUTH OF ZION WILL HOLD TO CHURCH. Occasionally someone arises who feels that it is his duty to inform the world that the old members of the Church are still faithful in the doctrines that were taught by the Prophet Joseph Smith, and by President Brigham Young, but that the rising generation is departing from such

---
[35]Conf. Rep., Oct., 1912, pp. 123-124.

things, that the children of these fathers are turning from the teachings of their fathers, as they put it. I am here to testify that this is not true. There may be, of course, and are, those among us who are not faithful, who do turn from the footsteps of their fathers. It has always been so. We may expect that in some cases it will continue.

But so far as the Latter-day Saints are concerned, *the majority of them will not turn from the faith of their fathers.* It is not destined that such should be the case, for when this gospel was restored, the Lord declared through his servants who came from the heavens with the message of salvation, that the gospel was restored for the last time, and that *it must grow and increase and the knowledge grow and spread until it shall fill the whole earth.* That is the destiny of the thing the world calls Mormonism. So they are wrong in their conclusions when they expect the children to depart from the teachings of their fathers.[36]

CHURCH ALWAYS TO PROGRESS. We are advancing, we are gaining in knowledge, in wisdom, and in power. This is as it should be, and as it will always be in the Church and kingdom of our Father; for there must be progression, there must be advancement. *Knowledge will be poured down upon this people, and the Lord will make known unto us from time to time, through revelation, and the Spirit of inspiration, many things that are for our good, when we are prepared and ready to receive them.* I speak generally of the Church.

But notwithstanding all our advancement, increase of faith and diligence, there is still great room for improvement. There are many among us who are not living up to their duties, accepting their callings and magnifying them as they should do. There are many among us who fall short and fail in various ways in keep-

---
[36]Conf. Rep., Apr., 1925, pp. 74-75.

ing the commandments of the Lord to that extent of which they are capable.[37]

ZION TO PROSPER. The Lord will bless Zion. He will pour out his Spirit upon the people. He will prosper them if they will remember him, if they will keep his commandments, if they will observe the covenants that they have made before him and not violate them, if they will hold themselves aloof from the world, and not be partakers of the sins of the world.

I do not mean to say that we ought not to associate at any time with those not of our faith, for there are many good people who have not embraced the gospel. We are not required to avoid them, for our mission in the world is with them, to convert them to the truth if we can. But we need not be partakers of the sins of the world. We need not follow the foolish fashions of the world. We need not corrupt ourselves because many in the world are corrupt.

We have received better things. We are walking in the knowledge and the understanding of the gospel of the Lord Jesus Christ, and are entitled to that inspiration which will warn us of danger and guide us in the path of duty, and give us power to resist and overcome evil. We have the right to call upon the Lord in prayer and in faith for help, for guidance, for the assistance of his Holy Spirit, and *we will receive it.*

UNITY IN THE KINGDOM. And I pray that we may be true to our covenants, true to each other; that we will cast out of our hearts all that is evil; that we will not speak evil one of another, or be given to backbiting or contention or strife, for the spirit of wickedness destroys faith and tends to divide and separate instead of uniting and strengthening the people. We must stand united as one —our purposes are the same, our aims are the same.

We are laboring in the direction of eternal life and progression. There is no variance among the teachers

---
[37]Conf. Rep., Apr., 1914, p. 90.

in Israel concerning the principles of the gospel. We are united concerning these things. There is no division among the authorities, and there need be no division among the people, but unity, peace, brotherly love, kindness and fellowship one to another. These are the blessings that we are entitled to, if we will live in accordance with the gospel, and the Lord will pour out other and greater blessings, even all that we are able to contain.[38]

PROPHESIES TRIUMPH OF ZION. I am very greatly impressed, this morning, with the many evidences that proclaim this to be in very deed the place—the place of Zion; that here are found the people of the Lord with whom he has made covenant, and who have made covenant with him to serve him and keep his commandments; that *Zion will grow and prosper until her fame shall fill the earth and her glory and majesty shall cover the face thereof.*[39]

---
[38]Conf. Rep., Oct., 1913, pp. 73-74.   [39]Conf. Rep., Apr., 1916, p. 69.

CHAPTER 15

ORIGIN AND DESTINY OF THE "REORGAN-IZED" CHURCH

ORIGIN OF EARLY APOSTATE CULTS

FALSE "REORGANITE" CLAIMS. The ministers of the "Reorganized" church,[1] or the "New Organization," as it was first called, declared that the Church at the death of the Prophet Joseph and Patriarch Hyrum Smith was badly divided, its members scattered to the four winds, and that the Church was rejected with its dead.

They also claim that the "Reorganization" is composed of the faithful who did "not bow the knee to Baal," but remained true to the "original faith" as revealed and practiced by the Prophet Joseph Smith.

In the words of their president: "The individuals who kept this covenant [the new and everlasting covenant] were accepted of him [the Lord] and were not rejected, nor their standing before God put in jeopardy by the departure of others from the faith. Whatever the office in the priesthood each held, under the ordinations ordered by the call of God and vote of the church, would remain valid. They could as elders, priests, etc., pursue the duties of warning, expounding, and inviting all to come to Christ, and by command of God could build up the church from any single branch, which, like themselves, had not bowed the knee to Baal, or departed from the faith of the Church as found in the standard works of the body at the death of Joseph and Hyrum Smith."

It is strongly implied in this quotation from the writ-

---

[1]President Joseph Fielding Smith has published three well-documented treatises on the "Reorganite" claims and heresies: *Origin of the "Reorganized" Church*; *Blood Atonement and the Origin of Plural Marriage*; and *The "Reorganized" Church vs. Salvation for the Dead*.

ings of the president of the "Reorganization" that all those who followed President Brigham Young and the Twelve Apostles, lost their priesthood and standing before the Lord, and that the founders of the "New Organization" and their followers were the only ones who remained true and steadfast to the truth.

APOSTATE ATTEMPTS TO DIVIDE THE CHURCH. The evidence in this regard is against them. *The truth is that the founders of the "Reorganized" church were the ones who followed every will-o-the-wisp, bowed the knee to Baal, and departed from the faith,* while the Twelve and the saints on the other hand, pursued an even course and were steadfast under all trials and difficulties even to the end.

It is not true that the Church was broken, scattered, and rejected following the martyrdom and that the "Reorganization" is a portion of the "original church." Their organization did not come into existence until some 16 years after the death of the Prophet and Patriarch and was an outgrowth of the movement under James J. Strang.

There was a movement on foot to divide the Church, following the assassination of the Prophet and Patriarch, but its range was not as extensive as has generally been supposed. The chief actors in this movement were Sidney Rigdon, James J. Strang and William Smith, each of whom aspired to lead the Church.

FALSE CLAIMS OF RIGDON, STRANG, AND WILLIAM SMITH. Mr. Rigdon based his claim to the presidency on the fact that he had been the first counselor to the Prophet Joseph Smith, and therefore by right should be the "guardian" of the Church. His claim was in conflict with the position of the Church and the teachings of the Prophet. He laid his case before the conference of the Church, August 8, 1844, and his claim was rejected by the saints almost unanimously. At the same conference

ORIGIN AND DESTINY OF THE "REORGANIZED" CHURCH 249

the Twelve Apostles were sustained as the presiding quorum of the Church.

Mr. Strang's claim to the presidency was based on his statement that the Prophet had appointed him as his successor by letter, a few days before the martyrdom. William Smith claimed the right of presidency by virtue of being the brother of the Prophet.

UNSTABLE NATURE OF "REORGANITE" FOUNDERS. Each of these men gathered around him a *few followers,* principally of that class of *restless, erratic individuals,* who never remain contented very long in any one place or under any circumstances; but none of them gathered many followers. Their organizations barely existed for a few years and then disappeared, *the fragments* becoming the nucleus of the "Reorganization."

The movement which resulted in the bringing forth of the "Reorganized" church, was of more recent date and was due principally to the efforts of two men, viz., *Jason W. Briggs and Zenas H. Gurley.*

Mr. Briggs was born June 25, 1821, at Pompey, Oneida County, New York. He joined the Church June 6, 1841, and members of the "Reorganization" declare that he was ordained an elder in 1842. His home was in Beloit, Wisconsin, from 1842 to 1854.

After the death of the Prophet, Mr. Briggs sustained the Twelve Apostles and the Church and was apparently true to them until the exodus in 1846. At that time he lost heart, *turned from the Church in its darkest hour and sought the favor of the world.* Some time subsequent to this he joined the movement under James J. Strang. In Strang's organization he did missionary work, received honors and organized a branch.

In 1850 he renounced Mr. Strang and joined with William Smith. In the latter organization he was "ordained" an "apostle." He soon tired of William Smith, and in 1851 joined with Zenas H. Gurley who was at that time a follower of James J. Strang. These two men then organized a church of their own which afterwards was known as the "Reorganized" church. In 1886 Jason W. Briggs withdrew from this organization of his own begetting, declaring that it was not the Church of Christ.

STATUS OF ZENAS H. GURLEY BEFORE HIS APOSTASY. Zenas H. Gurley was just as unstable as Mr. Briggs. He was born at Bridgewater, New York, May 29, 1801, joined the Church in April, 1838, and moved to Far West, from whence he was driven with the saints in the expulsion of 1838-39. After this expulsion he settled in Nauvoo, where in 1844 he was ordained a seventy, under the direction of President Joseph Young,[2] and on the 6th day of April, 1845, he was ordained senior president of the 21st quorum of seventy.

He sustained the Twelve and followed their teachings and remained with the Church until February, 1846 (the month of the exodus), when he also left the Church and shortly afterwards joined with James J. Strang. Mr. Gurley was endowed in the Nauvoo Temple with his wife January 6, 1846, and of that event the record of seventies states under date of January 10, 1846:

"President Zenas H. Gurley arose and said that the presidents of the quorum [21st] had received their endowment. He observed that it was remarkable for the unusual outpouring of the Holy Spirit." (Page 29.)

Again speaking of the authorities of the Church he said: "He remembered forcibly the sayings of the First Presidents of Seventy, that we should so live that no charge can be brought against us. A few years ago the men in high standing in this Church were as little as we are. They obtained their exaltation by patient submission to right, and minding their own business." (Page 29.)

On January 25th, 1846, he said: "The saints who have passed through the trials of the Church were gen-

---
[2]The *"Reorganized"* Church History states that Z. H. Gurley was ordained a seventy in Far West in 1838. This is an error; they have no original record of such an ordination. The original records of the seventies in the Historian's Office, Salt Lake City, give his ordination as stated here. J.F.S.

erally rooted and grounded in love and have a witness in their own hearts or they would not have remained." (Page 33.)

BRIGGS AND GURLEY DESERTED CHURCH IN DAY OF TRIAL. Within a very few days of this time *Zenas H. Gurley deserted the Church because he was unable to face the trials and hardships the saints were forced to undergo.* The Mormon people were journeying in a strange land, the prospects before them were dark and some of the members became faint-hearted and were unable to endure to the end. Of this number *Jason W. Briggs and Zenas H. Gurley were two who turned back and sought refuge in the apostate organization of James J. Strang.*

Indeed, it required a strong heart and a firm-rooted faith for men and women to give up all earthly comforts and undertake a journey of that kind. Death stared the saints in the face; they were poorly clothed, without shelter, save their ragged tents that would not shed the rain, and almost destitute of food; yet with the exception of *the few who sought the "fleshpots of Egypt,"* they patiently and determinedly pursued their way until crowned with the victory.

The opinion of the world at that time was that the exodus meant the end of Mormonism, and that the Latter-day Saints had gone to their destruction; for without the necessary means to support life, and isolated as they were from the rest of civilization, they must surely perish in the barren and distant West. Such, too, would doubtless have been the case had not the protecting hand of Jehovah guided them. Is it any wonder under such trying conditions that the hearts of those *weak in the faith* should fail them.

BRIGGS AND GURLEY JOIN TO FORM "REORGANIZED" CHURCH. In 1849, Mr. Gurley filled a mission for Mr. Strang and made a number of converts to that faith. In 1850, he organized the "Yellowstone branch" for the Strangite church. In 1852 he rejected the claim of Mr. Strang and joined with Mr. Jason W. Briggs, and these two men united their respective Strangite branches, those of Yellowstone and Beloit, and organized themselves into a new religious movement known today as the "Reorganized" church.

In 1853, the leaders of this movement called a number of men to the ministry, "ordained" seven "apostles," and began a proselyting movement. For several years they tried to get "young Joseph," the son of the Prophet Joseph Smith, who had never affiliated with the saints since the exodus from Nauvoo, to join them and become their president. In this they failed, but were diligent and finally, through their continued efforts and the persuasion of his mother, he accepted that position in 1860, was "ordained" president of their church by William Marks, Zenas H. Gurley, and William W. Blair, and he and his successors have continued in that position ever since.

Mr. Gurley remained with this movement till his death, but his family, together with Jason W. Briggs, voluntarily withdrew in 1886.

ONLY A FEW HUNDRED OF SAINTS JOINED "REORGANIZATION." In 1852, when Jason W. Briggs and Zenas H. Gurley combined their Strangite forces, the membership was about 100 souls, most of whom were converts made for Mr. Strang. *In 1860 when "young Joseph" assumed the leadership, the membership was 300 souls, most of whom were converts that had never belonged to the Church of Jesus Christ of Latter-day Saints.*

Of the members of the Church who were in fellowship in 1844-46, the "Reorganization" has received no more, and likely less than 1,000 converts, which fact shows that the apostasy was not so great in 1844-46, as has been pictured. These statements are based on the testimony of original members of the "Reorganization," as they testified before the U. S. Court of Appeals for the Western District of Missouri in 1894, in the Temple Lot suit, which was for the possession of property in the hands of the "church of Christ" or "Hedrickites."

Before that court Mr. William W. Blair, who for many years was a member of the presidency of the "Reorganization," and who was one of its oldest members, testified that *"1,000 was probably too high an estimate for the members of the original Church, that had joined the 'Reorganized' church."* He could "approximately say" that 1,000 had joined the " 'Reorganized' church, and possibly that estimate was too large." (Record pp. 180, 181.)

WILLIAM MARKS, APOSTATE, ORDAINED "YOUNG JOSEPH." William Marks was also one of those who joined the "Reorganization" in an early day. At the time of the martyrdom he was president of the Nauvoo Stake, but was *disfellowshipped for transgression* at the October conference, 1844, and *finally excommunicated.*

Afterwards he joined the organization under James J. Strang. In that organization he became a "bishop," was a member of the "high council," and later a member of the "first presidency." After the death of James J. Strang, he joined the organization of Charles B. Thompson, another apostate.

This is the same William Marks who "ordained" Joseph Smith, of Lamoni, president of the "Reorganization." In that ordination he was assisted by Zenas H. Gurley and William W. Blair. *Mr. Blair never belonged to the Church.*

COUNTERFEIT NATURE OF "REORGANIZED" CHURCH. *It is almost needless to add that these men held no divine authority and could not bestow the priesthood and officiate in the ordinances of the gospel, and, therefore, the pretentions of the "Reorganized" church are fraudulent. Judged by its history, doctrines and the unstable character of its founders, it is proved to be a counterfeit and nothing more.*

Considering the conditions under which the "Reorganization" came into existence, and the fact that in the beginning the original 100 members came from the Strangite church, and that during the existence of that organization from its foundation to 1894, not more than 1,000 members of the "original Church" (i.e. the Church of Jesus Christ of Latter-day Saints as it stood in 1844) had joined it, we are not to be blamed if we declare that *that church is not the successor, a faction or a portion of the "original Church"* founded by Joseph Smith the Prophet through the command of God, April 6, 1830.

And after following the history of its founders and pointing out their instability and the manner in which they followed after false leaders, receiving "ordinations" and honors under their hands, we can most emphatically declare that they were not the faithful who did "not bow the knee to Baal," and who kept the "everlasting covenant."[3]

SUCCESSION IN THE PRESIDENCY

TWELVE STAND NEXT TO PRESIDENCY. In the year 1835, when the Twelve Apostles were chosen and their duties defined, the Lord declared that they were equal with the Presidency as a quorum.[4] That is, *in case of the dissolution or destruction of the First Presidency of the Church, the Twelve should succeed to the Presidency,* and would thus act until such time and place as the Lord revealed that the First Presidency should be again organized. *And whenever the First Presidency should be disorganized, it would devolve upon the quorum of Apostles to set in order and direct the affairs of the Church.* . . .

When the First Presidency is disorganized, the Twelve Apostles become the presiding quorum of the Church until the presidency is again organized, and dur-

---

[3]*Blood Atonement and the Origin of Plural Marriage,* pp. 89-94.

[4]D. & C. 107:21-24; 112:14-34; Joseph Fielding Smith, *Teachings of the Prophet Joseph Smith,* p. 190.

ing that time they are virtually the presidency of the Church—the presiding quorum.

How Twelve are Equal to Presidency. If through some cause—which is not likely to arise—both these quorums should be destroyed, then it would devolve on the seventies to set in order the Church and they would become the presiding quorum. This is the law that God has revealed, and it is the only law and order of the priesthood that he has revealed for the guidance of the Church in succession. You may search the *Doctrine and Covenants* from beginning to end and will find no other law of succession.[5]

I think it must be conceded that *the apostles could not be equal in authority with the Presidency when the First Presidency is fully and properly organized.* There could not be two heads—or three heads—of equal authority at the same time, for such a thing would lead to confusion. Hence *the apostles are equal,* as has been stated, *in that they have power to assume control of the affairs of the Church* when the Presidency is dissolved by the death of the President.[6]

Law of Common Consent Governs Succession. In several of the revelations given to the Church in the beginning, the doctrine of common consent is made mandatory. In the revelation of April 6, 1830, the date of the organization of the Church, the Lord says: "The elders are to receive their licenses from other elders, by vote of the church [branch] to which they belong, or from the conferences. . . . No person is to be ordained to any office in this church, where there is a regularly organized branch of the same, without the vote of that church."[7] In section 26, verse 2: *"All things shall be done by common consent in the church,* by much prayer and faith, for all things you shall receive by faith."

---
[5]D. & C. 107:25-32.
[6]*Origin of the "Reorganized" Church,* pp. 52-54.
[7]D. & C. 20:63, 65; 28:13; 38:34; 41:9; 51:12; 72:7; 104:64, 71-72, 76; 124:144.

The saints, by vote, accepted the Twelve Apostles as the presiding quorum of the Church at this special conference on August 8, and again at the regular conference in October. *This fact settled the matter of succession according to the revelations.* These authorities and their successors have been sustained at each conference of the Church, twice a year, and at the quarterly conferences of the various stakes four times a year from that day to this.

SUCCESSION DETERMINED AT NAUVOO BY VOTE OF SAINTS. The question of succession was, therefore, settled at Nauvoo when the assembled saints voted to sustain the apostles as the presiding quorum of the Church. *The attempt of any party or parties, before any other body, to set up the Church and to ordain officers in conflict with the action of the Church on the dates previously mentioned, would be illegally done:* just as much so as if in the municipality, state or nation, after the majority of the citizens had elected officers (and that almost unanimously) to serve them, a few *disgruntled, defeated, candidates and their sympathizers should appoint another election, hold it by themselves, and then declare that the regularly and properly elected officers were rejected and unauthorized to serve.* Such a thing in the nation could be no more foolish or absurd than were the attempts of apostates to set up a *new organization* of the Church from a handful of disgruntled office-seekers and their sympathizers. In one case there would be as much authority as in the other and no more.[8]

ALL BUT A FEW MEMBERS FOLLOWED BRIGHAM YOUNG. At the time of the martyrdom the Church in and about Nauvoo, the headquarters, numbered *not to exceed 20,000 souls.* This information is based on the best possible authority. And while this was not all the Church membership in the United States, it was the great bulk of the saints. . . .

---
[8]*Op. cit.,* p. 12.

Now, in the exodus from Nauvoo these saints—the great bulk of the Church—continued to be true and faithful and followed the Twelve Apostles.

Governor Thomas Ford, in his *History of Illinois,* states that in 1846 there were 16,000 Church members with the Twelve on the plains of Iowa, while the 1,000 that remained, a small remnant, were those who were unable to sell their property, or who having no property to sell, were unable to get away. (*History of "Reorganized" Church,* 3:164.) And this remnant followed as soon as they were able.

In the census report for 1850—three years after the settlement of Salt Lake Valley, we learn that the population of Utah was 11,380, all Mormons. That same year the population of Pottawattomie county, Iowa, was 7,828, all Mormons, the Latter-day Saints at Kanesville.

Thus we see that *19,208 members of the Church, who had followed President Brigham Young in the exodus from Nauvoo, were located at these two places.* And that is not all, there were other settlements of the saints at Garden Grove, Mount Pisgah, St. Louis, and other places where temporary settlements for the saints were formed during that exodus. These also later gathered to Utah.

Thus we see that *almost the entire membership of the Church as it stood in 1844, is accounted for in the following of President Brigham Young and the Twelve.*

CHURCH NEVER THREATENED WITH DISSOLUTION. That the Church was not threatened with dissolution the following statistics will show—I have not at hand the increase of membership of the Church during that period in the United States, but the increase in Great Britain is as follows: *In the year 1844, the population of the Church in the British Isles was 7,797. Six years after the martyrdom—December, 1850—that membership had increased to 30,747. This does not show much of a dissolution or falling away!*

I do not intend to convey the idea that there was not a falling away, an apostasy, at the time of the martyrdom and the exodus from Nauvoo, for *there were many who forsook the cause, but compared with the Church membership, they were but few.* Who were they? *Did the faithful saints forsake the Church at that time?* Did those who risked their lives—who were shot at with the Prophet and Patriarch forsake the Church? No! We do not find the faithful Latter-day Saints, who had the gospel rooted in their hearts, turning away.[9]

BRIGHAM YOUNG ORDAINED PRESIDENT BY JOSEPH SMITH. By whom was President Young ordained to the Presidency of the Church? It appears that the emissaries of the "Reorganite" church have discovered in that question a fruitful source of sophistical controversy, and that they are triumphantly asking it wherever they go.

The proper reply is, *he was ordained by the Prophet Joseph to that calling, when the Prophet, prompted by the Holy Spirit, conferred upon the Twelve Apostles the power and authority he himself had received.* . . .

The Prophet Joseph earnestly desired that his brother Hyrum should live to succeed him in the Presidency of the Church. In the year 1841, by command of the Lord, he ordained him to this exalted position.[10] . . .

Shortly before the martyrdom, the Prophet tried with all his power to persuade Hyrum not to accompany him to Carthage knowing full well the fate that awaited them there. Had Hyrum stayed behind, and thereby remained in mortality, he would, by virtue of his position and the ordination received in 1841, have become the President of the Church. His brother thought that this should be,[11] but through his faithfulness to, and love for, his brother, Hyrum fell a martyr before the Prophet Joseph did.

PROPHET GAVE KEYS TO ALL THE TWELVE. Now

---
[9]*Op. Cit.,* pp. 9-10, 12-14.
[10]*D. & C.* 124:94-95.
[11]*Times and Seasons,* vol. 5, p. 683.

mark! *The Lord, who knew that Hyrum should receive a martyr's crown at Carthage, in the winter of 1843-4, commanded the Prophet to confer upon the heads of the Twelve Apostles, every key, power, and principle, that the Lord had sealed upon his head. The Prophet declared that he knew not why, but the Lord commanded him to endow the Twelve with these keys and priesthood, and after it was done, he rejoiced very much, saying in substance, "Now, if they kill me, you have all the keys and all the ordinances and you can confer them upon others, and the powers of Satan will not be able to tear down the kingdom as fast as you will be able to build it up, and upon your shoulders will the responsibility of leading this people rest."*[12]

In this manner the Prophet ordained the Twelve Apostles, which body constitutes the second quorum of the Church, equal in authority with the First Presidency,[13] with the keys of the kingdom. *Brigham Young was president of the Twelve, and upon him devolved the duty of presiding.*

NEW PRESIDENCY ALREADY HAD KEYS OF KINGDOM. Therefore, after the death of Joseph and Hyrum Smith, the Twelve assumed the authority of their office, the duty to preside over the Church. Later, when through revelation the quorum of the First Presidency was reorganized with three presidents—Brigham Young and Counselors Heber C. Kimball and Willard Richards— they claimed, and rightfully, that *since they were ordained under the hands of Joseph Smith, and from him had received all the keys and powers of the priesthood which the Prophet held, it would have been superfluous to have been ordained again.* They were in this capacity, however, set apart and sustained by the unanimous vote of the saints, which was essential to make such ordination of force in the Church.

There is an abundance of testimony to prove that

---

[12]*Ibid.*, vol. 5, p. 651.   [13]D. & C. 107:21-24.

the Prophet did so ordain the Twelve.[14] We repeat that *Brigham Young received all the keys, powers, authority and priesthood, that were held by Joseph Smith, that enabled him to preside over the High Priesthood, from the Prophet Joseph Smith in Nauvoo in the winter of 1843-4.*

How Question of Succession was Settled. This important question was *settled long ago by the entire body of the saints* who accepted the leadership of the Twelve, after the departure of the Prophet and Patriarch, and sustained President Young in his office. It was *settled by the approval of the Almighty* of the marvelous work he accomplished, and which could not have been done without divine aid and guidance.

To ascribe the mighty deeds Brigham Young performed through the power of the divine Spirit which rested upon him, to the spirit that is the originator of succession, rebellion, apostasy, and falsehood, is to come dangerously near blasphemy. What is it but a repetition of the sin of the adversaries of our Lord who, although they knew that "no man can do these miracles that thou doest, except God be with him,"[15] yet proclaimed to the people: "He hath an unclean spirit."[16] *What is it but to assail the disciple with a weapon that is in vain directed against the Master?*

There was some excuse for difference of opinion on the subject of succession, immediately after the martyrdom, because the people were not in possession of full information, but there is no excuse now. To use a familiar illustration: At the time of an election citizens are expected to have different opinions as to candidates for office; they are expected to work for those whose views and principles they support.

But when the question is settled at the polls, loyalty demands that all accept the verdict and work together

---

[14]*Times and Seasons*, vol. 5, pp. 651, 644, 698; *Millennial Star*, vol. 10, p. 115.

[15]John 3:2.
[16]Mark 3:30.

for the common interests of the community. *The body of the Latter-day Saints having accepted, as guided by the Holy Spirit, the leadership of the Twelve, there was no longer any valid reason for seeking the leadership of other shepherds.*

BRIGHAM YOUNG KNOWN BY HIS FRUITS. The trouble with some of our "Reorganized" brethren is that they look upon the members of the Church as a flock of sheep, that, like other property, can be inherited. This is entirely contrary to the fundamental principles of the gospel. The Church belongs to Christ. The leaders and officers are the servants of the Lord and the people of the Lord. It follows that the Lord raises up whoever *he* pleases, to perform the services necessary from time to time.

Brigham Young was in every way equipped for the peculiar work needed during his time. *Who could have done what he did?* Sidney Rigdon? Lyman Wight? James J. Strang? The founders of the so-called "Reorganized" church? Let the reader reflect on the facts history records: and then, decide for himself, remembering that *every tree is known by its fruit.*[17]

AVOID USING NAME "JOSEPHITES." The authorities of the Church have been trying for many years to get our people, especially writers, to *quit calling the "Reorganites" by the title "Josephites."* The members of this spurious organization like to be called "Josephites" and to call us "Brighamites," making a distinction between the Prophet Joseph Smith and Brigham Young, emphasizing their false claim that they are followers of Joseph Smith and we are not.[18]

FRUITS OF THE "REORGANIZATION"

MISSION OF "REORGANITES": TO ABUSE SAINTS. During the summer of 1906 and continuing until the

---

[17]*Origin of the "Reorganized" Church,* pp. 114-117; Matt. 7:15-20. [18]Pers. Corresp.

summer of 1907, a number of "Reorganite" ministers, who were engaged in missionary work in Salt Lake City and Ogden, were greatly encouraged by one or two apostates and the local anti-Mormon press. *Their method of proselyting was of the usual nature, a tirade of abuse and false accusation hurled at the authorities of the Church.*

Encouraged by the anti-Mormon help, they became extremely vindictive in their references to President Brigham Young and the present Church authorities. Their sermons were so bitter and malignant—which has been the character of most of their work from the beginning in Utah—that they raised considerable protest from many respectable citizens. Even non-Mormons declared that in no other community would such vicious attacks be tolerated.

"Reorganite" Proselyting Methods. It appeared at times that these missionaries were attempting to provoke the Mormon people to some act of violence, that it might be seized upon and published to the world through the anti-Mormon press that they had been mobbed, and thus capital for their cause be made of it. Fortunately they were not molested, to the credit of the people so constantly abused.

One of these meetings was attended by a prominent gentleman from the East who was somewhat acquainted with Utah and her people. He said, in conversation with the writer a few days later, that never in his experience has he witnessed such a thing before. "If that fellow"— referring to a "Reorganite" who has since been promoted in his church—"should come to our town and abuse the ministers of our church, calling them murderers, thieves and liars, as he did Brigham Young and your churchmen, we would kick him off the streets."[19]

False "Reorganite" Revelations. To presume to speak in the name of the Lord is a serious matter, and

---
[19]*Op. cit.*, p. 3.

wo be to the man who speaks in the name of the Lord, when he has not been commanded. It is far better never to receive a revelation than to follow after those who receive "revelations" that the Lord has not given. *The "revelations" given by the "Reorganite" president to the "Reorganized" church, need only to be read to convince one of their spurious character.* They are weak, puerile, and it takes a very little of the spirit of discernment to know of what source they are. However, if they are acceptable to the "Reorganization," that is their business. We are satisfied.[20]

DESTINY OF "REORGANITE" CHURCH. Without the divine guidance and the constant watchcare of Jehovah over the destinies of the Mormon pioneers, with Brigham Young at their head, the West today would be but a barren wilderness. Under the leadership of Brigham Young the Mormon people prospered, and he left them in a better condition temporally and physically, and spiritually more united and more firmly established in the faith than they ever were before.

Where among the so-called "factions" can you point to one that has accomplished the hundredth part of what the followers of Brigham Young have accomplished? They have all practically disappeared but one —gone to their destruction. And the one that remains will dissolve and disappear as surely as the sun shines. You cannot fight the work of God and prosper.[21]

THE "REORGANITES" VS. SALVATION FOR THE DEAD

"REORGANITES" CLAIM CHURCH REJECTED WITH ITS DEAD. The so-called "Reorganized" church, which is so bitter in its antagonism towards the Church of Jesus Christ of Latter-day Saints, has claimed from its beginning to be teaching and practicing the doctrines of the gospel as they were revealed from God through the Prophet Joseph Smith. Its officers declare that they

---

[20]*Op. cit.*, p. 108.   [21]*Blood Atonement and the Origin of Plural Marriage*, pp. 51-52.

are walking in the footsteps of the martyred Seer, hewing closely to the line, and observing in all things the commandments which were given from God through his instrumentality, without variation, change, or loss of power from all that pertains to the salvation of the human family in this dispensation of the fulness of times.

Their foundation is built upon the absurd and misty claim that the Church of Jesus Christ of Latter-day Saints, which was established April 6, 1830, through the labors of Joseph Smith the Prophet and the will of God, was "rejected with its dead for transgression of its members," and that the "Reorganized" church is a "new organization"[22] which God raised up to succeed the original—but as they would have us believe, "rejected"—Church.

NO TRUE CHURCH WITHOUT SALVATION FOR DEAD. It is not now my purpose to discuss the foolish question of the "rejection of the Church," but to examine the "Reorganite" position in regard to salvation for the dead; and to show their lack of harmony with the teachings of the Church of Jesus Christ of Latter-day Saints pertaining to the dead, as those teachings have been revealed through the latter-day Prophet.

It stands to reason that if the Lord rejected his Church with its dead, because of transgression, or any other cause whatever, that he would not raise up a substitute church to carry on his work on earth and still keep the dead—who could in no wise be held responsible for the rejection—in suspension: and deny to them the privilege of receiving the ordinances of the gospel by proxy according to the revealed plan of God, as it was ordained from before the foundations of the world were laid, as a means of salvation to those who die without

---

[22]In a number of articles by Zenas H. Gurley, one of the founders of the "Reorganized" church, in the *Saints Herald*, vol. 1, the "Reorganization" is referred to as "a new organization of the church." This agrees with the statement of the president of that church in the *Saints Herald*, Feb. 17, 1904. Said he: "The Church, using the words to mean the Church rejected, has not been again received." J.F.S.

a knowledge of the gospel. To any reasonable mind this truth would need no argument.

Yet the "Reorganized" church declares that the Lord did this very thing! And in the light of the revelations given to the Prophet Joseph, as well as those in the ancient scriptures, which bear on this subject of salvation for the dead, their declaration is fatal to their organization; it stamps it as fraudulent and their officers as impostors. *A church without salvation for the dead, according to the revealed will of God to the Prophet Joseph Smith, cannot be the Church of Christ.* . . .

"REORGANITES" REJECT SALVATION FOR DEAD. We will now consider the attitude of the "Reorganization" in relation to this grand and eternal principle of the redemption of the dead.

At first the founders of the "Reorganized" church *appeared* to favor it and declared that when the "Reorganization" was established that this principle would be practiced, for as the "rejection of the church produced an effect on the dead," said they, "as well as on the living, so will the reorganization."[23]

But when the "Reorganization" took place, the change that was promised in regard to the dead was not fulfilled, and since that time to the present day—over 75 years—baptism for the dead, and temple building and temple work, have never been, by that organization, practiced or entertained. In fact they have turned about face, and have *rejected* peremptorily the doctrine of baptism for the dead, and *now* declare that it is not binding on them.

"REORGANITE" DECLARATIONS ON SALVATION FOR DEAD. In a resolution adopted by that church, April 9, 1886, the following startling declaration was made:

"That as to the alleged 'temple building and ceremonial endowments therein,' that we know of no temple

---
[23]*History of the "Reorganized" Church,* vol. 3, p. 245.

building, except as edifices wherein to worship God, and no endowment except the endowment of the Holy Spirit of the kind experienced by the early saints on Pentecost day.

" 'Baptism for the dead' referred to belongs to those local questions of which the body has said by resolution:

" 'That the *commandments of a local character, given to the first organization of the church are binding on the "Reorganization" only so far as they are either reiterated or referred to as binding by commandment to this church.' And that principle has neither been reiterated nor referred to as a commandment."*²⁴

In February, 1904, the president of that "organization" declared that baptism for the dead was a *"permissive rite,"* and that it was *taken from the church,* "and if subsequently it was to be engaged in," said he, "and enjoyed by the same people, *it must be restored again by revelation and command,* and could not be assumed as being held over by sufferance. *We do not know of any revelation or command, authoritatively promulgated, renewing the privilege."*²⁵

"YOUNG JOSEPH" ADMITS KEYS OF ELIJAH NOT HELD. *His statement is a flat acknowledgment that he does not hold the keys of this work and that they can only be received by revelation.* That he does *not* hold the keys is true. *That he did not receive them from his father he admits,*²⁶ and William Marks, William W. Blair and Zenas H. Gurley, who "ordained" him to his office of president of the "Reorganized" church, *never* held them. They could only be obtained from the Prophet Joseph Smith, and from him, as has been shown, the Twelve received them in 1844.

---

²⁴Conference resolutions pamphlet of "Reorganized" church, p. 82.
²⁵Editorial in *Saints Herald,* Feb. 17, 1904.
²⁶In his testimony before the Circuit Court, at Kansas City, in the "Temple Lot" suit, he said: *"No sir, I did not state that I was ordained by my father as his successor; according to my understanding of the word ordain, I was not." Plaintiff's Abstract,* p. 79, para. 126. J.F.S.

"Young Joseph" might truthfully have gone further and declared that *if the privilege was taken away, before it could again be practiced with authority and power, that the keys of the priesthood which were held by Elijah would again have to be restored.*

His statement is an unqualified admission that the work of Elijah was performed in vain. He challenges the prophet's statement, that the time had "fully come." He acknowledges that, in spite of all the efforts of the "Reorganization" in the attempt to save souls, the whole earth is in danger of being "smitten with a curse," and "utterly wasted" at the coming of the great and dreadful day of the Lord, which is "near, even at the doors."[27]

"REORGANITES" FLOUNDER IN UNBELIEF AND IGNORANCE. *If* this statement of the president of the "Reorganized" church is true, then the members of his church stand in jeopardy every hour; darkness covers the face of the earth; there is no salvation for the children of men; *the word of the Lord has failed, and destruction awaits the earth and her inhabitants.*

In declaring that baptism for the dead was a *"permissive rite,"* he shows a willful lack of understanding pertaining to the great eternal plan of salvation which was revealed through his Prophet father. In declaring that baptism was a *local commandment* to the saints at Nauvoo, not binding on the members of the "Reorganization," the members of his church acknowledge that the hand of Jehovah is *not* guiding them; that they are floundering in the mire of unbelief and ignorance. They make light of one of the "most glorious subjects belonging to the everlasting gospel."

Yes, the authorities of the "Reorganized" church have declared by conference resolution that baptism for the dead is not binding on them because it was a "local commandment," and "has never been reiterated nor referred to as a commandment!"

---
[27]D. & C. 110:13-16.

Judged by the "Reorganite" standards of faith and doctrine, will this statement bear the light of investigation? Baptism a local commandment, not binding on the saints! . . .

REVEALED TRUTHS ABOUT SALVATION FOR DEAD. We learn from the revelations and teachings of the Prophet the following important facts pertaining to the salvation of the dead:

1. Salvation in behalf of the dead is the binding or sealing of the hearts of the fathers and children, the welding link.[28]

2. It is the most glorious subject belonging to the everlasting gospel.[29]

3. It is the greatest responsibility in this world that God has laid upon us—to seek after our dead.[30]

4. It is obligatory to man.[31]

5. Without it the whole earth and its inhabitants would be smitten with a curse.[32]

6. It is an eternal doctrine, prepared before the foundation of the world.[33]

7. It is the burden of the scriptures.[34]

8. If we neglect it, it is at the peril of our own salvation.[35]

9. Through it we become saviors on Mount Zion, and may save multitudes of our kin.[36]

10. We, without our dead, and our dead without us, cannot be saved with a perfect salvation.[37]

11. We cannot lightly pass this doctrine over as pertaining to our salvation.[38]

12. The time granted to the saints to redeem their dead and gather and seal their living relatives before

---

[28]D. & C. 128:18; "Reorganite" edition 110:18.
[29]D. & C. 128:17; "Reorganite" edition 110:17.
[30]Times and Seasons, vol. 6, p. 616.
[31]Ibid.
[32]Mal. 4:6; D. & C. 128:18; "Reorganite" edition 110:18.
[33]D. & C. 128:5, 8, 18; "Reorganite" edition 110:5, 8, 18.
[34]Times and Seasons, vol. 2, p. 578; "Reorganite" Church History, vol. 2, p. 546.
[35]Ibid.
[36]Ibid., pp. 577 and 545.
[37]D. & C. 128:18; "Reorganite" edition 110:18.
[38]D. & C. 128:15; "Reorganite" edition 110:15.

ORIGIN AND DESTINY OF THE "REORGANIZED" CHURCH 269

the earth shall be smitten with a curse, "is none too long."[39]

AWFUL FATE OF "REORGANITES" FOR REJECTING SALVATION FOR DEAD. Now, my "Reorganite" friends, in the face of this, how dare you presume to circumscribe, limit and profane this doctrine of salvation for the dead? Why do you call this eternal and most glorious principle a "permissive rite," a "local commandment," and declare before God that it is not binding on you?

God has declared it to be ordained before the foundations of the world were laid for the salvation of the dead who die without a knowledge of the gospel—an eternal principle, the burden of the scriptures, obligatory to man. Are you in harmony with the word of God? *Were your leaders inspired to declare, in the face of Jehovah's commands, that this eternal principle was a "local commandment," not given to them as a commandment? Binding only on the saints at Nauvoo?*

Do you not fear and tremble for your own salvation in neglecting the salvation of your dead? If the Jews who lived in the days of Christ will have to answer for "all the righteous blood shed upon the earth, from the blood of righteous Abel unto the blood of Zacharias, son of Barachias," *because they neglected the salvation of their dead as well as their own salvation,* pray tell, what will your punishment be?[40] Remember that you without your dead cannot be made perfect.

Confronted by this evidence, for you to declare that your leaders are inspired and that yours is the Church of Christ is most preposterous!

SALVATION FOR DEAD AN ETERNAL PRINCIPLE. That the salvation for the dead is a *Bible* doctrine practiced by the ancient saints, we learn from the writings of Peter,[41] and Paul,[42] and the Revelator John.[43] Isaiah

---

[39] *History of Joseph Smith,* Jan. 20, 1844.
[40] Matt. 23:35; *Times and Seasons,* vol. 3, pp. 760-761.
[41] 1 Pet. 3:18-20.
[42] 1 Cor. 15:29.
[43] Rev. 22:12.

prophesied of it,[44] and our Redeemer taught it to the Jews,[45] not as a "local commandment," but as an eternal truth and a principle of the greatest importance to the whole human family. And for that reason, "Christ also hath suffered for sins, the just for the unjust, that he might bring us to God, being put to death in the flesh, but quickened by the Spirit: By which also he went and preached [*not in vain*] unto the spirits in prison."[46]

A PRESIDENT WITHOUT KEYS IS AN IMPOSTOR. The keys of the priesthood belong to the presiding officer of the Church and *must* be held in order that the ordinances of a *perfect salvation* may be administered to the saints and in behalf of the dead. The keys of the priesthood could *only* be received from the one who held them, the Prophet Joseph Smith, who received them from the heavens.

Any man claiming to be president of the high priesthood, without these keys, is an impostor. We have been given a key by which the impostor may be detected, for we have the word of the Lord that: "The great and grand secret of the whole matter, and the *summum bonum* of the whole subject that is lying before us, consists in obtaining the powers of the Holy Priesthood. *For him to whom these keys are given there is no difficulty in obtaining a knowledge of facts in relation to the salvation of the children of men, both as well for the dead as for the living.*"[47]

"REORGANITE" PRESIDENT DOES NOT HOLD KEYS. This declaration from the Lord, through the Prophet Joseph Smith, is most explicit. We may ask: Has the president of the "Reorganized" church obtained this priesthood? No, he has not! Then there is no wonder that he cannot obtain "knowledge of facts in relation to the salvation of the children of men, both as well for the dead as for the living."

[44]Isa. 42:6-7; 61:1-2.
[45]John 5:28-29.
[46]1 Pet. 3:18-19.
[47]*D. & C.* 128:11; "Reorganite" edition 110:11.

If he had obtained the keys, would it be possible for him to lead his people for more than 45 years without a knowledge of this power which the Lord, through the Prophet, declares is *not difficult* for him who holds the keys and the powers of the holy priesthood to obtain, and which is the "sealing and binding power, and, in one sense of the word the keys of the kingdom, which consist in the keys of knowledge?"[48]

If he held these keys, would it be possible that this grand and glorious principle would have been neglected for so long a time, when his father, the Prophet, declared that in this day there was "not too much time to save and redeem" the dead, and gather the living relatives, that they also may be saved, before the consummation decreed falls upon the world?

Would it be possible, if he held these keys, for him to declare that this doctrine was a "local commandment," a "permissive rite," not binding on the saints? Verily no!

FULNESS OF PRIESTHOOD HAD ONLY IN TEMPLES. The Lord declared in 1842, that he was *about to restore* to earth many things pertaining to the priesthood,[49] and that *only in temples could the fulness of the priesthood be restored.*[50] Did the word of the Lord fail? Did the Lord make a mistake? If the contention of the "Reorganized" church is true, he did. But Latter-day Saints know better. On our part we will accept the word of the Lord.

Since the "Reorganized" church does *not* build temples, and knows of "no temple building except as edifices wherein to worship God and no endowment except the endowment of the Holy Spirit of the kind experienced by the early saints on Pentecost day," it is to be expected that their president should be *ignorant* of the "fulness of the priesthood" and therefore experience great "difficulty in obtaining knowledge."

---

[48]*D. & C.* 128:14; "Reorganite" edition 110:14.
[49]*D. & C.* 127:8; "Reorganite" edition 109:5.
[50]*D. & C.* 124:28; "Reorganite" edition 107:10.

ENDOWMENT CEREMONIES REVEALED. If the elders of that church had read in the 107th section of their *Doctrine and Covenants* they would have discovered that the doctrine of "ceremonial endowments" is there taught most plainly:

"Therefore, verily I say unto you, that your anointings, and your washings, and your *baptisms for the dead,* and your solemn assemblies, and your memorials for your sacrifices by the sons of Levi, and for your oracles in your most holy places wherein you receive conversations, and your statutes and judgments, for the beginning of the revelations and foundation of Zion, and for the glory, honor, and *endowment* of all her municipals, are ordained by the ordinance of my holy house, which my people are *always* commanded to build unto my holy name.

"And verily I say unto you, let this house [Nauvoo Temple] be built unto my name, *that I may reveal mine ordinances therein unto my people;*

"*For I deign to reveal unto my church things which have been kept hid from before the foundation of the world,* things that pertain to the dispensation of the fulness of times.

"*And I will show unto my servant Joseph all things pertaining to this house, and the priesthood thereof.*"[51]

REPENT O YE "REORGANITES." Now, if all the foregoing passages are true—and they must be if Joseph Smith was a prophet of God, which he was—then these things pertaining to the priesthood were revealed to him; and salvation for the dead is just as binding on us and just as important as salvation for the living. One depends upon the other, and they are binding on all the children of men. *The Church of Jesus Christ of Latter-day Saints cannot teach one without the other, for they are inseparable.* A house divided against itself cannot stand.

Repent, therefore, and receive the gospel; save

---
[51]*D. & C.* 124:39-42; "Reorganite" edition 107:12-13.

yourselves with your dead by becoming saviors on Mount Zion, before the consummation decreed falls upon the earth; and by hearkening to these things, you will not be "smitten with a curse," nor "utterly wasted" when the dreadful day of the Lord does come.[52]

---

[52]*The "Reorganized" Church vs. Salvation for the Dead*, pp. 3-5, 9-12, 18-23.

CHAPTER 16

THE LAW OF REVELATION

ETERNAL NATURE OF REVELATION

REVELATION BURSTS UPON AN APOSTATE WORLD. We believe that our Eternal Father is just as ready to converse with those who seek him now as he was in ancient days.

We believe that the *Bible* does not contain all the revelations given by divine manifestations; but that it contains only fragmentary accounts of the dealings of the Lord with his servants the ancient prophets.

We believe that when he was on earth in his ministry, our Savior, Jesus Christ, established his Church upon eternal principles, fundamental to the salvation of mankind.

We believe that following the death of the ancient apostles, these eternal principles were corrupted and became mixed with pagan philosophy.

We believe that the essential ordinances of the gospel were changed and modified by man's will and not by divine instruction, so that the time came when, as Isaiah declared, men were drawing near to the Lord with their mouths, and with their lips honoring him, but that their hearts were far removed from him.[1]

The church had become so corrupted and changed that it became necessary for the opening of the heavens, the coming of heavenly messengers, and a restoration of the primitive faith and divine authority.[2]

REVELATION BEGAN AGAIN WITH JOSEPH SMITH. After the days of the apostles, man refused to heed the Spirit of the Lord, therefore the Spirit was withdrawn

---
[1] Isa. 29:13.   [2] Pers. Corresp.

THE LAW OF REVELATION 275

and man was left without divine guidance. So the strange belief arose that the Lord no longer communed with man, but had given him in the written word all that was essential for his guidance. This was the universal belief when Joseph Smith announced his vision. As a youth he had been taught that there was no coming of angels, no revelation, or need of additional scripture.

But the Lord gave to Joseph Smith a revelation of the fulness of the gospel, "Proving to the world that the holy scriptures are true, and that God does inspire men and call them to his holy work in this age and generation, as well as in generations of old; Thereby showing that he is the same God yesterday, today, and forever."[3]

PROPHETS FORETOLD LATTER-DAY REVELATION. *Why should it be considered strange that the Lord should speak to man in this day,* either by his own voice or by the voice of angels? Is he less interested in man today? Or has man advanced so far that he has passed beyond the need of divine help?

One ancient prophet said, "Where there is no vision, the people perish,"[4] and another said, "Surely the Lord God will do nothing, but [i.e. until] he revealeth his secret unto his servants the prophets."[5] Yet another, speaking of the last days, said: "Your old men shall dream dreams, your young men shall see visions; And also upon the servants and upon the handmaids in those days will I pour out my spirit."[6]

Equally positive is the saying of an ancient Nephite prophet: "Have angels ceased to appear unto the children of men? Or has he withheld the power of the Holy Ghost from them? Or will he, so long as time shall last, or the earth stand, or there shall be one man upon the face thereof to be saved? Behold I say unto you, Nay; for it is by faith that miracles are wrought; and it is by faith that angels appear and minister unto men; where-

---

[3]*D. & C.* 20:11-12.
[4]Prov. 29:18.
[5]Amos 3:7.
[6]Joel 2:28-29.

fore, *if these things have ceased wo be unto the children of men, for it is because of unbelief, and all is vain."*[7]

Yes, it is very strange that the Latter-day Saints stand conspicuously alone in the belief that the Father may and does reveal himself and his truth to man, as proclaimed by ancient prophets that he should do in these latter days.[8]

REVELATION NEEDED TO FULFIL COVENANTS OF LORD. It is very strange, considering what is written in the *Bible,* that the idea ever should have become fixed in the minds of the people that the canon of scripture is full; that the Lord has no more counsel to give to man, no matter how great the need for further divine direction, and man must depend entirely for solace upon the word spoken to ancient Biblical prophets.

These prophets had no such understanding. They spoke of *covenants to be made between God and man in the last days.* How could this be done unless there was an opening of the heavens? If the heavens were so opened, would it not be a revelation, yes, even scripture? Voicing the word of the Lord to Israel in the last days, Ezekiel said:

"And they shall dwell in the land that I have given unto Jacob my servant, wherein your fathers dwelt; and they shall dwell therein, even they, and their children, and their children's children, forever. . . . Moreover *I will make a covenant of peace with them; it shall be an everlasting covenant* with them: and I will place them, and multiply them, and will set my sanctuary in the midst of them for evermore. My tabernacle also shall be with them: yea, I will be their God, and they shall be my people."[9]

EVERLASTING COVENANT REVEALED THROUGH JOSEPH SMITH. Jeremiah also bears this same witness and adds that the people shall not teach "every man his

[7]Moro. 7:36-37.
[8]*Church News,* May 30, 1931, p. 2.
[9]Ezek. 37:25-27.

neighbour, and every man his brother, saying, Know the Lord: for they shall all know me, from the least of them unto the greatest of them, saith the Lord: for I will forgive their iniquity, and I will remember their sin no more."[10]

Because of this ancient promise it should not be strange that a prophet should come declaring the introduction of the new and everlasting covenant. In this day the Lord said to Joseph Smith: "Wherefore, I the Lord, knowing the calamity which should come upon the inhabitants of the earth, called upon my servant Joseph Smith, Jun., and spake unto him from heaven, and gave him commandments: . . . *That mine everlasting covenant might be established;* That the fulness of my gospel might be proclaimed by the weak and the simple unto the ends of the world, and before kings and rulers. Behold, I am God and have spoken it."[11]

REASONABLE TO RECEIVE NEW REVELATION. If a man will permit reason to guide him in the path of common sense, he will be forced to conclude that there is no justification for the belief that all scripture is enclosed within the cover of the *Holy Bible.* Such a doctrine closes the mouth of the Almighty, denying him power to speak. Nor can it be consistently stated that there is no need for further revelation. It is equally inconsistent to say that the Lord did not have interest enough in *other peoples,* outside of Palestine, to speak to them and guide them by his word.

Alma, a Nephite prophet living before the days of Christ, uttered this truth: "For behold, the Lord doth grant unto *all nations,* of their own nation and tongue, to teach his word, yea, in wisdom, all that he seeth fit that they should have; therefore we see that the Lord doth counsel in wisdom, according to that which is just and true."[12]

---

[10] Jer. 31:34.
[11] *Church News,* June 13, 1931, p. 2; D. & C. 1:17, 22-24.
[12] Alma 29:8.

TWO NATIONS STAND AS WITNESSES FOR CHRIST. Nephi, an earlier prophet, by command recorded, "Know ye not that there are more nations than one? Know ye not that I, the Lord your God, have created all men, and that I remember those who are upon the isles of the sea; and that I rule in the heavens above and in the earth beneath; and *I bring forth my word unto the children of men, yea, even upon all the nations of the earth?*

"*Wherefore murmur ye, because that ye shall receive more of my word? Know ye not that the testimony of two nations is a witness unto you that I am God, that I remember one nation like unto another?* Wherefore, I speak the same words unto one nation like unto another. And when the two nations shall run together the testimony of the two nations shall run together also."[13]

This was spoken by prophecy to the gentiles of the present day. It should be remembered also, that the law given to Israel was that "the testimony of two men is true,"[14] providing they are honorable witnesses. Here *the Lord applies the law to nations.* Why should it not be so?

If the word of the Lord is to be established by two chosen witnesses, then we may well look for *two chosen nations to stand as witnesses for Jesus Christ.* One such nation was Israel in Palestine, the other was Israel in America, Judah speaking from the Old World and Joseph from the New. Today these two testimonies for God and his truth have run together.[15]

LATTER-DAY SCRIPTURE CLARIFIES BIBLE. There is not one principle pertaining to the salvation of men that is so clearly stated in the Bible, as it has come down to us, that men do not stumble over—not one thing. There is not one principle they can be united on that has been so clearly stated that they do not find their interpretations of it conflicting.

---

[13] 2 Ne. 29:7-8.
[14] John 8:17.
[15] *Church News,* June 20, 1931, p. 2.

THE LAW OF REVELATION

Do you want to know about the resurrection of the dead? Who is going to be saved in the celestial kingdom of God? Then read your *Book of Mormon.* Read your *Doctrine and Covenants.* The 76th section of the *Doctrine and Covenants,* known as the Vision, is the clearest, most concise statement regarding salvation that I know anything about, and I doubt if the Lord ever gave to any people, at any time upon the face of the earth, anything clearer than this revelation.

Do the people of the world know where they are going when they die? No. They sing about a beautiful isle of somewhere. They do not know. Can they find out in the *Bible?* Yes, we can find it. They could find it if they had the right inspiration. But with the added help that we obtain from the records the Lord has given us, we do not stumble over that.

We do not stumble over baptism and how it should be performed and by whom. We have a clear and perfect understanding of the nature of God. Now, I can find that in the *Bible;* so can you. So can they, if they would search for it in the spirit of faith; but they stumble over it; and yet they are not willing to accept the revelations of the Lord given in the day and dispensation in which they live that would set forth clearly to them all these principles of eternal truth. How greatly are we blessed![16]

SEEING THINGS THAT ARE PAST. It is a common known fact in science that the light from the stars has taken thousands of years to reach the earth and we see them as they were thousands of years ago and not as they are today. That being true, if we could get in the right place we could see things as they were at any previous period of time.[17]

REVELATION IN THE CHURCH TODAY

REVELATION SINCE DAY OF JOSEPH SMITH. *The Presidents of the Church from the Prophet Joseph until*

---
[16]Conf. Rep., Sept., 1950, pp. 11-12.   [17]Pers. Corresp.

now have received revelations from the Lord for the guidance of his people. While all these revelations have not been placed in the *Doctrine and Covenants*, they are none the less true. Not all the revelations given to Joseph the Seer were placed in the *Doctrine and Covenants* in his day; we have added many of his revelations to that volume since his death.

And there are others that have not been placed in it. Some of them were for the Church and *not for the world*, and therefore, are given only to the saints. But *many revelations have been given to the Church since the death of Joseph Smith. Some of these have been published; some have not.* It has been my privilege to read and handle a number of them that are still in the manuscript and have not as yet been given to the world for a wise purpose in the Lord. But they are on file and will be preserved.[18]

CHURCH LED BY REVELATION TODAY. The Church today is led by revelation. Not all of the revelations given to the Prophet are in the *Doctrine and Covenants;* but everything in it is essential to our salvation. It is not necessary that we add other revelations wherein there is no new doctrine revealed, but such as are merely guidance and counsel, to that volume of scripture.

All of the presidents of the Church have had revelation; some of these by Brigham Young,[19] John Taylor,[20] Wilford Woodruff,[21] and Joseph F. Smith, have been published. You will find one by President Smith in *Gospel Doctrine*.[22]

We need not get alarmed, for *if we have the spirit of discernment, we will know that the Spirit of the Lord is guiding the authorities of the Church.*

Revelation from the Lord is binding upon us whether

---

[18]*Origin of the "Reorganized" Church,* p. 107.
[19]*D. & C.* 136.
[20]B. H. Roberts, *Seventy's Course in Theology,* First Year Book, pp. 15-16.
[21]G. Homer Durham, *Discourses of Wilford Woodruff,* pp. 213-218.
[22]Joseph F. Smith, *Gospel Doctrine,* 5th ed., pp. 472-476.

THE LAW OF REVELATION 281

we receive it or not; and if we reject it, we will be punished.[23]

The Lord has not left us to wander; he has not left us alone in the world to grope in darkness, but the Church which he has founded is guided by the spirit of revelation, and *the inspiration of the Lord rests upon those who stand at the head.* They are not doing this work in their own name; they are not endeavoring to establish themselves; but to carry out the plan which the Lord has revealed; and to make known unto the children of men the great desire of our Father, that all men may be saved through obedience to the gospel and receive a place and standing in his kingdom.[24]

REVELATION GIVEN AT GENERAL CONFERENCE. The remark is sometimes made by thoughtless and unobserving persons that the spirit of revelation is not guiding the Latter-day Saints now as in former times. This thought can hardly be entertained by the members who crowded the Tabernacle during the three days of conference. To all who possess the spirit of discernment and the enlightenment of the Holy Spirit, it was very apparent that the Lord was pouring out his Spirit and giving to the members of the Church commandment and direction, which is most timely and needful in these days of increased disobedience and wickedness, which pervade the world.[25]

REVELATION GIVEN TO THE BRETHREN. *The Lord blesses this people through the inspiration that comes to his servants, as they direct, and teach, and expound the scriptures.* The statement is often made by the enemies of the people, and we hear it upon the streets of this city, from time to time, that there is no revelation in the Church. I say to you that *there is revelation in the Church.*

The Lord not only blesses the men who stand at the

---
[23]Pers. Corresp.   [25]*Era*, vol. 40, p. 700.
[24]Conf. Rep., Apr. 1921, p. 39.

head and hold the keys of the kingdom, but *he also blesses every faithful individual with the spirit of inspiration.* He gives his people revelation for their *own* guidance, wherein they keep his commandments and serve him. That is a blessing promised and within their power to receive.

We are blessed with revelation; the Church is built upon that foundation. All the revelations given do not have to be written. The inspiration may come to the brethren, stating what shall be done, or what shall not be done, as the Lord directs them. It does not have to be printed in a book. We have revelations that have been given, that have been written; some of them have been published; some of them have not.[26]

MORE REVELATIONS NEEDED IN EARLY DAYS OF CHURCH. In the days of the Prophet Joseph Smith the Lord gave revelations to the Church covering every principle which was essential to a proper understanding of gospel principles and Church procedure. As the members had just come out of the world and had been taught in all its religious concepts and traditions, they required guidance on all things. The receiving of revelation for their guidance lessened as the years passed so that in the last four or five years of the Prophet's life, the Lord did not need to reveal information in regard to fundamental principles.

However, he did say that the saints should be "crowned with blessings from above, yea, and with commandments not a few, and with *revelations* in their time —they that are faithful and diligent before me."[27] This promise and the word of the Lord to the Church in section 104:58, has been literally fulfilled and is being fulfilled constantly. It is not necessary for the Lord to require that all of his revelations to the Church be published in a book and given to the people. He speaks to his servants

---

[26]Conf. Rep., Oct., 1910, pp. 40-41.   [27]*D. & C.* 59:4.

THE LAW OF REVELATION

and reveals his will, and then they impart the instruction to the people.[28]

REVELATIONS LIMITED BY MAN'S CAPACITY TO RECEIVE. Revelation is promised us through our faithfulness; so, also, is knowledge pertaining to the mysteries and government of the Church. *The Lord withholds much that he would otherwise reveal if the members of the Church were prepared to receive it.* When they will not live in accordance with the revelations he has given, how are they entitled to receive more? The people in the Church are not living in full accord with the commandments the Lord has already required of them.

We find ourselves, therefore, much like the Nephites when Nephi spoke of revelation: "And now, I, Nephi, cannot say more; the Spirit stoppeth mine utterance, and I am left to mourn because of the unbelief, and the wickedness, and the ignorance, and the stiffneckedness of men; for they will not search knowledge, nor understand great knowledge, when it is given unto them in plainness, even as plain as word can be."[29]

Further reasons why the Lord does not give the people more revelations are given by Mormon and Moroni in the *Book of Mormon*.[30]

We have little occasion to clamor for more revelation when we refuse to heed what the Lord has revealed for our salvation. However, the authorities are directed by revelation, and this is apparent to all who have the spirit of discernment. The Lord has not forsaken his people, although they have not always put their trust in him.[31]

FALSE SPIRITS AND FALSE REVELATIONS

THE PRESIDENT: SOLE SOURCE OF REVELATION FOR CHURCH. There is but one at a time who holds the keys and the right to receive revelation *for the Church,* and that man is *the President of the Church.* And when the First Presidency is disorganized through the death of

---
[28] D. & C. 68:3-5.
[29] 2 Ne. 32:7.
[30] 3 Ne. 26:6-12; Ether 4:4-12.
[31] Pers. Corresp.

the President, then, according to revelation, the Twelve Apostles become the presiding quorum of the Church, and then, if the Lord has any revelations to give to his people they will come through the proper channel—*the President of the Twelve.*

If we will keep this in mind, it will be a *key* to us as the Lord intended that it should be, by which we may *gauge and weigh the pretended revelations* of men. When we see this man, or that man, or perhaps that woman, or child, giving revelations as was the case in the "Reorganized" church when Jason W. Briggs, Zenas H. Gurley, Henry H. Deam and the daughter of Zenas H. Gurley, received "revelations" bearing on the organization of their cult, we will know assuredly that *these things are not of God.*

The Lord will never ignore the presiding officer and quorum of the Church, for he respects authority, as he requires us to respect authority. And it will always be a key to us, if we will bear it in mind, that *whenever he has a revelation or commandment to give to his people that it will come through the presiding officer of the Church.* This is plainly taught in the revelations.[32]

TEST OF TRUTH OF REVELATIONS. If the Lord has a revelation or a commandment to give to his people, it is going to come from the head, and when someone else comes among the people professing to have revelations and to give commandments we can test that matter very readily. *We do not have to go into any details or make an extended examination of the claims.* There is no need of any investigation whatever, because the Lord has given us the key as a law to the Church by which we are to be governed.[33]

KEY WHEREBY TRUE REVELATIONS MAY BE KNOWN. We have a key given us by revelation by which false spirits may be known, by which false revelation

---
[32]*Origin of the "Reorganized" Church,* pp. 76-77; D. & C. 43:1-10.   [33]Conf. Rep., Oct., 1948, p. 98.

THE LAW OF REVELATION

may be known. There is *only one man* in this Church, at a time, who has the right to receive revelation for the Church. The Lord has said that his house is a house of order, not a house of confusion, and therefore one is appointed to speak. One has the right to receive the word of the Lord and give it to the Church.

We all have the right to receive *revelation for our own guidance*. A president of a stake has the right of revelation for the guidance of his stake. But no man has the right to receive revelation for this Church, except the one whom the Lord has called.

If he receives a revelation it will be declared without question, if it is intended for the Church, in a manner by which we may all know the source from whence it comes. And when we find people secretly distributing to the Church what are said to be revelations, or visions, or manifestations, that have not come from nor received the approval of the authorities of the Church, we may put it down that *such things are not of God.*

We do not need to write to ask questions in regard to these things. We do not need to question them for a moment, because the Lord is not going to give a revelation to any high priest, any elder, or seventy, for this Church. It will come through the one who is so appointed. And if the Lord is not going to choose those who have standing in the quorums of the priesthood, you may be certainly assured that he is not going to choose someone who does not hold the priesthood at all. So our minds may be at rest in regard to matters of this kind....

FALSE SPIRITS DECEIVE THE UNFAITHFUL. If we will follow the spirit of light, the spirit of truth, the spirit that is set forth in the revelations of the Lord; if we will, through the spirit of prayer and humility, seek for the guidance of the Holy Ghost, the Lord will increase our light and our understanding so that we shall have the spirit of discernment; we shall understand the truth; we shall know falsehood when we see it, and we shall not be deceived.

Who is it that is deceived in this Church? Not the man who has been faithful in the discharge of duty; not the man who has made himself acquainted with the word of the Lord; not the man who has practiced the commandments given in these revelations; but the man who is not acquainted with the truth, the man who is in spiritual darkness, the man who does not comprehend and understand the principles of the gospel. Such a man will be deceived, and when these false spirits come among us, he may not understand or be able to distinguish between light and darkness.

FAITHFUL NOT DECEIVED BY FALSE REVELATIONS. But if we will walk in the light of the revelations of the Lord, if we will hearken to the counsels that are given by those who stand in the councils of the Church, empowered to give the instructions, we will not go astray....

"*And whoso treasureth up my word, shall not be deceived.*"[34] Therefore let us go to with our might in the labor of this Church, and in the study and understanding of the principles of the gospel, these principles of light; and as we study them, the Lord will reveal to us further light, until we shall receive the fulness, in due time, of the perfect day; and we shall not be under the necessity of being subject to doubt and seeking for advice when confronted by matters of this kind, because *the Spirit of the Lord itself will teach us.*

The day is coming, so Jeremiah says, when it will not be necessary for one man to teach his neighbor, saying, "Know the Lord,"[35] for they all shall know him, from the greatest to the least. And that will come when we, in all full purpose of heart, are willing to serve the Lord and keep his commandments and hearken to the counsels that come to us from those who preside.[36]

---
[34]Joseph Smith, 1:37.
[35]Jer. 31:34.
[36]Conf. Rep., Apr., 1931, pp. 70-72; D. & C. 50:1-3, 21-24.

THE LAW OF REVELATION

SAINTS ENTITLED TO SPIRIT OF DISCERNMENT. There is no reason in the world why each member of the Church should not have a thorough understanding of the principles of the gospel, of the order of the Church, and the government of the Church, so that none need be led astray by any wind of doctrine, or notion that prevails among the children of men, which may come to his attention.

If we are firmly grounded in the faith and built upon the rock, we will know the truth, the truth which will make us free. There is a lying spirit abroad in the land. . . .

If you understand the Church articles and covenants, if you will read the scriptures and become familiar with those things which are recorded in the revelations from the Lord, it will not be necessary for you to ask any questions in regard to the authenticity or otherwise of any purported revelation, vision, or manifestation that proceeds out of darkness, concocted in some corner, surreptitiously presented, and not coming through the proper channels of the Church.

TRUE REVELATIONS WILL BE PUBLICIZED BY CHURCH. Let me add that when a revelation comes for the guidance of this people, you may be sure that it will not be presented in some mysterious manner contrary to the order of the Church. *It will go forth in such form that the people will understand that it comes from those who are in authority,* for it will be sent either to the presidents of stakes and the bishops of the wards over the signatures of the presiding authorities, or it will be published in some of the regular papers or magazines under the control and direction of the Church, or it will be presented before such a gathering as this at a general conference. It will not spring up in some distant part of the Church and be in the hands of some obscure individual without authority, and thus be circulated among the Latter-day Saints. Now, you may remember this."[37]

---
[37]Conf. Rep., Oct., 1918, pp. 54-57.

MANIFESTATIONS FOR INDIVIDUAL, NOT THE CHURCH. There have been individuals, from time to time, who have been invited to go into the wards, in the sacrament meetings, priesthood classes, Sunday Schools and Mutual Improvement organizations, and at times, for their special benefit, cottage meetings have been held where they might come and relate remarkable visions or revelations claimed by these individuals to have been given to them. *All this is wrong.* . . .

Now, the Lord will give revelations to this Church; and he will give commandments to this Church from time to time, and as it is necessary; but always in accordance with his own law; and we do not have to run around and invite individuals who are without authority to relate unto us purported visions, or revelations or commandments, for the guidance of this people.

Everything in the Church is done in order. Everything pertaining to the kingdom of God is in order, because it is obedient to law. . . .

If a man comes among the Latter-day Saints, professing to have received a vision or a revelation or a remarkable dream, and the Lord has given him such, he should keep it to himself. It is all out of order, in this Church, for somebody to invite him into a sacrament service to relate that to the Church, because the Lord will give his revelations in the proper way, to the one who is appointed to receive and dispense the word of God to the members of the Church. . . .

SAINTS WILL NOT FOLLOW FALSE REVELATIONS. Now, these stories of revelation that are being circulated around are of no consequence, except for rumor and silly talk by persons who have no authority. The fact of the matter is simply this: *No man can enter into God's rest until he will absorb the truth, insofar that all error, all falsehood, all misunderstanding and misstatement he will be able to sift thoroughly and dissolve, and know that it is error, and not truth.*

When you know God's truth, when you enter into God's rest, you will not be hunting after revelations from Tom, Dick and Harry all over the world. You will not be following the will-o'-the-wisp of the vagaries of men and women who advance nonsense and their own ideas. When you know the truth, you will abide in the truth, and the truth will make you free. It is only the truth that will free you from the errors of men and from the falsehoods and misrepresentations of the evil one, who lies in wait to deceive and to mislead the people of God from the paths of righteousness and truth.[38]

[38]Conf. Rep., Apr., 1938, pp. 64-67; D. & C. 46:7-9.

CHAPTER 17

GAINING THE KNOWLEDGE THAT SAVES

NATURE OF SAVING KNOWLEDGE

No Salvation in Ignorance of Gospel. There never was a time, I suppose, in the history of the world when so much knowledge was in the possession of men. Surely knowledge has been increased, but at the same time, the doctrine taught in this prophetic saying by Paul is true: men are ever learning, but apparently never able to come to a knowledge of the truth.[1]

We have been informed that it has been said that our present system of education has taken man apart. It has done more. It has made a brute of him, and given him a brute ancestor, instead of placing him on the platform as a son of God, the offspring of God, where he properly belongs. . . .

The Prophet did say that a man cannot be saved in ignorance, but in ignorance of what? He said that *a man could not be saved in ignorance of the saving principles of the gospel of Jesus Christ.*[2] Not many of the great and the mighty, those who form and control the thoughts of the people of today, are going to find salvation in the kingdom of God. Why? Because they have not found the way; they are not walking in the light of truth. They may have knowledge, but they lack intelligence.

Intelligence is the light of truth, and we are informed that *he who has intelligence or the light of truth will forsake that evil one.*[3] A man who has intelligence will wor-

---
[1] 2 Tim. 3:7.
[2] Joseph Fielding Smith, *Teachings of the Prophet Joseph Smith*, pp. 297, 301, 324, 331, 332.
[3] D. & C. 93:36-37.

GAINING THE KNOWLEDGE THAT SAVES

ship God and repent of his sins; he will seek to know the will of God and follow it. . . .

Now I understand that knowledge is very important, but *there is a great fund of knowledge in the possession of men that will not save them in the kingdom of God. What they have got to learn are the fundamental things of the gospel of Jesus Christ.* They have got to learn to have faith in God. They must learn to obey him. They have got to learn his commandments, his ordinances, and keep them, and *unless* they do, all their learning and all their knowledge will be of little benefit to them. . . .

EXALTED BEINGS EVENTUALLY WILL KNOW ALL THINGS. Now I say it boldly, all the knowledge that a man can gain in this world or beyond this world, independent of the Spirit of God, the inspiration of the Almighty, will not lead him to a fulness.[4] . . .

So with all our boasting, with all our understanding, with all the knowledge that we possess—and let me say that this great knowledge that has been poured out upon men, and all that is truth, has come from God—but with it all, unless we humble ourselves, and put ourselves in harmony with his gospel truth, and seek for the light which comes through the Spirit of truth, which is Jesus Christ, we will never gain a fulness of knowledge.

I realize that it must eventually come to pass in the case of *those who gain the exaltation and become sons of God, that they must, in the eternities, reach the time when they will know all things.* They must know mathematics; they must know all the principles of science; they must be prepared in all things—by learning, by study, by faith—to comprehend these principles of eternal truth, even as our Father in heaven comprehends them; and *unless men will put themselves in harmony with him and his Spirit and seek the light which comes through that Spirit, they never will reach the goal of perfection in these*

---
[4]*D. & C. 93:26-27.*

things. *It is, however, knowledge of the principles of the gospel that will save men in the kingdom of God.*[5]

GOSPEL TRUTH GREATER THAN SCIENTIFIC TRUTH. Brother Joseph F. Merrill never lost sight of the kingdom of God. Nothing that he ever received in his secular training ever influenced him against the fundamental teachings of the gospel of Jesus Christ. He learned to evaluate truth. He knew that not all truth was of the same importance—that some things were of far greater importance than others. No matter how great a truth may be, or how important it may be to the benefit of the human family, *there is nothing that can be obtained through the secular education that can take the place of a knowledge of the kingdom of God.*

The fact that Jesus Christ is the Only Begotten Son of God and the Redeemer of the world is worth more than all that Brother Merrill learned in relation to electricity, or the physical sciences, as important as they are; and he realized that.

To know how atoms are constructed is a wonderful thing, and to know how many elements there are; but that knowledge will not take a man into the kingdom of God, although it may be, and is, important.

To learn to control electricity and make it serve man, to give him light and power and heat, and otherwise become useful, is important; but it never will be as important in this world as to know that a man must repent and be baptized for the remission of his sins.

TESTIMONY MORE IMPORTANT THAN WORLDLY LEARNING. Brother Merrill learned these truths, and to him the kingdom of God and the way to eternal life were far more important than all the learning, the training, that he received in the great colleges of the land.

I marveled at his energy. Apparently he never got tired; he loved the truth. He loved the truth of science, but he loved *more* the truths of the gospel of Jesus Christ.

---
[5]*Millennial Star*, vol. 102, pp. 514-516.

Before his brethren he has stood on his feet and borne testimony that God lives, that Jesus Christ is the Redeemer of the world, the Only Begotten Son of God. He has informed us of how he obtained that testimony. He knew that Joseph Smith was and is a Prophet of God. He knew that the gospel of Jesus Christ has been restored, and *in all the years of his training in physics and electrical energy he never lost sight of the kingdom of heaven,* and he was always active in some capacity in the Church.

It is not every man, you know, that can take courses such as were taken by Brother Merrill in the great colleges of this land, and still hold faithful and true to the fundamental teachings of the gospel of Jesus Christ. Some of them fail. They fall by the wayside. They let the philosophies of man warp their better judgment. They cease to pray. They begin to forget the Lord, and before they are aware, they are out of touch with the things of a spiritual nature. They have lost the Spirit of the Lord. *No man in this Church can afford to take a course that would deprive him of the guidance of the Holy Spirit.*[6]

GAINING TRUTH AND LIGHT FROM THE SPIRIT

How to Gain a Testimony. *There is no reason in the world why any soul should not know where to find the truth.* If he will only humble himself and seek in the spirit of humility and faith, going to the Lord just as the Prophet Joseph Smith went to the Lord to find the truth, he will find it. There is no doubt about it. There is no reason in the world—if men would only hearken to the whisperings of the Spirit of the Lord, and seek as he would have them seek, for the knowledge and understanding of the gospel of Jesus Christ—for them not to find it: no reason, except the hardness of their hearts

---
[6]*Church News*, Feb. 13, 1952, pp. 3-4. These expressions were made at the funeral service of Elder Joseph F. Merrill of the Council of the Twelve.

and their love of the world. *"Knock, and it shall be opened unto you."*[7]

UNFAITHFUL EASILY DECEIVED. The nearer we approach God, the better we endeavor to keep his commandments and the more we search to know his will as it has been revealed, the less likely it will be for us to be led astray by every wind of doctrine, by these false spirits that lie in wait to deceive, and by the spirits of men. We will be protected; and we will have the power to understand, to segregate truth from error; we will walk in the light, and we will not be deceived.

Now the man who is dilatory, the man who is unfaithful, the man who is not willing to keep the commandments of the Lord in all things, lays himself open to deception, because the Spirit of the Lord is not with him to lead and direct him and to show him the way of truth and righteousness; and therefore, some error comes along and he absorbs it because he cannot understand and realize the difference between truth and error.[8]

OBEDIENCE OPENS DOOR TO GOSPEL KNOWLEDGE. I have been asked the question, what evidence we have that there is a life after death. One rather prominent educator has recently declared that we have no evidence whatever of a life after death, because no one has ever returned. I dispute that statement and declare that it not true.

The best evidence that we have or that we may receive of eternal life, of the resurrection or restoration of the spirit and body after death, is that which *comes to us through obedience to the gospel and the testimony of the Spirit of the Lord.* There is no greater evidence than this.

The Savior said: "My doctrine is not mine, but his that sent me. *If any man will do his will, he shall know of the doctrine,* whether it be of God, or whether I speak of myself."[9]

---

[7]Conf. Rep., Apr., 1951, p. 59; Matt. 7:7-11; Jas. 1:5.
[8]Conf. Rep., Apr., 1940, pp. 98-99; D. & C. 50:2-35.
[9]John 7:16-17.

That is a key that unlocks the door to knowledge of our eternal existence. If men will follow that instruction, they will know the truth, and they will realize that Jesus Christ is indeed the Son of God and the Redeemer of the world; that he arose from the dead and on the third day after his resurrection appeared to his disciples. Not only that, but that the graves were opened, as the scriptures say, "And many bodies of the saints which slept arose, And came out of the graves after his resurrection, and went into the holy city, and appeared unto many."[10]

KEY TO UNDERSTANDING THE SCRIPTURES. Christ has also given us this counsel: "It is the spirit that quickeneth; the flesh profiteth nothing: the words that I speak unto you, they are spirit, and *they are life.*"[11]

Then again he said this: "*I am the light of the world: he that followeth me shall not walk in darkness, but shall have the light of life.*"[12]

And that is the burden of these scriptures. That is the testimony of the disciples of the Lord. John, in writing to the saints, declares in his first epistle:

"*And hereby we do know that we know him, if we keep his commandments.* He that saith, I know him, and keepeth not his commandments, is a liar, and the truth is not in him. But whoso keepeth his word, in him verily is the love of God perfected: hereby know we that we are in him."[13]

Now these passages of scripture, I say, form a *key* by which the mysteries of eternal life are unlocked. There is no need for any man being in darkness or declaring that he has no evidence of life after death, and that no one has ever returned.

Instead of being the statement of someone wise and learned, such statement as that is a statement of *ignorance*. *We may all know the truth; we are not helpless.* The Lord has made it possible for every man to know

---
[10]Matt. 27:52-53.
[11]John 6:63.
[12]John 8:12.
[13]1 John 2:3-5.

the truth by the observance of these laws, and through the guidance of his Holy Spirit—who is sent purposely to teach us when we comply with the law, so that we may know that truth which makes us free. So this is the *best way* in which to learn the truth of immortality and the resurrection of the dead.[14]

MYSTERIES OF GOD KNOWN ONLY THROUGH SPIRIT. There are in the gospel such things as mysteries. A mystery is, of course, some truth which is not understood. All the principles of the gospel and all truth pertaining to the salvation of men are simple when understood. Until it is understood, however, a simple truth may be a great mystery.

Gospel truths appeal more to the spirit, that is, they are spiritually discerned. A man may know a thing to be true by the teaching of the Spirit, but he may not be able to explain it to others. This may not be in keeping with modern worldly teaching, but it is true nevertheless. Revelations through the Spirit of the Lord, many times, cannot be explained.

"And no tongue can speak, neither can there be written by any man, neither can the hearts of men conceive so great and marvelous things as we both saw and heard Jesus speak; and no one can conceive of the joy which filled our souls at the time we heard him pray for us unto the Father."[15]

HIDDEN MYSTERIES KNOWN TO FAITHFUL. *The best educated man in the world may not be able to comprehend the simple truths of the gospel because his soul is not in tune; he has not been enlightened by the Spirit of the Lord.* He, therefore, fails to *see* and *feel* the significance of these principles. They cannot be seen except through the *touch of the Holy Ghost*. For this reason Alma explained to Zeezrom how gospel light may be known. Said he:

---
[14]*Church News,* June 3, 1933, p. 5; [15]3 Ne. 17:17.
John 14:26; 15:26-27; 16:13-14.

"It is given unto many to know the mysteries of God; nevertheless they are laid under a strict command that they shall not impart only according to the portion of his word which he doth grant unto the children of men, according to the heed and diligence which they give unto him.

"And therefore, he that will harden his heart, the same receiveth the lesser portion of the word; and *he that will not harden his heart, to him is given the greater portion of the word, until it is given unto him to know the mysteries of God until he know them in full.*

"And they that will harden their hearts, to them is given the lesser portion of the word until they know nothing concerning his mysteries; and then they are taken captive by the devil, and led by his will down to destruction. Now this is what is meant by the chains of hell."[16]

The Lord promised the saints that he would reveal to them the mysteries of his kingdom on certain conditions, as we read in the *Doctrine and Covenants,* section 76:1-10. *These truths cannot be understood except by obedience to the law of the gospel on which the reception of this knowledge is based.* It was for the same reason the Lord told Nicodemus, "Except a man be *born again,* he cannot *see* the kingdom of God."[17]

SPIRIT LEADS TO A FULNESS OF TRUTH. *To understand spiritual things, a man must have spiritual discernment, that is, guidance by the Holy Ghost.* For this reason we are confirmed and receive the gift of the Holy Ghost.

The Lord expects us to use our faculties and has given us *reason as a measuring rod to measure truth under certain conditions.* Primarily in the search after gospel truth, there must be the teaching of the Spirit— *Spirit speaking to spirit—*and this comes only through obedience to gospel law.

The man who will not "do his will" may search

---
[16]Alma 12:9-11.   [17]John 3:3.

forever, *but in vain;* but cannot find it! It is not to be found in psychology, in biology, or sociology, no matter what *other* truth may be found therein. When we hearken to the Spirit who guides into all truth, we will see that the truth revealed is reasonable and consistent with all other truth.

Only by the aid of the Holy Ghost, and through obedience to the principles of the gospel, will a man eventually attain to the knowledge of all truth. In other words, those who will not make their lives conform in every particular to the Divine Life; who will not adjust their lives through faith and repentance and obedience to all divine law, will *never* be in a position to comprehend truth in its fulness. Therefore, *only in the celestial kingdom will the fulness of the truth be attained.*[18]

All who will not place their lives "at-one" with the Father and the Son cannot comprehend the things of God. They are foolishness unto them.[19] For this reason so many of the learned men in the world fail to comprehend the gospel and teach theories and philosophies at variance with revealed truth which they cannot understand. We are in that day when the people are "ever learning, and never able to come to the knowledge of the truth."[20]

TRUTH: NEW AND EVERLASTING. If we love the truth, we never get tired of hearing it. *No matter how many times we hear the truth expressed, if we love it, it is always new.*[21]

The truth endures forever. It is always new. It grows brighter with use. We love it the more we come in contact with it, *which is not the case with falsehood.*[22]

Every institution of learning, no matter where it is or what it is, should be teaching eternal truth, and whatever is taught that does not conform to truth must eventually perish. Further, that which we learn in all the

[18]D. & C. 50:23-28; 93:26-28.
[19]1 Cor. 1:17-31; 2:1-16.
[20]Pers. Corresp.; 2 Tim. 3:7.
[21]*Church News*, May 31, 1947, p. 1.
[22]Conf. Rep., Oct., 1924, p. 99.

experiences of life, should be with the ultimate aim of eternity in view. . . .

The man who is guided by the Holy Spirit and who keeps the commandments of God, who abides in God, will have the clearest understanding and the better judgment always, because he is directed by the Spirit of truth. And the man who relies upon himself, or the knowledge of other men, will not have as clear a vision as will the man who abides in the truth and is directed by the Holy Spirit.

FULNESS OF TRUTH GAINED ONLY THROUGH THE CHURCH. A man cannot receive the fulness of truth except in the kingdom of God, in other words, if you please, the Church of Jesus Christ of Latter-day Saints. *No man*—no matter how great his education, no matter how much he studies in the things of the world, no matter what he does in the eternities to come—*will ever reach the goal of perfection in truth or the fulness of light and understanding outside of the kingdom of God.* And when I say the kingdom of God, I have reference to the celestial kingdom.

Let me read this verse: "And no man receiveth a fulness unless he keepeth his commandments. He that keepeth his commandments receiveth truth and light, until he is glorified in truth and knoweth all things."[23] And that is the promise that is made to us as members of the Church if we will walk in the light of the Spirit of truth, or the Comforter, and in the fulness of the gospel of Jesus Christ, keeping the commandments of God.

You can not get a fulness anywhere else. Men may search; they may study; they may learn, of course, a great many things; they may lay up a great fund of information; but they will never be able to come to the fulness of truth and the brightness spoken of in this revelation unless they are guided by the Spirit of truth, the Holy Ghost, and keep the commandments of God.

[23]D. & C. 93:27-28.

MORE TRUTH TO LEARN IN THE RESURRECTION. The man who seeks God and is guided by the Spirit of truth, or the Comforter, and continues in God, will grow in knowledge, in light, in truth, until eventually there will come to him the perfect day of light and truth. Now, *we will not get all that in this life.* It is impossible for a man to reach that goal in the few years of mortal existence. But what we learn here, that which is eternal, that which is inspired by the Spirit of truth, will continue with us beyond the grave, and then we shall go on, if still continuing in God, to receive light and truth until eventually we shall come to that perfect day.[24]

PLACE OF REASON IN THE SEARCH FOR TRUTH. *Reason is all right when intelligently used.* There is not a principle of the gospel that will not appeal to the reason of man, for every principle of the gospel of Jesus Christ is reasonable, clear and easily understood with the aid of the Spirit of truth. But *man cannot determine, upon the strength of his own reason, unaided by the Spirit of God, the power and saving grace of the gospel principles and expect to find out God.* He cannot do it![25]

While the principles of the gospel are reasonable and we can employ reason in the discussion of them all, and while all truth is in perfect accord with all other truth—whether it is taught in philosophy, biology, or sociology, or in any other branch of science—yet we must understand that *we must walk by faith as well as by sight in the discovery of truth.* This is true in any field of research. There is no scientific study where those engaged do not walk by faith. Moreover, in all our consideration of the principles of the gospel and the salvation of men, we must not lose sight of the fact that *the things of God are known only by the aid of the Spirit of God, and cannot be discerned by the spirit of man.*[26]

One can learn more and get nearer to the truth by heeding the testimony of the servants of the Lord and

---

[24]*Church News*, Mar. 30, 1940, pp. 1, 4-5; D. & C. 50:23-28.
[25]Conf. Rep., Apr., 1916, p. 71.
[26]Pers. Corresp.; 1 Cor. 2:1-16.

hearkening to the teachings of the Spirit of the Lord, than one can possibly do by following the commandments and the teachings of men who have received their understanding and their learning in the spirit and in the wisdom of man.[27]

TRY THE SPIRITS. We are to try the spirits. We should prove them to know from what *source* they come.

How are we going to prove the spirits and understand which are right and which are wrong unless we ourselves are walking in the light? Unless we have been studying and pondering over the principles of the gospel, we may be deceived. If we have not had in our hearts the spirit of prayer, of faith, of humility, and have been obedient to our Eternal Father, then how are we going to distinguish between these spirits and discover what comes from God and what comes from man or from some evil source? . . .

There is no need for men to shut their eyes and feel that there is no light, only as they may depend upon their reason, for the Lord has always been willing to lead and direct and show the way. He has sent messengers from his presence. He has sent revelation. He has commanded that his word be written, that it be published, so that all the people might know it.[28]

SEARCH THE SCRIPTURES

KNOWLEDGE OF GOSPEL PRECEDES OBEDIENCE. *There is not anything in this world of as great importance to us as obedience to the gospel of Jesus Christ.* Let us search these scriptures. Let us know what the Lord has revealed. Let us put our lives in harmony with his truth. Then we will not be deceived, but we will have power to resist evil and temptation. Our minds will be quickened and we will be able to comprehend truth and segregate it from error. The man who can not segregate

---

[27]Conf. Rep., Oct., 1917, p. 69.   [28]Conf. Rep., Oct., 1931, p. 15; 1 John 4:1; 1 Tim. 4:1.

truth from error, is the man who has not kept himself in harmony with the Spirit of God.[29]

It is a requirement that is made of us, as members of this Church, to make ourselves familiar with that which the Lord has revealed, that we may not be led astray, for the Lord has said there are many spirits abroad in the land. Some of them are the spirits of men. Some are the spirits of devils; but he has given unto us his Spirit, if we will receive it, and that Spirit leads and directs in all truth. *How are we going to walk in the truth if we do not know it?*[30]

STUDY ALL THAT HAS BEEN REVEALED. We declare, "We believe all that God has revealed, all that He does now reveal, and we believe that He will yet reveal many great and important things pertaining to the Kingdom of God."[31] This being true, it becomes necessary for us to understand all that he has revealed, and that which he is now revealing; otherwise we are not in touch with his work and cannot know his will concerning us, for we do not comprehend it.

There is no valid excuse on the part of any member of the Church for a display of ignorance of the fundamental principles of the gospel as they are now revealed and published for the benefit of the world, for our attention has been forcibly called to them, and we have been commanded to make ourselves familiar with them *by study* and also *by faith*. They are accessible and within the reach of all.

It is a thing most desirable, in order to bring to pass the exaltation of the saints, that all the members of Church should become acquainted, intelligently, with *all* that the Lord has revealed through his servants the prophets. By so doing we may become acquainted with his will and understand the reason for each of the commandments he has given, and learn to be obedient to the

---
[29]*Church News*, May 6, 1939, p. 8; John 5:39; *D. & C.* 1:37.　[30]Conf. Rep., Oct., 1934, p. 65.　[31]Ninth Article of Faith.

laws and ordinances which have been prepared for our salvation.

IMPOSSIBLE TO BE SAVED IN IGNORANCE. *The Lord hates inexcusable ignorance concerning the life-giving principles of the gospel,* which, from time to time, since the beginning, he has declared to a perverse people through his chosen prophets, that all who would repent and receive the truth might be instructed in all things which are essential to their education in heavenly things.

The Lord is greatly pleased with his children when they devote their time and energies in study and reflection, with the desire to gain a perfect knowledge of these great principles and commandments, for without a knowledge of them, and obedience to them, we cannot be saved.

The promise has been made to all those who will receive the light of truth and through their research and obedience endeavor to acquaint themselves with the gospel, that they shall receive line upon line, precept by precept, here a little and there a little, until the fulness of truth shall be their portion; even the hidden mysteries of the kingdom shall be made known unto them; "For every one that asketh receiveth; and he that seeketh findeth; and to him that knocketh it shall be opened."[32] All these are heirs of salvation, and they shall be crowned with glory, immortality, and eternal life, as sons and daughters of God, with an exaltation in his celestial kingdom.

WHY PAUL EXHORTED SAINTS TO STUDY SCRIPTURES. "For whatsoever things were written aforetime were written for our learning, that we through patience and comfort of the scriptures might have hope."[33] Thus the Apostle Paul wrote in his epistle to the saints of Rome in reference to the inspired writings of the ancient prophets.

Again, to Timothy he wrote: "All scripture is given

---
[32]Matt. 7:8; *D. & C.* 76:1-10; 98:11-15; 121:26-32; 128:21; Isa. 28:9-13.   [33]Rom. 15:4.

by inspiration of God, and is profitable for doctrine, for reproof, for correction, for instruction in righteousness."[34]

For these reasons he advocated that the saints of his day should study the prophetic writings of the servants of the Lord that they might increase their knowledge of the sacred scriptures and grow in grace before the Lord, in the understanding of the doctrines of the Church, and thereby receive comfort in the hope of eternal salvation. . . .

DIFFICULTIES OF STUDY IN PRIMITIVE CHURCH. In that day when Paul wrote to Timothy and the Roman saints, copies of the *Bible* were not to be had, for the books which compose our holy scriptures had not been compiled. Neither could they all be found in the archives of each of the churches. Fortunate, indeed, were the members of any branch of the Church, in that day, who possessed a full set of the books of Moses, the writings of the ancient prophets, and a very limited sprinkling of the epistles of the apostles. The four gospels had not been written, and the saints depended almost solely upon the testimony of the living witnesses for the teachings of the Son of God.

Such books as they had were written by hand on parchment and in the form of a scroll. These were usually kept and guarded very sacredly by the learned scribes or priests, who confined such writings with jealous care within the sacred precincts of the synagogues, where they were not exhibited to the public gaze of the common people, or subject to their profane touch.

GOSPEL SCHOLARS AMONG PRIMITIVE SAINTS. The art of printing was unknown in that day, and the writing of the sacred books required a great deal of patience, time, and skill, in order that they might be produced even for use in the synagogues, or meeting places of the people. Therefore, the study of the scriptures—such as they were

---
[34] 2 Tim. 3:16.

fortunate enough to have—by the people at large, in that day, was a privilege that was great indeed.

The art of reading and writing was not then universal, but was confined almost exclusively to the class of scribes who copied the sacred writings, and were considered also to be the interpreters of the sacred word, and to the priests and teachers who were trained to be instructors of the people.

Yet, with their limited opportunities, the saints were commanded by the apostles of old, and even by the Lord our Redeemer himself, to make themselves familiar with the writings of all the prophets; and, with the great handicap under which they labored, many of the primitive saints became exceedingly skilled in the knowledge of the gospel of the Lord and zealous advocates of the written word.[35]

How to Treasure Up Word of Lord. It would be well if we would follow the counsel the Lord has given us, which is: "And whoso treasureth up my word, shall not be deceived."[36] Treasuring up his word is far *more than merely reading it. To treasure it one must not only read and study, but seek in humility and obedience to do the commandments given, and gain the inspiration which the Holy Spirit will impart.*[37]

Leave the "Mysteries" Alone. *We should keep our feet on the ground and not get off in the realm of the mysterious, the speculative, the things which the Lord has not yet made plain.* There are so many important matters pertaining to our duties and salvation which are clearly and positively revealed; it is with these that we should spend our time and to which we should give our thoughtful study.

The discussion of mysteries and doctrines only partly revealed can await the coming of the Lord, for then "he shall reveal all things—Things which have passed, and

---
[35]*Young Women's Journal*, pp. 591-592.
[36]Joseph Smith 1:37.
[37]*Era*, vol. 45, p. 780.

hidden things which no man knew, things of the earth, by which it was made, and the purpose and the end thereof."[38]

The fundamental prinicples of the gospel—all that has to do with the salvation of man—are very clear and can be understood by those with ordinary intelligence. To spend time discussing useless questions which have no bearing on our salvation, and have no relationship to the commandments and obligations required of us by the plan of salvation, is just a useless pastime.

Whether we are right or wrong in the field of the mysteries, will make no difference so far as our individual acts are concerned, and will neither exalt nor damn us, providing we do not make a fetish of our notions or get off on a tangent and destroy ourselves.

GOSPEL ANSWERS WILL NOT SATISFY ALL. I realize that it is impossible to satisfy every soul in regard to many questions. The Savior failed to satisfy all who heard his teachings. To many he was inconsistent: he was the friend of publicans and sinners; he was a winebibber, he healed the sick by the spirit of Beelzebub; some of his habits, for instance, nonconformity with Jewish ceremonial washing before eating, were condemned.

If we will seek the Spirit of the Lord for guidance in humility, with "a broken heart and a contrite spirit,"[39] we will not find many difficulties that we cannot surmount, the *apparent inharmonies will vanish away*, and we will be able to see the wisdom of the Almighty in all that he has revealed.[40]

---
[38]D. & C. 101:32-33.　　　　[40]Pers. Corresp.
[39]D. & C. 59:8.

CHAPTER 18

TEACHING THE GOSPEL

RAISING THE WARNING VOICE

OUR TWO GREAT RESPONSIBILITIES. The Church has two great responsibilities, that is the members of the Church have these responsibilities. . . . *It is our individual duty to preach the gospel* by precept and by example among our neighbors. In section 88 of the *Doctrine and Covenants* we are informed that even those who are warned are under the obligation to receive the message and also to warn their neighbors.[1]

The people who are living are entitled to hear the message, so this responsibility to teach the world is an outstanding one. We cannot get away from this obligation. The Lord declared that his coming is nigh at hand and that he would cut short his work in righteousness. It is our duty, then, to do all we can, and the Lord will bring to our aid other forces besides our missionaries that his work may advance and his words be fulfilled.[2]

I speak of this responsibility at this time for fear there may be some who think the work they are doing is the great work of this dispensation. The people engaged in the Relief Society, the Sunday School, and the Mutual work, feel that they have great responsibilities, and they have, but their work does not overshadow this great duty of preaching the gospel to the world.

The other great responsibility which is placed upon each of us individually is to *seek after our dead.*[3]

PREACH TO A WICKED WORLD. Now there are many debts which we owe to the Lord. There is the

[1]*D. & C.* 88:81.
[2]*D. & C.* 84:97-98; 109:59.
[3]*Gen. & Hist. Mag.*, vol. 22, pp. 109-110.

debt of preaching this gospel to a wicked and a perverse generation, and those are the words of the Lord, so do not accuse me of calling the world wicked.[4] It is. I can testify to that from what I have seen of it, and I have seen of the wickedness but a small part, I assure you.

But the world today is filthy, drunken, saturated and stinking with tobacco. The world is full of immorality. It is a fallen world. It has been a fallen world since Adam was driven from the Garden of Eden, and yet we are in it, and the Lord has given us the mission of assisting him, of being his agents in this world, to regenerate it, as far as it is possible to bring to pass that regeneration. It will never be fully accomplished, so far as we are concerned. We are not going, by our preaching, to save very many souls.[5]

The Lord has given unto men their agency. They may act for themselves, they can choose to do good, or they can choose to do evil.[6] The Lord said that men love darkness rather than light because their deeds are evil.[7] Yet our mission, I say, is, so far as it is within our power, to regenerate, to bring to repentance, just as many of the children of our Father in heaven as it is possible for us to do. That is one of our debts; that is an obligation the Lord has placed upon the Church, and more particularly upon the quorums of the priesthood of the Church, and yet this obligation belongs to every soul.

It is the duty of every member of this Church to preach the gospel by precept and by example.[8]

OUR MESSAGE TO WORLD. *We are witnesses of the truth. It is the mission of every man holding the priesthood in this Church to preach Christ and him crucified.* That is our message to the world; and the message is sorely needed in the face of these false doctrines taught by the power of men. When men are turning from the

---
[4]*D. & C.* 33:2; 36:6; 88:75; 121:23.
[5]Matt. 7:13-14; 1 Ne. 14:12.
[6]*D. & C.* 29:39; Moses 6:33; 2. Ne. 2:27.
[7]John 3:19.
[8]Conf. Rep., Apr., 1944, pp. 50-51.

Lord and seeking to find everlasting truth without his aid, our mission becomes all the more urgent in calling men to repentance and to a belief in the redemption brought to pass through the atonement of the Son of God, whose blood was shed for the sins of the world. . . .

It is our message and our mission to the world to preach this truth, and to establish faith in the hearts of the people, and endeavor to get them to believe in Jesus Christ as their Redeemer and as the Son of God.[9]

Men love darkness today rather than light, just as they did in the days of the Redeemer. They are blinded against truth and righteousness; they see it not. Our mission is to proclaim it.[10]

WARNING THE WICKED. We all know that the world is in distress because of wickedness. People in every land reject the gospel, and the judgments of the Lord have been poured out upon them. These judgments are continuing and will continue if the people will not repent. The Lord has said that he will come to set things in order when the cup of iniquity is full. The missionaries of the Church have been sent out to *warn* the people and *to gather* out of the nations and out of our own land all who are willing to repent and receive the gospel. They are also commanded to warn others that they might escape the calamities and the judgments which are bound to continue if people will not receive the gospel.[11]

When we see evil lurking, when we see dangers confronting the people, and especially the Latter-day Saints, it is *our duty to raise the warning voice,* and not only in behalf of the Latter-day Saints, but to warn all people, for our mission is one that is world-wide, and we should warn all men and give them the opportunity of repentance, of serving the Lord and keeping his commandments if they will. If they will not, yet we have

---

[9]Conf. Rep., Apr., 1924, pp. 42-43.
[10]*Millennial Star,* vol. 96, p. 353; John 3:19.
[11]Pers. Corresp.; *D. & C.* 1:1-16; 43:15-28; 84:61-98; 88:77-91.

saved our souls. We are clear from the blood of this generation. That is our duty.[12]

DUTIES OF WATCHMEN ON TOWERS. We are watchmen on the towers of Zion. The Lord has placed in our hands great and wonderful responsibilities. No men anywhere in all the earth, no matter what their calling, hold responsibility equal to that which we have received, for we have had conferred upon us the priesthood of God. We are possessed of divine authority and have been set apart as his servants and watchmen upon the towers of Zion.

Our duty is to teach, to guide and direct the members of the Church in the path of righteousness. Our duty is to set examples before the world, that they seeing our good works may glorify our Father in heaven, and have faith and confidence in us. It is our duty to warn all men and endeavor to teach them the truth, so that *those who will not hearken may be left without excuse.*[13]

GIVE HEED TO WARNING OF CHURCH AUTHORITIES. *It is the duty of the authorities of the Church to speak by inspiration and revelation.* If the membership, or any part thereof, should fail to heed the warning or accept the counsel, the instruction which these men in authority give—and especially the one who holds the keys of authority—still it is the duty of these men to give that instruction, even though they may feel it will not be followed. And then the responsibility rests upon the shoulders of those who hear it, and if they refuse to receive it the sin is upon their own heads, and they will have to answer for it.

The Lord said: "Whether [it be] by mine own voice or by the voice of my servants, it is the same."[14] I read this in the preface to this wonderful book President Rudger Clawson has been telling us about:

"The arm of the Lord shall be revealed; and the day cometh that *they who will not hear the voice of the Lord,*

---
[12]Conf. Rep., Oct., 1933, p. 61; Ezek. 3:17-21. [13]Conf. Rep., Oct., 1929, p. 60 [14]*D. & C.* 1:38.

neither the voice of his servants, neither give heed to the words of the prophets and apostles, shall be cut off from among the people."[15]

Those members of this Church who criticize and say we hear too much of this or that, and *thus* confess their sins, should take heed and repent, for if they refuse to accept the counsels that are given, then the responsibility of that disobedience is theirs, and they will have to answer for it.[16]

PREPARE TO DEFEND TRUTH. We must be prepared to defend the truth, and as men holding the holy priesthood which was restored by the opening of the heavens and the laying on of hands by holy messengers sent from the presence of the Lord, be prepared to protect the members of the Church against the cunning devices that are being employed in opposition to the gospel, to wean away our members who are not sufficiently informed and who lack the abiding testimony which faithfulness and obedience will ensure to every soul.

War, quietly, insidiously, and with some fear because of the spread of the truth, is being waged against the restoration of divine truth.[17]

TEACHING IN THE CHURCH

QUALIFICATIONS FOR CHURCH TEACHERS. The matter of teaching is one of the greatest importance. We cannot estimate its value when it is properly done; neither do we know the extent of the evil that may result if it is improperly done. Whether in the Church schools, the seminaries, auxiliary organizations, or in the priesthood quorums, *the greatest qualification required of a teacher is that he have faith in the principles of the gospel;* that he believe in the principles of revealed truth as they have come through inspired prophets in our own day as well as in times of old; and that he shall exercise his privilege as a teacher in the spirit of prayer and faith.

---
[15]D. & C. 1:14.
[16]Conf. Rep., Oct., 1937, p. 114.
[17]Preface, vol. 2, *The Divine Church* by James L. Barker.

I am in full accord with the commandment as it is written in this revelation.[18] *Unless a man does have a knowledge of the truth, has faith in the word of the Lord and his power, and is guided by the Spirit of the Lord, he should not teach.* We are commanded "to give diligent heed to the words of eternal life." For we "shall live by every word that proceedeth forth from the mouth of God. For the word of the Lord is truth, and whatsoever is truth is light, and whatsoever is light is Spirit, even the Spirit of Jesus Christ."[19]

FAITH OF MORE WORTH THAN EDUCATION FOR TEACHERS. In this day of wonderful educational privileges and opportunities for the gaining of knowledge, as the world understands it, we may feel that the greatest thing required of a teacher is that he possess a liberal education. It is very essential that men with the responsibility that teaching brings be educated; that they have knowledge in a general way; but *it matters not what a man's training or what his schooling may be—how many degrees he holds—if he has not faith in the gospel of Jesus Christ and has no testimony received from the Spirit of the Lord of the divine truth which has been revealed, he is not qualified to teach in any organization within the Church.*

Sometimes those who are serving as bishops and presidents of stakes, and in other leading positions, I fear, may overlook this fact, and in the choosing of teachers in classes, as teacher trainers, or wherever it may be, think of the man's educational qualifications as they would be looked upon in the world and forget *the spiritual and doctrinal qualifications which are more essential.*

A teacher should not be called primarily because of his schooling, or educational attainments, without taking into consideration his humility, his faith and his integrity to the cause of truth which he is supposed to

---
[18]D. & C. 42:13-14; 50:13-22. [19]D. & C. 84:43-45.

represent. This training does not come through the study of science, art or literature, but through prayer and faith and the promptings of the Spirit of the Lord. It cannot be stated too forcefully that the man or the woman without faith in the gospel as it has been revealed in the day in which we live should not teach. The Lord has made it very emphatic.

WORTH OF SOULS ALREADY IN THE CHURCH. This is a very important age in which we live, and our message and our authority in the world are the most important things in the world. The souls of members of the Church are just as precious in the sight of the Lord as are the souls of the people in the world unto whom our missionaries go with the plan of salvation. In fact, if a choice is to be made, a soul already in the Church—one who is in the covenant—is just a little dearer to the Father, if possible, than is one who is on the outside. Of course, the Lord is no respecter of persons, and all souls are precious in his sight, but *he no doubt loves those who obey his voice and who are willing to walk in his truth, more than he does those who fail to do so.*

We should spend our time and give diligent attention to the training of members of the Church. Teachers who are filled with the spirit of the Lord and who are tried and true, should be called to act in this capacity, and those who are not so tried and proved, should not be called to instruct the members.

What do we accomplish if we spend our time and means preaching in the world to make converts to the gospel, if we place instructors before the youth in the stakes and wards who destroy the faith in the hearts of the young people in the divine message intrusted to our care?[20]

AWFUL SIN OF LEADING SOULS AWAY FROM TRUTH. How careful our instructors in our schools, institutes, seminaries, priesthood classes and auxiliaries should be

---
[20]Conf. Rep., Apr., 1928, pp. 64-66.

to guard the revealed truth from heaven! How fearful we should be lest we teach that which is false and thereby lead souls astray, in paths that lead to death and away from the exaltation in the kingdom of God. *"And the Spirit shall be given unto you by the prayer of faith; and if ye receive not the Spirit ye shall not teach,"* the Lord has said.[21] *There is no greater crime in all the world than to teach false doctrines and lead the unsuspecting astray, away from the eternal truths of the gospel.*[22]

We are all going to be judged according to our works, every soul. I have often thought of my place and responsibility in this Church. What a dreadful thing it would be to be going forth to teach, to lead men, to guide them into something that was not true. *I think the greatest crime in all this world is to lead men and women, the children of God, away from the true principles.* We see in the world today philosophies of various kinds, tending to destroy faith, faith in God, faith in the principles of the gospel. What a dreadful thing that is.

The Lord says if we labor all our days and save but one soul, how great will be our joy with him; on the other hand *how great will be our sorrow and our condemnation if through our acts we have led one soul away from this truth.*[23]

He who blinds one soul, he who spreads error, he who destroys, through his teachings, divine truth, truth that would lead a man to the kingdom of God and to its fulness, how great shall be his condemnation and his punishment in eternity. For *the destruction of a soul is the destruction of the greatest thing that has ever been created.*[24]

SAINTS THIRST FOR GOSPEL KNOWLEDGE. My experience has taught me that the people of the Church are hungry for gospel themes. I think they have been "fed up" on philosophy and ethical ideas, and they are

---

[21]D. & C. 42:14.
[22]*Church News*, June 12, 1949, pp. 21-22.
[23]Conf. Rep., Apr., 1951, p. 153; D. & C. 18:10-16; 2 Ne. 28:15.
[24]*Church News*, Mar. 30, 1940, p. 4.

crying for the fundamental things of the gospel of Jesus Christ.[25]

Throughout the length of the land the cry has been raised that churches are empty; pulpits are being deserted; houses of worship are for sale, or being transformed into buildings for other purposes. Ministers who profess to be Christians stand before their congregations without a blush and confess that they have no faith in the divine mission of Jesus Christ. They accept him merely as a great moral and ethical teacher, but not as the Only Begotten Son of God.

APOSTASY COMES WHEN TRUTH NOT TAUGHT. Modern education declares that there never was such a thing as the fall of man, but that conditions have always gone on in the same way as now in this mortal world. Here, say they, death and mutation have always held sway as natural conditions on this earth and everywhere throughout the universe the same laws obtain. It is declared that man has made his ascent to the exalted place he now occupies through countless ages of development which has gradually distinguished him from lower forms of life.

Such a doctrine of necessity discards the story of Adam and the Garden of Eden, which it looks upon as a myth coming down to us from an early age of foolish ignorance and superstition. Moreover, it is taught that since death was always here, and a natural condition prevailing throughout all space, there could not possibly come a redemption from Adam's transgression, hence there was no need for a Savior for a fallen world.

Is it any wonder, *under such circumstances*, that churches are deserted; that more than half of the population of this country has become indifferent, if not antagonistic, to religion? This, also, is just as true of other lands.

We cannot take the attitude which destroys faith

---
[25]*Church News*, Apr. 1, 1939, p. 1.

in God and which casts a doubt upon his work, and then receive the beneficent guidance of his Spirit. From the attendance at places of worship the people have transferred their allegiance to places of amusement, and all men know that much that is received in these places is of a most unwholesome if not unsavory character.[26]

TEACHING OUR CHILDREN

PARENTS TO TEACH CHILDREN. *Parents will be responsible for the actions of their children, if they have failed to teach their children by example and by precept.*

If parents have done all in their power to teach their children correctly by example and precept and the children then go astray, the parents will not be held responsible and the sin will be upon the children.[27]

The Father has never relinquished his claim upon the children born into this world. They are still his children. He has placed them in the care of mortal parents with the admonition that they be brought up in light and truth.[28] The primary responsibility, and fundamentally so, is upon the parents to teach their children in light and truth.

CHURCH TO TEACH CHILDREN. This commandment does not preclude or deny the Church the privilege of taking the children and aiding in their training. For this reason we have in the Church the auxiliary organizations given by inspiration and commandment of the Lord. Chief among these organizations for teaching children is the Deseret Sunday School Union, which has accomplished a wonderful work in the past in training the members of the Church. Parents should avail themselves of the services of this great organization in the training of their children.

There are two vital things in this training of the children in the Church: first, to see that nothing but the

---
[26]*Era,* vol. 40, p. 310.   [28]*D. & C.* 93:40-50.
[27]Pers. Corresp.; *D. & C.* 68:25-28.

fundamental and established doctrines are incorporated in the lessons; second, that only those who are filled with the Spirit of the Lord and who have a testimony of the truth are called to teach the classes.[29]

Our great Mutual organization has adopted as a motto, "The Glory of God is Intelligence," and sometimes I have regretted that they stopped there. We have been teaching the people everywhere that the glory of God is intelligence, stopping our quotation in the middle of a sentence, and perhaps getting some misunderstanding out of it. But the Lord continues and says "or in other words light and truth." So, if we bring up our children in light and truth they will not be so much troubled with that evil one, because light and truth forsake him, and he has no place with light and truth.[30]

TEACH BY PRECEPT AND EXAMPLE IN THE HOME. There should be prayer and faith and love and obedience to God in the home. It is the duty of parents to teach their children the saving principles of the gospel of Jesus Christ, so that they will know why they are to be baptized and that they may be impressed in their hearts with a desire to continue to keep the commandments of God after they are baptized, that they may come back into his presence.

Do you, my good brethren and sisters, want your families, your children? Do you want to be sealed to your fathers and your mothers before you? *Do you want to have this family unit perfect when you, if you are permitted, shall enter the celestial kingdom of God?* If so, then you must begin by teaching at the cradle-side. You are to teach by example as well as precept. You are to kneel with your children in prayer. You are to teach them in all humility of the mission of our Savior, Jesus Christ. You have to show them the way, and the father who shows his son the way will not say to him:

---

[29]*Instructor*, vol. 84, pp. 206-207.   [30]*Rel. Soc. Mag.*, vol. 18, pp. 683-684; D. & C. 93:36-39.

"Son, go to Sunday School, or go to Mutual, or go to the priesthood meeting," but he will say: "Come and go with me." He will teach by example.

DOCTRINES SHOULD BE TAUGHT IN HOME. Family prayer will be in the home. In the morning when the family arises for the day, the father will gather his family, kneel in prayer, and thank the Lord for his blessings. At night he will have them assemble again, and in the family unit they will kneel again to pray. And all these things will be taught in the home, because we want to have the home intact. We do not want it destroyed when we cross to the other side. . . .

Are you teaching your children these truths, my brothers, my sisters? Are you training them so that when they are married, they will want to go to the house of the Lord? Are you teaching them so that they will want to receive the great endowment which the Lord has in store for them? Have you impressed upon them the fact that they can be sealed as husbands and wives and have bestowed upon them every gift and every blessing that pertains to the celestial kingdom, and thus they shall become the sons and the daughters of God, and have you impressed upon them that great truth that if they are not married for time and eternity that they will come forth in the resurrection of the dead separately and singly, to be servants for those who belong to the family of God. Have you done that? Are you doing that?[31]

PREPARE WAY FOR WARD TEACHERS. There is much that we can do individually as members of the Church, without the necessity of being taught by our instructors. The Lord expects it of us. It ought not to be necessary for the teachers to come into my home to teach me the law of tithing. It should not be necessary for them to come to me and my family and teach us the word of wisdom. It should not be necessary for them to call upon us to teach us the necessity of prayer, or of

---
[31]Conf. Rep., Oct., 1948, pp. 153-154.

fasting, or any other of these simple and fundamental principles of the gospel.

We ought to know enough from what we have constantly been taught and the knowledge we have from our natural understanding of the scriptures as we are guided by the Spirit of the Lord, to do these things without being taught or commanded more than to follow the general commandment as it is written in the scriptures.

While it is necessary, of course, that the teachers visit in the homes of the people, to see that there is no iniquity in the Church, no backbiting, fault finding, no envy, no strife, and that all the members do their duty,[32] yet I say we should so live that when they come to us to teach us, we can tell them with a clear conscience that we are performing these labors and accepting these principles with an eye single to the glory of God. I feel this to be our duty as members in the Church.

WE SHOULD TEACH OURSELVES. It should not be necessary that we be continually taught and admonished in these simple truths in the gospel of Jesus Christ. We ought so to prepare ourselves through study and through faith, through observance of the law of the gospel, through attendance at meetings and the magnifying of our callings generally, to know what the Lord expects at our hands without the necessity of someone telling us.

The Lord has promised that *the time shall come when every man shall be his own teacher, that is, he will know because of righteous living what to do.*[33] He will be so filled with the Spirit of the Lord that he will be guided and directed in doing right without the necessity of someone coming into his home to set it in order. Now is a good time for us to begin.

Let every man set his house in order, and see that his family is taught the principles of the gospel of Jesus Christ; that they abstain from the use of strong drink, from the use of tea, from the use of coffee, tobacco and

---
[32]*D. & C.* 20:46-59.   [33]Jer. 31:31-34.

320   DOCTRINES OF SALVATION

other stimulants and narcotics which tend to destroy and to break down rather than to build up the system. Let them teach in their homes faith in God—for we all know it is necessary that faith should be taught among the people.³⁴

TESTING TRUTH OF ALL TEACHINGS

FAULT OF PRESENT DAY EDUCATION. *The education of the present day is very largely knowledge without the accompanying intelligence, or light and truth. It is bound to be so, and much of the knowledge will be mixed with error, where faith in God and in his revelations is eliminated, and only the cold and many times barren conclusions of mind and reason are the guide. Such learning leads to spiritual death, not to spiritual life.*³⁵

I regret exceedingly that courses in study in the public schools, in the colleges and places of learning throughout the land, are in conflict with fundamental truths of the Christian faith; and, for one, I desire to express my feelings, and to declare that I consider it an outrage against the liberties of the people, when we are denied the privilege of teaching principles of eternal truth in the realm of religion; when we are denied the privilege of praying to our Heavenly Father in the schools, or referring to the Supreme Being for fear that we will offend someone; and at the same time instructors are permitted to advocate that, in the schools, which the teachers themselves profess and declare to be in conflict with the fundamentals of the faith which I believe, and which thousands of others accept throughout this nation and other nations of the world as divine truth.³⁶

MODERN SCIENTIFIC FICTION. The world is full of philosophy. One prominent and intelligent writer has called these theories "scientific fiction." I think he is right. We have the theories of evolution, of higher criticism, the ideas that prevail in the schools throughout our

---
³⁴Conf. Rep., Apr., 1914, pp. 91-92.   ³⁶Conf. Rep., Oct., 1921, p. 185.
³⁵*Young Women's Journal*, vol. 36, p. 339.

land that are dangerous, that are striking at the fundamentals of the gospel of Jesus Christ, trying to destroy the faith in the minds of the students who attend the schools. We are troubled with it to some extent even in our own state, and the colleges throughout the country are full of it, and the professors teach it; they believe in it, at least they profess to believe in it; and it seems to me that the sole purpose of it is to undermine and destroy the gospel of Jesus Christ.

I want to say to the Latter-day Saints that it is our duty to put our faith in the revealed word of God, to accept that which has come through inspiration, through revelation unto his servants the prophets, both ancient and modern. And *whenever you find any doctrine, any idea, any expression from any source whatsoever, that is in conflict with that which the Lord has revealed and which is found in the holy scriptures, you may be assured that it is false;* and you should put it aside and stand firmly grounded in the truth in prayer and in faith, relying upon the Spirit of the Lord for knowledge, for wisdom, concerning these principles of truth.

SPIRITUAL KNOWLEDGE PARAMOUNT TO ALL OTHER. If you will walk in the light, and will receive the doctrines of our Redeemer, he will grant unto you, through the inspiration that will come from the Spirit of the Lord, a testimony of the truth. You need not walk in darkness nor in doubt, but may have a clear and a distinct comprehension and understanding of the truth which will make you free. It is our duty to seek the Lord, to obey his laws, to keep his commandments, to put away from us light-mindedness, foolishness, and the false theories, notions, and philosophies of the world, and to accept with fulness of heart and in humility these solemn, God-given principles which will bring unto us eternal life in the celestial kingdom.[37]

There is no knowledge, no learning that can com-

---
[37]Conf. Rep., Apr., 1917, pp. 64-65.

pensate the individual for the loss of his belief in heaven and in the saving principles of the gospel of Jesus Christ. An education that leads a man from these central truths cannot compensate him for the great loss of spiritual things.[38]

CHURCH JUDGED BY APPROVED DOCTRINES. The Church of Jesus Christ of Latter-day Saints is not responsible for the sayings or doings of any individual in conflict with that which has been received as a standard by which the Church is to be governed. We are to be judged by our authorized doctrines and deeds, and not by the whims or notions of men. But the ministers of the "Reorganization" have not been willing from the beginning to permit us to stand on this platform, but insist that we stand on the platform they have prepared for us.

The *Bible, Book of Mormon, Doctrine and Covenants,* and the *Pearl of Great Price,* including the Articles of Faith, have been received by the vote of the Church in general conference assembled as the standard works of the Church. On this platform we stand. *The Church is not responsible for the remarks made by any elder or for the numerous books that have been written.* The authors of the words or books must be responsible for their own utterances.

ALL TEACHINGS MUST CONFORM TO REVELATIONS. It is not to be supposed from this that all that has been written outside of the standard works of the Church is discarded and rejected, for these things are profitable as helps in the government of the Church, and to promote faith in the members. The point is this, if in these books mistakes are found, "they are the mistakes of men," and the Church as an organization is not to be held accountable for them, but for that which is received from time to time by vote of the Church, as it comes through the President of the High Priesthood. When the Lord re-

[38]*Church News,* June 19, 1937, p. 4.

TEACHING THE GOSPEL 323

veals his mind and will, it is to be received, "whether by mine own voice or by the voice of my servants, it is the same," but we are not to be judged by unauthorized sayings or deeds.[39]

If I should say something which is contrary to that which is written and approved by the Church generally, no one is under obligation to accept it. Everything that I say and everything that any other person says must square itself with that which the Lord has revealed, or it should be rejected.[40]

KEY TO JUDGE TRUTH OF ALL TEACHINGS. If members of the Church would place more confidence in the word of the Lord and less confidence in the theories of men, they would be better off. I will give you a *key for your guidance. Any doctrine, whether it comes in the name of religion, science, philosophy, or whatever it may be, that is in conflict with the revelations of the Lord that have been accepted by the Church as coming from the Lord, will fail.*

It may appear to be very plausible; it may be put before you in such a way that you cannot answer it; it may appear to be established by evidence that cannot be controverted; but all you need do is to bide your time. *Time will level all things.*

You will find that every doctrine, theory, and principle, no matter how great it may appear, no matter how universally it may be believed, if it is not in accord with the word of the Lord, it will perish. Nor is it necessary for us to try to stretch the word of the Lord to make it conform to these theories and teachings. The word of the Lord shall not pass away unfulfilled.

I realize that we are all weak, and at times may place false interpretations upon the written word, but the revelations are so clear regarding Adam, the fall, the atonement, the resurrection, the redemption of the earth when it shall again be proclaimed "good," and so

---

[39]*Origin of the "Reorganized" Church,* p. 81; *D. & C.* 1:38.   [40]Conf. Rep., Oct., 1943, p. 97.

many other things which fall under the ban of present-day teaching, that we need not be led astray. *The theories of men change from day to day. Much that is taught now will tomorrow be in the discard, but the word of the Lord will endure forever.*[41]

---

[41]*Gen. & Hist. Mag.*, vol. 21, pp. 155-156.

[END OF VOLUME I]

INDEX

A

Aaron, witness of truth borne by, 205.
Aaronic Priesthood, details of restoration of, 195-197.
Abihu, death of, 135.
Abinadi, teaches how Christ is the Father, 29-30; teachings of, about seed of Christ, 25.
Abominable Church, dark ages power of, 175, 177.
Abraham, dispensation had by, 161; Elias of day of, 174; Father did not eat with, 16-17; God's covenant with, 164-166; gospel known by, 160; knowledge of astronomy had by, 147-148; other witnesses in days of, 204-205; pre-existent greatness of, 59; witness of truth borne by, 204.
Abrahamic Covenant, continuation of, with Israel, 165; nature of, 164-165.
Achan, death of, 135.
Adam, all life affected by fall of, 92-93; Ancient of Days is, 93; atonement beyond power of, 122, 126-127; celestial body of, 97; celestial time used by, 79; Christ is Redeemer of, 104-105; Christ not fathered by, 105; Christ superior to, 98-100; creation of, 90-91; creative powers of, 90, 93; death entered world through, 107-113; dispensation had by, 161; doctrine of fall of, 107-120; dust of earth formed body of, 90-91; duty of, to replenish earth, 93-94; Edenic status of, 91; evolutionists do not believe in, 141; fall of, brought death, 82; fall of, foreordained, 109-110, 121; Father present with, in Eden, 26; first man, 93; first man and first flesh, 77-78; God creator of, 100; God parent of, 101; godhood of, 96-99; gospel knowledge had by, 95-96; gospel known by, 160; government of, 93-94; greatness of, 90, 93-96; immortal creation of, 77; intelligence of, 94-96; keys of salvation held by, 99-100; language of, 107; language and writing of, 95; language of God spoken by, 26; Lord appeared to, 100; nature of body of, 91-93; nature of immortal creation of, 91; no evolutionary origin for, 141; no worship of, 106; participation of, in creation, 74-75; perfect nature of, 140; physical creation of, 76-78; post-fall status of, 111-116; pre-existent status of, 90; pre-fall status of, 107-111; rank of, as Ancient of Days, 106; status of, as our father and God, 96, 98-100; superior intelligence of, 144-145; ten commandments known to, 96; time since day of, 79-81; transgression of, 92-93, 104, 111-116; truth of doctrine about, 116-117; visits of Father to, 103-104.
Adam-God Theory, discussion of, 96-106; source of, 96.
Adam - ondi - Ahman, appearance of Lord at, 100; coming of Christ at, 106.
Advocate: See Christ.
Advocate, status of Christ as, 26-27.
Agency, dark ages denial of, 175; eternal progression by, 70; exercise of, by Judas and Cain, 61; exercise of, in both estates 70-71; gospel preached because of, 70; mortal man receives gift of, 60; no exaltation without, 70; no salvation without, 70; pre-existent spirits granted gift of, 58-59, 64-65; rebellion in heaven because of, 64; universal nature of, 62; unrighteous use of, 71.
Agnostics, millennial status of, 86.
Alma, quoted—revelation for all nations, 277.
Ananias, Paul baptized by, 198.
Ancient of Days, Adam's position as, 93, 106.
Angels, limitations on administration of, 195-196, 198; mortals sometimes have title of, 17; reaping of earth by, 241-242; restoration brought to pass by, 191-192; so-called guidance from, 54.
Animals, atonement applies to, 137; creation of, antedates Adam, 77-78; creation of, for man, 62-63; form of spirits of, 63-64; no death for, before fall, 107-109; physical creation of, 75-76; pre-existence of, 62-64; redemption of, 73-74; souls of, 63-64; spirit creation of, 75-76; spirits of, 63-64.
Animal Sacrifice: See Sacrifice.
Answers, all not satisfied by, 306.

Apostasy, failure to teach truth brings about, 315-316; gospel lost by, 161-162; revelation needed because of, 274.
Apostate cults, origin of, 247-254.
Apostles: See Quorum of Twelve.
Apostles, nature of Godhead known by, 2; organization of, 232.
Assistant President, no present need for, 222; office of, 212; status of Oliver Cowdery as, 211-213.
Astronomy, Abraham's knowledge of, 147-148.
Atonement, Christ becomes Father through, 28-29; doctrine of, 121-138; earth and all life affected by, 73-74, 137; fall of Adam basis of, 119-123; foreordained nature of, 121; how Christ worked out, 127-129; infinite scope of, 137; infinite suffering of 129; justice makes demand for, 122-123; lack of gratitude for, 131-133; mankind bought with a price through, 125-126; murderers not forgiven through, 134-137; nature of, 137; ransoming power of, 123-127; salvation comes through, 133-134; some sins not forgiven through, 133-134; twofold nature of, 123; vicarious nature of, 126; voluntary nature of, 127.
"At-one-ment," attaining of, 125.
Authorities, duty of, to speak by revelation, 310-311; revelation received by, 280-284; saints safe in following counsels of, 243.

B

Baptism, damned for rejecting covenant of, 157; everlasting covenant of, 152.
Baptism for Dead, false "Reorganite" teachings about, 265-268; revelation basis of, 272.
Baptist, John: See John the Baptist.
Baptist, John, mission of, as an Elias, 171-172.
Beasts, pre-existence of, 62-64.
Bell, inspiration given to, 180.
Benjamin, King, teachings of, about seed of Christ, 25-26.
Bible, latter-day revelation gives clarification of, 278-279.
Birth, pre-existence determines nature of, 59-61.
Bishopric, first organization of, 232.
Black, James W., David Whitmer's standing endorsed by, 224-225.
Blair, William W., a "Reorganite" founder, 253.
Blasphemy, Christ accused of, 97-98; exaltation in, by sons of perdition, 49; nature of, 47; prevalent nature of, 12-14; "Reorganites" approach sin of, 260.
Blatchford, Robert, quoted—fall of man, 119.
Blood, mortal body quickened by, 76-77.
Blood Atonement: See Atonement.
Blood Atonement, Church did not engage in practice of, 136-137; doctrine of, 133-138; universal practice of, 136.
Bodies, denial of, to devils, 65; gaining of, 66-68.
Book of Mormon, details of translation of, 197-198; doctrine of fall taught in, 108-109; historicity of Jesus shown by, 35-36; witnesses of, 222-228.
Brazen Serpent, raising of, in similitude of Christ, 22.
Briggs, Jason W., apostasy of, 249-251; biography of, 249-252; false revelations of, 284.
Brother of Jared, appearance of Christ to, 37.
Buchanan, George W., David Whitmer's standing endorsed by, 224-225.

C

Cain, agency had by, 61; status of, as son of perdition, 49.
Calamities, prevalence of, in last days, 85.
Calvin, Lord gave inspiration to, 174-175.
Cantwell, L. C., David Whitmer's standing endorsed by, 224-225.
Capital Punishment, law of, 136-137.
Catholics, millennial status of, 86.
Cave-Man, Adam not a, 140; degeneration of man to state of, 148.
Celestial Beings, this earth prepared for, 72.
Celestial Bodies, resurrection of, 86.
Celestial Body, special definition of, 97.
Celestial Day, length of, 78-81.
Celestial Earth: See Earth.
Celestial Time, earth created on, 78-81; nature of, 78-81.
Child, Jacob O., David Whitmer's standing endorsed by, 224-225.
Children, Church responsibility for teaching of, 316-317; parental responsibility for teaching of, 316-319; teaching of, 316-320.
Christ, Adam subordinate to, 98-100; animal sacrifice a similitude of, 22-

INDEX

23; appearance of, to Brother of Jared, 11, 37; atoning power of, 127-129; brazen serpent a similitude of, 22; Church organized by, 238-239; creation of many worlds by, 74; creative powers of, while a Spirit, 18; death had no power over, 127-129; demands of justice satisfied by, 122-123; doctrines of, always same, 159-160; earth and all life redeemed by, 74; enemies admit historicity of, 34-35; everlasting nature of, 11-12; evolutionistic denial of, 142-143; Father of, immortal, 128; Father puts his name on, 27-28; footsteps of Father followed by, 32-33; foreordained mission of, 15-16; fulness of Father gained by, 33; gospel restored in days of, 162-163; Holy Ghost not father of, 18-20, 101-102; infinite sacrifice of, 122; ingratitude to, 131-133; inherent power of, to live or die, 127-129; Isaiah foretells life and mission of, 23-25; keys of resurrection gained by, 128-129; law of witnesses obeyed by, 206-207; life in himself possessed by, 31; light and truth gained by, 32; man in debt to, 131-133; manner of appearance of, to various prophets, 37; mission of, based on fall, 119-120; modern prophets receive visits from, 36-37; mortal probation of, 32-33; name Shiloh (Shilo) applies to, 20-21; nature of, as personage of spirit and tabernacle, 6-7; no reincarnation for, 18; outward appearance of, 23; part Holy Ghost played in birth of, 18-20; personal testimony of, 208; position of, as God of Israel, 27; position of, as Mediator and Advocate, 26-27; position of, as Son, Mediator, and Only Begotten, 1; power of immortality had by, 30-31; power over death had by, 31; price paid by, 129-131; priestly status of, 99; prophecies concerning advent and mission of, 20-26; putting open shame upon, 49; ransom paid by, 123-127; righteous visited by, 36-37; second coming of, 173; seed of, 25-26; shedding of blood of, 133; sorrows and sufferings of, foretold, 23-25; status of, as Father and Son, 27-30; sudden appearance of, 194; sufferings of, 129; teach true status of, 33-34; two nations stand as witnesses for, 278; unbelieving receive no personal ministration of, 209-210; use of name of, as a title, 15-16; wickedness to end with coming of, 82-84; working out salvation of, 32-33.

Christ, Light of: See Light of Christ.

Church: See Kingdom.

Church, apostate attempts to create division in, 248; approved basis of judgment of, 322; children to be taught by, 316-317; Christ set up, 274; Christ's personal organization of, 238-239; devotion of Joseph F. Merrill to, 292-293; doctrine of salvation for dead essential to divinity of, 264-265; enduring nature of, 240-246; evolution not in harmony with, 143; first bishopric in, 232; first conferences of, 230-231; first members of, 230; first missions in, 232-234; fulness of truth gained through, 299; guarantee of progress of, 244-245; individual manifestations not for, 288; keep name of, above reproach, 237-238; members of, called saints, 234-236; millennial position of, 168; minor nature of early apostasy from, 256-258; nature of, 229-246; perpetuity of, 241; position of, as kingdom of God on earth, 229-234; preparation for defense of, 311; qualifications for teachers in, 311-313; restoration of, 167-168, 240; restoration of, in days of Christ, 163; rise or fall of, 188; revelation in, 279-283; revelation given to, 279-284; setting up of, 230-234; study in meridian, days of, 304-305; teachings in 311-316; teaching responsibility of, 307-320; true revelations publicized by, 287; two great responsibilities of, 307; warning voice to, 310-311; watchmen give guidance to, 310; worth of souls now in, 313; youth to remain true to, 243-244.

Civilization, ages of, 149-151; evolution and devolution of, 148-151; prophets foresaw day of, 146; rise and fall of, 147-151.

Columbus, source of inspiration of, 53.

Comforter: See Holy Ghost.

Comforter, second, nature of, 55.

Commandments, essential nature of, 155, 157.

Common Consent, law of, 255-256, 260-261.

Condemnation, slothful saints to receive, 237.

Conferences, beginning of, in Church, 230-231; revelation given at, 281.

Conscience, Light of Christ acts as, 51.

Constitution, way for restoration prepared by, 179.

Cornelius, account of conversion of,

198; receipt of Holy Ghost by, 41-42.
Corruption, mortality a state of, 67.
Council of Twelve: See Quorum of Twelve.
Councils, pre-existent spirits participated in, 57-58.
Covenant, children of, 164; discussion of, 152-166; essential nature of, 155; examples of, 152-153; Joseph Smith restorer of, 276-277; Lord stipulates terms of, 154; new and everlasting nature of, 152-153; penalty for rejection of, 156-157; prophets foretold establishment of, 153-154; purpose of, 155; rejection of, by Israel, 165; renewal of, in last days, 165-166; restoration of, 166-167; revelation needed for establishment of, 276; withdrawal of, 154-155.
Cowdery, Oliver, angels seen by, 213; Christ seen by, 36; desertion of Joseph Smith by, 214; keys and priesthood received by, 211-213, 217; loss of blessings by, 217-218; ordination of, as assistant president, 213; return of, to Church, 227-228; status of, as assistant president, 211-213, 217-219; status of, as joint witness, 217-222; testimony of, 226-228.
Creation, endless nature of, 61-62; Lord's blueprint of, 74-75; millions of years not involved in, 80-81; nature of, 72-81; no death in days of, 77; order of events in, 75-78; planning of, 75; physical nature of, 75-78; revealed account of, 75-78; temporal and spiritual status of, 77; those who participated in, 74-75; time element in, 78-81.
Creations, God progresses through, 7, 10.
Creator, status of Christ as, 30.
Creators, those who acted as, 74-75.
Cults, apostate origin of, 247-254.

D

Dark Ages, evil church dominated in, 175; ignorance prevailed in, 178; pall of darkness in, 177.
Davis, James A., David Whitmer's standing endorsed by, 224-225.
Deam, Henry H., false revelations of, 284.
Death, atonement destroys power of, 123-124; Christ not subject to, 128; Christ only had power over, 30-31; claim of, paid by Christ, 123-127; earths pass through, 72-74; Edenic creatures not subject to, 77; essential nature of, 68; fall results in, 107-113; importance of, 66, 116; merciful nature of, 115-116; millennial abolishment of, 86-87; sins unto, 135-136.
Deity, proper use of names of, 12-16; reverence for, 12-16; some hymns profane name of, 14; use names of sparingly, 16.
Devil: See Satan.
Devil, evolution doctrine of, 148-149.
Devils, bodies denied to, 65; bodies stolen by, 65; casting out of, 65.
Devolution, status of man result of, 148-151.
Discernment, saints entitled to spirit of, 287.
Disciples of Christ, dispensation had by, 161.
Discoveries, withholding of, until last days, 145-146.
Disobedience, covenants withdrawn because of, 154-155; ungrateful nature of, 131-133.
Dispensation, definition of, 160-161.
Dispensations, names and nature of, 160-164; number of, 162; partial list of, 161; restoration of keys of, 173-174; witnesses sent in, 203.
Dissolution, Church never threatened with, 256-258.
Doctrines, judgment of Church by, 322; teaching of, in home, 318.
Doniphan, A. W., David Whitmer's standing endorsed by, 224-225.
Drake, Durant, quoted—fall of man, 118.
Dunn, George W., David Whitmer's standing endorsed by, 224-225.
Dust of Earth, Adam created from, 90-91.

E

Earth, Adam assisted in creation of, 90; age of, 78-81; age of, since Adam, 79-81; atonement has effect upon, 137; burning of, 85-86; celestial destiny of, 87-89; celestial status of, 87-89; cleansing of, 85-86; creation and destiny of, 72-89; curse came upon, 92-93; death and resurrection of, 72-74, 82, 84, 87-88; division of, in days of Peleg, 85; fall brought mortality to, 77; heaven pertaining to, 73; inheritance of, meek, 88; living status of, 72-74; mortal probation of, 110; mortality of, 82; paradisiacal glory of, 169; paradisiacal status of, 84-87; post millennial status of, 87; renewal of,

INDEX

84-87; restoration of, 84-87, 169; stages of, existence, 82; telestial status of, 82-84; temporal continuance of, 79-81; terrestrial status of, 84-87.

Earths, creation of, 61-62; creation of, by Christ, 74; creation and salvation of, 72-75; death and resurrection of, 72-74; inhabitants of, 62; life upon, 139-140; mortal status of, 73; passing away of, 72-73; probationary status of, 73; resurrection of, 88-89.

Editor, David Whitmer's standing endorsed by, 224-226.

Education, fault of, 320; value of, 292.

Edison, inspiration given to, 180-181.

Elder Brother: See Christ.

Elder Brother, position of Christ as, 15-16.

Elders, early ordination of, 231.

Elements, use of, in creation, 75-76.

Elias, Abrahamic prophet by name of, 174; office and calling of, 172; participation of, in restoration, 170-174; restoration effected through, 174; witness of truth borne by, 204.

Elijah, linking of dispensations through, 170-171; participation of, in restoration, 170-174; prophetic position of, 188.

Elohim, human family created by, 103; position of, 96-97; worship accrues to, 106.

End, time of, 87.

End of World, meaning of, 82-84.

Endowments, revealed nature of, 272.

Enoch, assistance of, in creation, 75; dispensation had by, 161.

Environment, mortal existence affected by, 60.

Er, death of, 135.

Eternal Life, fall essential to, 113-115; knowledge of God essential to, 20.

Eternity to Eternity, meaning of, 12.

Everlasting Covenant: See Gospel.

Everlasting Covenant, provisions of, 157-158; discussion of, 152-166.

Everlasting Covenants: See Covenants.

Everlasting Covenants, discussion of, 152-166.

Evil Spirits: See Devils.

Evolution, apostasy comes from teachings of, 315-316; Christ denied by, 142-143; Church denied by, 143; debasing nature of, 141; devil author of, 148-149; false theory of, 140; Fatherhood of God denied by, 143-144; gospel does not harmonize with 141-142; religion does not harmonize with, 141-144; teachings about, 139-151; true doctrine of, 148.

Evolutionists, doctrine of atonement denied by, 118; doctrine of fall denied by, 117-118; God and religion ridiculed by, 117-120.

Exaltation, all knowledge part of status of, 291-292; fulness of gospel leads to, 160; mortality essential to, 91; status of, 97-98; straitness of way leading to, 69-70.

Ezekiel, quoted — everlasting covenants, 154.

F

Faith, belief in omnipotence of God required for, 6-7; damned for rejecting covenant of, 157; false teachings lead to loss of, 321; God seen by, 3; knowledge gained by, 302-303; teachers must have gift of, 311-313.

Faithful, false revelations not deceiving to, 286; mysteries known to, 296-297.

Fall of Adam, all life affected by, 62, 92-93; atonement comes because of, 121-127; blessings of, 113-116; death came through, 82, 107-113; doctrine of, 107-120; evolutionistic denial of, 143; foreordained nature of, 109-110, 121; immortality and eternal life came through, 113-115; mortality entered world through, 77-78; mortality result of, 111; no death before, 72-78; no sex sin in, 114-115; rejoicings of Adam and Eve in, 115; spiritual and temporal death came through, 122; truth of doctrine about, 116-117; truths about, yet to be revealed, 110-111; twofold nature of, 122.

False Revelation: See Revelation.

False Spirits: See Spirits (false).

False Spirits, unfaithful deceived by, 285-286.

False Teachers, sorrow and punishment of, 33-34.

Father, Adam dwelt in presence of, in Eden, 26; creation directed by, 74; Father of, 11-12; fulness of, explained, 6-7; glorious body of, 66-67; limitation on visits from, 4; men spirit children of, 1; name of, placed on Son, 27-30; nature of, as personage of spirit and tabernacle, 6-7; personal testimony of, 208; sole reason for appearance of, 27; status of, as a witness for Christ, 206-208; work and glory of, 7.

Fatherhood of God, evolutionistic denial of, 143-144.
Fear, nature of, of Lord, 4-5.
Fiction, truth replaced by, 320-321.
Final Battle, time of, 87.
Firstborn: See Christ.
Firstborn, place of Christ as, 18.
First Comforter: See Holy Ghost.
First Estate: See Pre-existence.
First Estate, nature of life in, 56-66; why no remembrance of, 60.
First Flesh, Adam created as, 92; how Adam became, 77-78; meaning of, 92; mortal nature of, 77-78.
First Man, Adam's place as, 93.
First Presidency, equality of twelve with, 255; first organization of, 232; order of succession in, 220-221; Peter, James, and John acted as, 173-174; succession in, 254-261.
First Vision, Holy Ghost overshadows prophet at, 42-43; knowledge of God restored by, 2; position of Christ as Mediator shown by, 28.
Fish, redemption of, 73-74.
Fisk, John, quoted—fall of man, 117.
Ford, Thomas, quoted—Church membership, 257.
Foreordination, nature of, 59-61.
Fowls, redemption of, 73-74.
Fraud, Joseph Smith's work without, 190-191.
Free Agency: See Agency.
Fulness of Times, inventions reserved for, 182-183.

G

Garner, H. C., David Whitmer's standing endorsed by, 224-225.
Gentiles, times of, 166.
Gethsemane, Christ's greatest suffering in, 130.
Gift of Holy Ghost: See Holy Ghost.
Gift of Holy Ghost, nature of, 38-43.
Gifts, nature of, in Church, 239-240.
God, Adam offspring of, 101; Adam taught by, 95; Adam visited by, 103-104; all life comes from, 139-141; apostate concepts of, 2; appearance of, to Abraham, 16-17; body and personage of, 102-103; body of flesh and bones had by, 56-57; character, attributes, and perfections of, 1-17; covenant of salvation offered by, 152; everlasting nature of, 11-12; evolutionist ridicule of, 119-120; exalted beings to gain knowledge of, 3; existence of, from eternity to eternity, 12; false teachings about progression of, 7-8; Fatherhood of, 1; gaining knowledge about, 3; how men walk with, 4: inventors inspired by, 147; Joseph Smith restored knowledge of, 2; law given all things by, 10; Light of Christ is power of, 152; man created in image of, 3; modern knowledge of, 1-5; no laws superior to, 10; obedience brings personal visitation from, 3-4; omnipotence of, 5-10; others than saints used by, 181-182; perfection of, not "relative," 8; pre-existent spirits lived in presence of, 56-57; progression of, 5-10; reverence for, 12-16; scriptures prove omnipotence of, 9-10; some hymns profane name of, 14; status of, as a Man, 18; terms of covenants stipulated by, 154; unalterable nature of laws of, 154.
God of Israel: See Christ.
God of Israel, Christ known as, 27.
Godhead, grand Presidency of, 15; members of, compared, 38-39; nature of personages in, 103; position of, as supreme governing council, 1; rank of members of, 1, 18-20; separate personages of, 1-2.
Gods, exalted beings become, 97-98; plurality of, 97-98.
Gospel, Abraham had knowledge of, 160; Adam had knowledge of, 95-96, 111-112, 160; all covenants embraced in, 158-159; all not satisfied by answers in, 306; apostasy from, 161-162; blessings of birth among those having, 236; definition of fulness of, 160; dispensations of, 160-164; evolution denies truth of, 141; knowledge of, precedes obedience, 301-302; meridian dispensation of, 163; nature of covenant of, 152-160; new and everlasting covenant of, 156; no salvation in ignorance of, 290-291; Noah had knowledge of, 160; obedience brings knowledge of, 294-295; restoration of, 167; saints seek knowledge of, 314-315; spiritual appeal of, 296; superior status of truths of, 292-293; teachers must have knowledge of, 311-312; teachings of, 307-324; unchangeable nature of, 159-160.
Gospel Covenants: See Covenants.
Gospel Covenants, nature of, 152-156.
Governments, preparation of, for restoration, 178-179.
Grant, Heber J., prophetic position of, 188.

INDEX 331

Gratitude, Christ deserving of, 131-133.
Graves, millennial abolishment of, 87.
Guardian Angels, so-called guidance from, 54.
Gurley, Zenas H., apostasy of, 251; biography of, 250-252; false revelations of, 284; false revelations received by daughter of, 284; pre-apostate status of, 250-251.

H

Harris, Martin, angel appeared to, 213; desertion of Joseph Smith by, 214; testimony of, 226.
Heaven, no neutrals in, 65-66; war in, 64-66.
Hell, claim of, paid by Christ, 123-127.
High Priests, early ordination of, 231-232.
Historicity of Jesus, outline of, 34-37.
Holman, W. R., David Whitmer's standing endorsed by, 224-225.
Holy Ghost, Adam inspired by, 95, 100; all prophets led by, 45-47; all things done by power of, 18-19; avoid speculating on destiny of, 39; blasphemy against, 47-49; Christ not begotten of, 101-102; Christ not Son of, 18-20; constant companionship of, 39-45; false nature of evolution taught by, 140; fulness of truth comes from, 297-298; gaining guidance from, 43-44, 47-48; gaining light and truth from 293-301; gift of, 38-43; gift of, and Holy Ghost compared, 41; gift of, comes by laying on of hands, 38-39; gift of, defined, 40; gift of, in a future eternity, 46; gift of, spoken of as "it," 50; guidance and protection from, 54; Holy Spirit of Promise known as, 45; Light of Christ an agency of, 54; man returned to presence of God by, 41; manner of bestowal of, 39-40; ministry of, when Christ was here, 45-46; mission of, 38, 42-45, 47-48; mysteries revealed by, 296-297; obedience precedes receipt of, 43; obtaining gift of, 40-42; omnipresence of, 40; operation of, through Light of Christ, 40; personage and gift of, compared, 40-42; personage and personality of, 38-39; personage of, spoken of as "he," 50; prophecy and revelation come from, 38; prophets guided by, 185-187; sin against, 47-49; Spirit personage of, 1-2; testimony comes from, 42-45, 47-48; testimony of, to non-church member, 42; truth-seekers receive testimony from, 42, 44-45; world does not receive gift of, 42-43.
Holy Spirit: See Holy Ghost.
Holy Spirit of Promise, definition and nature of, 45, 55; Holy Ghost known as, 45; sealing power of, 45.
Home, doctrines taught in, 318; teaching in, 317-319.
Hughes, C. J., David Whitmer's standing endorsed by, 224-225.
Hughes, J. S., David Whitmer's standing endorsed by, 224-225.
Hughes, James, David Whitmer's standing endorsed by, 224-225.
Human Family, God first of, 102-103.
Hymns, Deity profaned by, 14.

I

Ignorance, cannot be saved in, 303; no excuse for, 302-303.
Immortal Body, spirit quickening power of, 76-77.
Immortality, Adam created in, 91; Christ only had power of, 30-31; denial by "soul-sleepers" of, 30; earth to be renewed in, 73; fall essential to, 113-115; fall of Adam basis of, 120; free gift of, through atonement, 123-124; light and hope of, 31.
Indians, former civilization of, lost, 151.
Ingratitude, sin of, 131-133.
Innocence, children born in, 66.
Intelligence, ancient people had high state of, 144-148; definition of, 290-291; pre-existent development of, 145.
Inventions, non-church source of, 182; prophecy of Joel includes making of, 180; reservation of, for era of restoration, 179-180, 182-183; Spirit of Lord guides in, 178-179; way for restoration prepared by, 177-179; withholding of, until last days, 145-147.
Inventors, inspiration received by, 147; Lord makes use of, 180-181.
Investigators, source of guidance received by, 42, 52-53.
Isaiah, life and mission of Christ foretold by, 23-25; quoted — everlasting covenants, 153; quoted — rebellion of Lucifer, 64.
Israel, Abrahamic covenant had by, 165; cause of scattering of, 165; pre-existent status of, 59; restoration of kingdom to, 172-173.

J

Jacob, blessing of, by messenger, 17; Lord seen by, 17; Shiloh teachings of, 20.
Ja-oh-eh, time measurement of Kolob, 79.
Jaredites, decay of civilization of, 150-151; dispensations had by, 162.
Jehovah: See Christ.
Jehovah, all revelation comes from, 27; position of, 96-97.
Jeremiah, pre-existent greatness of, 59; quoted—everlasting covenants, 153-154.
Jesus: See Christ.
Jesus, historicity of, 34-37.
Jews, cause of scattering of, 165-166.
Joel, inventions help fulfil prophecy of, 180; quoted—Lord to pour out Spirit on all flesh, 175-176.
John, quoted—how to know God, 295.
John the Baptist, details of appearance of, 195-197; dispensation had by, 161; mission of, as an Elias, 171-172; position of, as a messenger before the Lord, 194-195; prophetic position, 188.
Joseph (Son of Jacob), Shiloh teachings of, 20-21.
"Josephites," avoid use of name of, 261.
Judas, agency had by, 61.
Justice, atonement satisfies demands of, 122-123.

K

Kelley, William H., false "Reorganite" teachings of, 20.
Keys, falsity of "Reorganized" church shown by absence of, 270-271; holding of, by two witnesses, 216-222; possession of, not claimed by "Reorganites," 266-267; restoration of, 173-174; Twelve received all of, 258-260; two witnesses required in restoration of, 210-211, 216-222.
Keys of Salvation, Adam possessor of, 99-100.
King Benjamin, teachings of about seed of Christ, 25-26.
Kingdom: See Church.
Kingdom, building up of, 237; dual nature of, 229; ecclesiastical nature of, 229-230; enduring nature of, 240-246; millennial status of 229-230; nature of, 229-246; organization and gifts of, 238-240; political nature of, 229-230; restoration of, 240; setting up of 230-234; status of Church as, 229; unity in, 245-246.
King Follett Sermon, quotations from, 10-12.
Knowledge, extent of, in last days, 145; fulness of, gained by exalted being, 291-292; gaining of, 290-306; God has fulness of, 5-10; obedience comes because of, 301-302; obedience required for attainment of, 294-295; preeminence of, in spiritual fields, 321-322; saints thirst for, 314-315.
Knox, Lord gave inspiration to, 174-175.
Kolob, status of, 78-81; time reckoning of, 78-81.

L

Lamech, witness of truth borne by, 204.
Language, Adam had knowledge of, 95.
Last Days, calamities in, 85.
Learning, importance of, 292-293.
Life, creation, fall, and redemption of, 144; God sole source of, 140-141; knowledge about origin of, 142; no beginning for, 139-140; origin of, 139-141; transplanting of, from other worlds, 74, 139-141.
Light, Christ's attainment of, 32; gaining of, 293-301.
Light of Christ, all flesh recipients of, 53; all men endowed with, 42; Columbus led by, 53; every man guided by, 50-54; Holy Ghost operates through agency of, 40, 54; impersonal nature of, 49; investigators led by, 52-53; inventions come by, 178-179; inventors guided by, 53, 176, 178, 180-183; nature of, 49-53; no guardian angels except, 54; omnipresent nature of, 49-54; pouring out of, on all flesh, 176; power of God exercised through, 52; strivings of, with man, 53.
Light of Truth: See Light of Christ.
Lodge, Oliver, quoted — fall of man, 118.
Lord: See God.
Lord, the, fear and love of, 4-5.
Lost Tribes, dispensation had by, 162; scattering of, 165.
Lucifer: See Satan.
Luther, Lord gave inspiration to, 174-175.

M

Major, H.D.A., quoted — fall of man, 117.

INDEX

Major Prophets, false classification of, 187-188.
Man, all creations presided over by, 62-63; intelligence of, 144-148; origin of, 139-141; transplanting of, from other worlds, 74.
Manifestations, individual nature of, 288.
Marconi, inspiration given to, 180.
Marks, William, "Young" Joseph ordained by, 253.
Marriage, everlasting covenant of, 153.
Mary, Christ the son of, 19.
Mary Magdalene, devils cast out of, 65.
Matthew, quoted — recounts resurrection of saints, 30.
McBride, E. W., quoted—fall of man, 117.
McCabe, Joseph, quoted — historicity of Jesus, 34-35.
McGinnis, Thos., David Whitmers standing endorsed by, 224-225.
Mediator: See Christ.
Mediator, position of Christ as, 1; status of Christ as, 26-27.
Meek, inheritance of earth by, 88.
Melchizedek, witness of truth borne by, 204.
Meridian of Time, definition of, 81, 163; gospel dispensation in, 163; meaning of, 81.
Merrill, Joseph F., love of truth of, 292-293.
Message, sending of, to world, 308-309.
Messenger, prophecy concerning, 193-195.
Messiah: See Christ.
Methusaleh, witness of truth borne by, 204.
Michael, Adam known as, 76, 90, 93; hosts of heaven led by, 87; intelligence of, 93-94; position of, 96-97.
Millennium, little season to come after, 82; nature of death during, 86-87; nature of kingdom of God during, 229-230; non-church members during, 86-87; paradisiacal conditions in, 84; restoration during, 168-169; those to inhabit earth during, 85-87.
Minor Prophets, false classification of, 187-188.
Missions, first organization of, 232-234; opening of, in many nations, 232-234.
Mohammedans, millennial status of, 86.
Moroni, quoted—gaining testimony by Holy Ghost, 42; quoted—Light of Christ, 50-51; visit of, to Joseph Smith, 198-199.
Mortal Body, blood quickening power of, 76-77.
Mortality, bodies gained through, 66-67; corruption attends state of, 67; effect of pre-existence on, 59-61; exaltation comes through, 91; fall brought blessings of, 111; fall brought status of, 107-116; importance of, 69; nature of, 66-71; people on other earths passing through, 62; pre-existent spirits taught about, 57-58; probationary nature of, 66-71; testing ground of, 69-70; two purposes of, 66.
Mosaic Law, preparatory nature of, 162-163.
Mosby, W. W., David Whitmer's standing endorsed by, 224-225.
Moses, dispensation had by, 161; other witnesses in days of, 204-205; quoted—pre-existent status of Israel, 59.
Mount of Transfiguration, manifestations on, 171-172.
Murder, death penalty for, 134-137.
Mysteries, spirit reveals nature of, 295-297; obedience precedes knowledge of, 295-297.
"Mysteries," avoidance of, 305-306; relationship of, to salvation, 306.

N

Nadab, death of, 135.
Negro, pre-existence determined status of, 61, 65-66.
Nehor, death of, 135.
Nephites, decay of civilization of, 151; dispensations had by, 162.
Neutrals in Heaven, none had status of, 65-66.
New and Everlasting Covenant: See Gospel.
New and Everlasting Covenant, discussion of, 156-159.
New Earth: See Earth.
New Heaven: See Earth.
Noah, assistance of, in creation, 75; dispensation had by, 161; gospel known by, 160; other witnesses in days of, 204.

O

Obedience, all truth gained only through, 298; debt of, 131-133; door to truth and knowledge gained by, 294-295; full blessings of atonement come because of, 129-131; gospel

knowledge lays foundation for, 301-302; no salvation without, 69-70; remission of sins through, 133.
Onan, death of, 135.
Only Begotten: See Christ.
Only Begotten, place of Christ as, 18; relationship of, to the Father, 1.
Organic Evolution: See Evolution.
Organization, nature of, in Church, 239-240.

P

Paradisiacal Earth, glory of, 169.
Paradisiacal Glory, gaining of, by earth, 84-87.
Parents, children to be taught by, 316-319.
Passion of Christ, suffering of, in Gethsemane, 130.
Passover, institution of, 22-23.
Paul, enemies admit historicity of, 34-35; nature of Godhead known to, 2; quoted — calling Church members saints, 235; quoted — Christ only hath immortality, 30; q u o t e d — church organization, 239-240; quoted —condition of Sons of Perdition, 48; quoted—pre-existent status of nations, 59; quoted—resurrection, 123-124; quoted—scriptural study, 303-304; quoted—sons of God, 98.
Peleg, earth divided in days of, 85.
Perdition, Sons of: See Sons of Perdition.
Peter, quoted—Sons of Perdition, 48-49.
Philosophy, dangerous nature of, 320-321.
Physical Creation: See Creation.
Pilate, no appearance of Christ to, 209-210, 215.
Pit, atonement ransoms from, 126-127.
Plan of Salvation, nature of, 58; pre-existent presentation of, 58; status of other earths in, 72.
Plants, physical creation of, 75-76; spirit creation of, 63-64, 75-76.
Pratt, Orson, quoted—celestial destiny of earth, 89.
Pratt, Parley P., quoted—death for all life came by fall, 113.
Prayer, improper use of Lord's name in, 14-15; offering of, for children of Joseph and Hyrum, 199-200; use of Lord's name in, 14-15; use of name of Christ in, 14-15.
Preaching, Church responsibility for, 307-320.

Pre-Adamites, none such, 77-78.
Predestination, false nature of, 61.
Pre-existence, Adam's status in, 90; agency had by spirits in, 58-59, 64-65; all creatures created in, 62-64; councils held in, 57-58; effect of, on mortality, 60-61; inequality in, 58-59; intelligence developed in, 145; Israel foreknown in, 59; life in presence of God in, 66-67; nature of life in, 56-66; plan of redemption presented in, 58, 64; plan of salvation presented in, 58, 64; probationary nature of, 58-59, 64-66, 70-71; progression in, 58-59; prophets chosen in, 184; purpose of mortality known in, 57-58; races accounted for because of, 61; saints have knowledge of, 56; why no remembrance of, 60.
Pre-existent Spirits, God seen by, 56-57.
President, revelation for Church comes through, 283-285.
Presidency: See First Presidency.
Presidency, first organization of, 232; order of succession in, 220-221; Peter, James, and John acted as, 173-174; succession in, 254-261.
Priesthood, Adam holds keys of, 99; cannot see God without, 4; eternal nature of, 99; fulness of, had only in temples, 271; two witnesses required in restoration of, 210-211, 216-222.
Probation, importance of, 69; mortality a state of, 66-71; people on other earths passing through, 62; pre-existence a state of, 58-59, 64-66.
Profanity, vulgar nature of, 12-13.
Progenitor, God's place as, 103.
Progress, Church will always maintain state of, 244-245.
Progression, nature of, of God, 5-10.
Prophets, definition of, 185-186; false labeling of, as major and minor, 187-188; intelligence of, 145-146, 147-148; last days seen by, 146; latter-day covenants foretold by, 153-154; latter-day revelation foretold by, 275-276; mission and calling of, 184-188; pre-existent choosing of, 184; pre-existent foreordination of, 59-60; position of saints as, 185-186; restoration to come through, 169-170; saints always to be guided by, 242-243; teachings of, conform to revelation, 187; testimony of Christ given by, 36.

INDEX

Protestants, millennial status of, 86.
Punishment, severity of, for false teachers, 33-34.

Q

Queensbury, W. R., David Whitmer's standing endorsed by, 224-225.
Quorum of Twelve, acceptance of, as presiding authority, 256; keys of kingdom conferred on, 258-260; rank of, 254-255.

R

Race, Adam parent of, 93.
Races, pre-existence accounts for, 61.
Ransom, payment of, through atonement, 123-127.
Redeemer: See Christ.
Redemption, gaining of, through Christ, 123-127; nature of, 123-127; plan of, presented in pre-existence, 58, 64; vicarious sacrifice basis of, 126.
Reincarnation, false doctrine of, 18.
"Reorganites": See "Reorganized" church.
"Reorganites," abuse of saints by, 261-262; apostate status of, 248; baptism for dead rejected by, 265-268; destiny of, 269; false claims of, 247-248; false claims of, 263-264; false revelations of, 262-263; false teachings of, 19-20; keys of sealing not held by, 266-267; proselyting methods of, 262; repentance enjoined upon, 272-273; salvation for dead rejected by, 265-268; temple building unknown to, 271; unbelief and ignorance of, 267-268; unstable nature of founders of, 249-254.
"Reorganized" church: See "Reorganites."
"Reorganized" church, counterfeit nature of, 253-254; creation of, 251-252; destiny of, 263; few saints joined with, 252-253; fruits of, 261-263; origin and destiny of, 247-273.
Replenish, meaning of, 93-94.
Reyburn, A. K., David Whitmer's standing endorsed by, 224-225.
Rigdon, Sidney, angels appeared to, 213; Christ seen by, 36; leadership of Church claimed by, 248-249; position of, 211.
Reason, place of, in search for truth, 300-301.
Rebellious, penalty for own sins paid by, 131; things of Spirit unknown to, 296-297.

Redemption, evolution not in harmony with plan of, 143.
Reformers, inspiration given to, 174-175; Joseph Smith's work compared with, 191.
Religion, creation of, by man, 189; evolution does not harmonize with, 141-144; evolutionist ridicule of, 119-120.
Renaissance, way for restoration prepared by, 177.
Repentance, atonement offers forgiveness on conditions of, 129-131; damned for rejecting covenant of, 157; "Reorganites," must submit to law of, 272-273.
Restoration, Aaronic Priesthood part of, 195-197; angelic ministration resulted in, 191-192; constitution prepares way for, 179; earth subject to, 169; glorious doctrine of, 167-183; governments prepare way for, 178-179; inventions prepared way for, 177-179; inventions to come forth in era of, 179-180; manner of bringing about of, 167; millennial era of, 167-168; need for, 167; part of Elias and Elijah in, 170-174; part witnesses played in, 210-211; perfect structure resulted from, 170; prophet needed for, 169-170; reformers prepared way for, 174-175; renaissance prepared way for, 176-177; second coming preceded by, 173; the dispensation of, 164; time of, 172-173; world-wide scope of, 174-183.
Resurrection, all earths attain unto, 88-89; ancient saints came forth in, 30; animals to come forth in, 62; atonement brings about, 123-124; Christ gained fulness of Father in, 33; Christ gained keys of, 128-129; earth and all life attains unto, 74; earths pass through, 72-74; exaltation available only in, 33; evolutionistic denial of, 143; gaining knowledge of, 294-296; gaining of truth after, 300; time of, 86; time of, of wicked, 87.
Retrogression, savages attain their state through, 149.
Revelation, apostasy brought need for, 274; Christ source of, 27; conference an occasion for, 281; covenants restored through, 276-277; doctrine of salvation for dead came by, 268-269; endowment ceremonies came by, 272; eternal nature of, 274-283; faithful not deceived by,

when false, 286; false nature of, among "Reorganites," 262-263; false principles of, 283-289; individual nature of, 288; Joseph Smith recipient of, 274-275, 282-283; law of, 274-289; limitation on receipt of, 283; personal nature of, 185-186; prophets foretold coming of, 275-276; publicizing of, 285; publicizing of, when of God, 287; reasonableness of receipt of, 277-278; receipt of, by Church today, 279-283; saints not deceived by, when false, 288-289; source of, for Church, 185-186, 283-285; study of, 302-303; teachings must conform to, 322-324; test of, 283-289; writing of, not always necessary, 281-282.
Revelations, prophetic utterances conform to, 187.
Reverence, law of, 12-16.

S

Sabbath, everlasting covenant of, 152-153.
Sacrifice, Christ offers himself as, 122; law, nature, and manner of, 22-23; performance of, in similitude of Christ, 22-23; vicarious nature of, 126.
Saints, acceptance of Brigham Young by vote of, 256-257; authorities give safe counsel to, 243; Brigham Young followed by, 256-258; condemnation for, if slothful, 237; false revelations not acceptable to, 288-289; gospel knowledge sought by, 314-315; gospel scholars among, 304-305; knowledge of pre-existence had by, 56; majority of, to remain true, 240-241; message of salvation had by, 181; peculiar status of, 234-236; privileges and duties of, 236-238; prophetic calling of, 185-186; prophets will always give guidance to, 242-243; "Reorganite" abuse of, 261-263; resurrection attained by, 30; some revelations reserved for, 280; spirit of discernment had by, 287; study expected of, 301-306; superior status of, 236; use of name by, 234-236.
Salvation, acceptance of Joseph Smith essential to, 189-190; Adam holds keys of, 99-100; all covenants essential to, 158-159; Christ worked out his, 32-33; evolution denies plan of, 141-142; fall of Adam basis of 120; gaining knowledge that brings, 290-306; gaining of, not predestined, 61; God offers covenant of, 152; gospel knowledge essential to, 290-291; knowledge leads to, 303; nature of knowledge that brings, 290-293; relationship of "mysteries" to, 306; saints have message of, 181; twofold nature of, 133-134.
Salvation for Dead, eternal nature of, 269-270; no true church without, 264-265; "Reorganite" declarations on, 265-266; "Reorganites" reject doctrine of, 265-268; "Reorganite" stand with reference to, 263-273; true doctrine of, 268-269.
Sanhedrin, no appearance of Christ to, 210, 215.
Satan, banishment of, 87; defeat of, 87; rebellion of, in heaven, 64; supremacy of, in telestial earth, 82-83.
Savages, retrogression brings to state of, 149.
Saving Knowledge: See Knowledge.
Saving Knowledge, gaining of, 290-306; nature of, 290-293.
Savior: See Christ.
Scripture, definition of, 186; value of, given in latter-days, 278-279.
Scriptures, key to gaining knowledge of, 295; prophetic utterances conform to, 187; reason for study of, 303-304; searching of, 301-306; teachings judged by standard of, 323-324; teachings must conform to, 322-324; treasuring up of, 305.
Second Comforter, denial of, 55; nature of, 55.
Second Coming, messenger to prepare way for, 193-195; restoration to come before, 173; temple appearance in connection with, 193-194.
Second Death: See Spiritual Death.
Second Elder, status of Oliver Cowdery as, 211-213.
Second Estate: See Mortality.
Second Estate, nature of, 66-71.
Second President, position of Hyrum Smith as, 220-221; status of Oliver Cowdery as, 211-213.
Seed of Christ, faithful become, 25-26.
Serpent, brazen, raising of, in similitude of Christ, 22.
Seventies, organization of, 232; presiding position of, 255.
Shiloh (Shilo), promised Messiah to be called, 21; prophecies concerning, apply to Christ, 20-21.
Shiloh Prophecy, fulfillment of, 21; nature of, 20-21.
Sign Seekers, witnesses rejected by, 214-215.

INDEX

Sin, commission of, by false teachings, 313-314; evolutionists deny power to, 120.
Sin of Adam: See Adam; Fall; Transgression of Adam.
Sin unto Death, nature of, 47-49.
Sins, some slain to atone for, 134-137.
Sins unto Death, nature of, 134-137.
Slaughter, Lewis, David Whitmer's standing endorsed by, 224-225.
Smith, Frederick M., removal of bones of Joseph and Hyrum by, 200-201.
Smith, Hyrum, blessings of Oliver Cowdery received by, 218; God's perfection and omnipotence taught by, 5; Joseph Smith held keys with, 216-222; Joseph Smith joint witness with, 216-222; keys held by, 218-219; keys of kingdom held by, 258; position of, as joint President of Church, 218-219; prayer for children of, 200; prophets tribute to, 219-220; quoted—omnipotence of God, 5; removing bones of, 200-201.
Smith, Joseph, an Elias, 184; ancient promises fulfilled through, 192; appearance of Christ to, 194; assistance of, in creation, 75; blood atonement teachings of, 135-136; Brigham Young ordained president by, 258; Christ seen by, 36; Church rises or falls with, 188; covenants revealed by, 276-277; details of translation of *Book of Mormon* by, 197-198; details prove divinity of, 195-199; divine mission of, 188-202; failure of attacks on, 189; Father and Son seen by, 4; first vision shows divinity of, 28; foreordination of, 184-185; God's perfection and omnipotence taught by, 6-7; Hyrum Smith held keys with, 216-222; Hyrum Smith joint witness with, 216-222; keys conferred upon Hyrum Smith by, 218-219; knowledge of God had by, 3; law of witnesses obeyed by, 205-206, 210-222; Moroni's visit to, 198-199; no fraud found in work of, 190-191; other witnesses shared burden of, 213; overshadowing of, by Holy Ghost, 43-44; penalty for rejecting testimony of, 189-190; personal sentiments about, 199-202; plurality of Gods taught by, 98; position of, as messenger before Lord, 194-195; prayer for children of, 199-200; prophetic calling of, 184-202; quoted —Adam's status, 93; quoted—distinction between Holy Ghost and Gift of Holy Ghost, 40-42; quoted —God an exalted man, 10-12· quoted—how God progresses, 7 quoted — nature of God and the Godhead, 6-7; quoted — priesthood and power of Adam, 99; quoted — restoration of the earth, 84-85; reformers work compared with, 191; removing bones of, 200-201; restoration came through, 169-170; revelation began with, 274-275; revelation in day of, 282-283; revelation since day of, 279-283; salvation comes through, 189-190; status of Adam revealed to, 100; testimony concerning, 201-202; the p r o p h e t, knowledge of God restored by, 2; tribute of, to Hyrum Smith, 219-220.
Smith, President Joseph F., quoted — how Holy Ghost operates, 40; revelation received by, 280.
Smith, Lucy Mack, quoted—three witnesses view plates, 210-211.
Smith, William, leadership of Church claimed by, 248-249.
Son, the: See Christ.
Son of God: See Christ.
Sons of God, exalted beings to become, 12, 96-97.
Sons of Perdition, apostates do not always become, 45; gathering of, by Satan, 87; how men become, 47-49; punishment of, 48-49; repentance denied to, 48-49.
Sorrows, Christ a man of, 23-24.
Souls, creation of animals as, 63-64; false teachings lead to destruction of, 313-314; worth of, 313.
Spirit: See Holy Ghost.
Spirit, gaining light and truth from, 293-301; knowledge comes through, 291-292; no effective teaching without, 311-312; spiritual body quickened by, 76-77; wisdom of men guided by, 299.
Spirit (Light of Christ), inventions come by, 178-179; inventors guided by, 176, 178, 180-183; pouring out of, 176-177.
Spirit Creation: See Creation.
Spirit of Christ: See Light of Christ.
Spirit of God: See Holy Ghost; Light of Christ.
Spirit of Lord: See Holy Ghost; Light of Christ.
Spirit of Prophecy, definition of, 185.
Spirit of Truth: See Holy Ghost.
Spirits, creation of animals as, 62-64; creation of plants as, 63-64; degrees of intelligence among, 58-59; in-

nocence of, in beginning, 66; testing for, whether false or true, 301; time of creation of, 75-76.
Spirits (false), deception comes from, 285-286; false revelations from, 283-289.
Spirits (pre-existent), God seen by, 56-57.
Spiritual Body, nature of, 6 (footnote).
Spiritual Bodies, physical nature of, 76-78.
Spiritual Creation: See Creation.
Spiritual Death, nature of, 48-49, 111-112.
Spontaneous Generation, theory of, 139-141.
Stars, redeemed status of, 88-89.
Stephenson, inspiration given to, 180.
Stone Age, civilization followed by, 149.
Strang, James J., leadership of Church claimed by, 248-249.
Study, all revelation subject of, 302-303; difficulties of, in primitive Church, 304-305; exhortation of Paul to, 303-304.
Suffering, infinite, involved in atonement, 129-131.
Sun, celestial status of, 88-89.
Sunday School, gospel taught by, 316.
Succession, common consent a governing principle of, 255-256; law of, in Presidency, 254-261; Nauvoo settlement of, 256; order of, in presidency, 220-221; settlement of question of, 260-261.

T

Taylor, John, quoted — death for all life came by fall, 113; revelation received by, 280.
Teachers, qualifications of, 311-313.
Teachers (false), sorrow and punishment of, 33-34.
Teaching, children subject of, 316-320; Church performance of, 311-316; Church responsibility for, 307-320; manner of, by example and precept, 317-318; personal nature of, 319-320; key to judge truth of, 322-324; test of truth of, 320-324.
Telestial Beings, earths prepared for, 72.
Telestial Earth: See Earth.
Ten Commandments, Adam had knowledge of, 96; everlasting covenant of, 153; fundamental nature of, 96.
Ten Tribes: See Lost Tribes.

Terrestrial Beings, earths prepared for, 72.
Terrestrial Bodies, resurrection of, 86.
Terrestrial Earth: See Earth.
Testators, requirement for death of, 222-223.
Testimony, daily renewal of, 44; disobedience causes dimming of, 44-45; gaining of, 201-202, 293; Holy Ghost source of, 42-45, 47-48; pre-eminence of, 321-322; sure nature of, 47-48; value of, 292-293.
Theistic Evolutionists, dilemma of, 142-143.
Theories, truth of, determined by scriptures, 323-324.
Three Witnesses: See Witnesses.
Three Witnesses, adherence to testimony by, 222-228; facts concerning, 222-228; impossibility of collusion among, 222-223.
Temporal, meaning of, 80.
Temporal Death, nature of, 111.
Time, end of, 81; meridian of, 81.
Transgression of Adam, nature of, 107-116.
Trigg, George W., David Whitmer's standing endorsed by, 224-225.
Truth, apostasy comes from lack of teaching of, 315-316; Christ's attainment of, 32; degrees of, 292; eternal nature of, 323-324; faithful receive, from Holy Ghost, 47-48; fulness of, comes only from Spirit, 297-298; fulness of, comes only through Church, 299; gaining of, 293-301; gaining of, after resurrection, 300; God has fulness of, 5-10; Holy Ghost reveals knowledge of, 42-45, 47-48; new and everlasting nature of, 298-299; preparation for defense of, 311; reason only a partial guide to, 300-301; sin of leading away from, 313-314; sin of leading from, 313-314; Holy Ghost sure witness of, 43-45, 47-48; test of, 320-324; treasuring up of, 305; triumphant destiny of, 241; utimate triumph of, 320-321.
Twelve: See Quorum of Twelve.

U

Unfaithful, deception of, 294; deception of, by false spirits, 285-286.
Unity, kingdom maintained in state of 245-246.

V

Visions, how past events may be seen in, 279.

W

War in Heaven, nature of, 64-66.
Ward Teachers, family to prepare way for, 318-319.
Warning Voice, duty to give heed to, 310-311; raising of, 307-316; responsibility for raising of, 309-310.
Wassen, George I., David Whitmer's standing endorsed by, 224-225.
Watchmen, duties of, 310.
Wealth, purpose of, 68-69.
Wesley, John, quoted — fall of man, 119.
Whitmer, David, endorsement of standing of, 224-226.
Whitmer, D. P., David Whitmer's standing endorsed by, 224-225.
Whitmer, David, angel appeared to, 213; desertion of Joseph Smith by, 214; testimony of, 223-226.
Wicked, warning of, 307-310.
Williams, Frederick G., position of, 211.
Witnesses: See Three Witnesses.
Witnesses, assistant president one of, 211-213; *Book of Mormon* and law of, 222-228; burden of prophet shared by, 213; Christ obeys law of, 206-207; death of, 221; divine law of, 203-228; divine nature of law of, 208-209; Father obeys law of, 206-208; Joseph Smith obeys law of, 205-206; keys and priesthood received by, 210-211; law of, applied to nations, 278; men condemned for rejection of, 215; nature and history of law of, 203-210; no collusion among, 213-214; Noah aided by, 204; penalty for rejection of, 228; rejection of, by sign seekers, 214-215; responsibility for acceptance of, 215-216; sending of, in all dispensations, 203.
Woodruff, Wilford, quoted — angels now reaping earth, 241-242; revelation received by, 280.
Woodson, T. D., David Whitmer's standing endorsed by, 224-225.
World, end of, 83-84; Holy Ghost not received by, 42-43; our message to, 308-309; preaching to, 307-308; wicked nature of, 307-308.
Worlds: See Earths.
Writing, Adam had knowledge of, 95.

Y

Young, Brigham, fruits of, 261; leadership of Church conferred upon, 256-261; ordination of, as president, 258-260; revelation received by, 280; status of Adam known by, 100-101; quoted — Adam-God Theory, 96, 97, 102; quoted — celestial destiny of earth, 89; quoted — death for all life came by fall, 112-113; quoted — fall of Adam, 92-93; quoted — position of Hyrum Smith, 220; quoted — teachings about Adam, 101-105.
Youth, Church always to be supported by, 243-244.

Z

Zemnarihah, death of, 135.
Zion, assurance of prospering of, 245; prophesies triumph of, 246; watchmen on towers of, 310.